GOSPEL HOUSES

HOW EVERYDAY CHRISTIANS CAN MAKE DISCIPLES AT HOME

ART THOMAS

FOREWORD BY JOEL COMISKEY

SUPERNATURAL TRUTH PRODUCTIONS, LLC
Practical Training for Spirit-Filled Living
www.SupernaturalTruth.com

Gospel Houses: How Everyday Christians Can Make Disciples at Home
Art Thomas

While many of the testimonies are shared with permission, some of the names have been changed for the sake of maintaining privacy for those involved.

Disclaimer: Nothing in this book should be considered legal advice. The author is simply sharing what he has seen to be healthy and practical in certain contexts. Be sure to check with a qualified lawyer within your own state or country to ensure that following any advice herein would not violate any laws.

ISBN: 978-1-959547-01-3

ENDORSEMENTS

The declaration of the gospel and the ministry of discipleship are personal, relational, and interactive. When you partner with the Holy Spirit to reach those within your circle of influence, even your home can become an epicenter for salvations, healings, miracles, deliverance, spiritual growth, and meaningful connections with other believers. In *Gospel Houses*, Art Thomas will expand your perspective of church community and accelerate true disciple making right under your own roof.

Daniel Kolenda
President, Christ for All Nations
CfAN.org

The Church is the primary agency that God is using to expand his kingdom here on earth. In his book *Gospel Houses*, Art shares a model of Great Commission church planting through house-church networks. He writes from the perspective of a healthy practitioner, not just a theorist. Art has a deep passion to see the church of Jesus grow and expand through disciple making in the home.

Doug Clay
General Superintendent, Assemblies of God
AG.org

With the wisdom of a pastor, the heart of an evangelist, the fire of a revivalist, the clarity of a prophet, and the theological accuracy of a Bible scholar, Art Thomas, with his years of experience in leading a house-church network, brings us back to a pure and simple devotion to Christ. *Gospel Houses* is more than a handbook on how to form a house church; it's a timeless and anointed mentor in a movement that God's Spirit is exploding around the globe. We can either embrace or reject God's move upon the hearts of believers to make disciples as expressed in house churches. I embrace it.

Jamie Morgan, D.Min.
Director, Trailblazer Mentoring Network
Mentor to women called to ministry
TrailblazerMentoring.com

At Iris Ministries, we have huge respect for the house-church model. It's the primary way our friends and neighbors in Mozambique receive pastoral care. In Southeast Asia, where we also lived and worked for years, house churches remain some of the most beautiful and committed gatherings we have ever seen. In the west, we saw home gatherings beginning to thrive in a special way during the pandemic. If you are seeking to work for the kingdom in this way, Art Thomas has written a book of strong practical advice. *Gospel Houses* is well worth reading for anyone who feels called to the ministry of making disciples, whether as a leader or simply as a faithful follower of Christ.

Heidi G. Baker, Ph.D.
Co-founder and Executive Chairman of the Board, Iris Global
IrisGlobal.org

I am always inspired by individuals who focus on making disciples through keeping it simple. In *Gospel Houses,* Art Thomas does just that. Without dismantling the church through criticism of what she is not doing, Art chooses to lift up our eyes to see the harvest is ripe and ready, and we need all hands on deck.

I have known Art for years and have admired his passion to equip the body of Christ to become fruitful and fulfill the Great Commission. From firsthand experience of planting churches in Africa and America, Art longs to see the everyday Christian discover they, too, can make disciples. And after gleaning from his insights in *Gospel Houses,* I find myself inspired to be more effective in making disciples who will, in turn, make disciples.

If you have bitterness in your heart toward the church and are looking for a book that will justify your bitterness, well, this is not that book. But if your heart is tender and soft to the rest of the body of Christ and you're seeking how you, too, can be part of the house-church movement, this book will encourage you. *Gospel Houses* offers keys that will help you take steps toward being a fruitful disciple maker.

Chris Overstreet
Founder, Compassion to Action
Author, *A Practical Guide to Evangelism Supernaturally* and *Faith That Sees*
CompassionToAction.com

ENDORSEMENTS

No one I know—and I mean no one—lives out the realities of house churches like Art, his family, and his team. This book comes from their years of experience, trials, and errors. It contains a word for the planter, the skeptic, and the proficient alike and perhaps a prophetic word to the body of Christ concerning the shift back to our ancient future. You'll enjoy the simple yet profound stories that come from open hearts and open doors.

Jim Weigand
Church-Planting Director, AG Michigan Ministry Network
Lead Pastor, Freedom Center—Fenton, MI

If you are serious about fulfilling the Great Commission and seeking wisdom for both starting and growing in your Christ-centered journey, then *Gospel Houses* by Art Thomas is a must read.

Having traveled a similar path, I can relate to his journey of gaining wisdom every step of the way. Art does an excellent job of guiding you on a faith journey toward sharing the good news of Jesus Christ, leading people to salvation, connecting them to the church, being the church, and discipling them to live fruitful lives within the body of Christ.

Although there are various approaches to being the church, I appreciate the way Art expresses it as both practical and doable. Manmade traditions have complicated being the church, and Art thoroughly uncomplicates it for all believers.

Art shares in detail the raw reality of his experiences obeying the Great Commission, not only in *starting* a church but also in *being* the church. When you are faced with these same situations, you will be grateful you took the time to be mentored through these stories.

Jesus said, "Follow me," and that is a reality in Art's life, ministry, and in the Roots Church network. Throughout the book, there is no wasted space or filler, and Art writes about his experiences in a way that is both informative and inspiring. Each word, each topic, and each chapter builds on the others and will be useful for you if you choose to obey Jesus Christ and begin this great adventure of being the church Jesus has called us to be.

Greg Lancaster
Greg Lancaster Ministries
GregLancaster.org

Art Thomas has a way of challenging, if not upending, the church's status quo without pride or prejudice. Littered with historical documentation and fruit-filled anecdotal evidence, this book challenges us to reexamine the merits of traditional meeting models. With intelligence, wit, and wisdom, Art inspires *every* saint to be equipped and empowered to carry Christ's gospel torch.

Josh Adkins
Director of School of Ministry, Kingdom Church—St. Louis, MO
Founder, Loft Church—Herrin, IL
JoshAdkins.org

It's not often that you find a book that can both challenge us to rethink our current understanding of church and provide the practical steps to moving toward the vibrant life God designed for his people. Art has done that here in *Gospel Houses*—a resource that is just as valuable to the brand-new believer as it is to the seasoned church planter. By getting into the DNA of the church, Art shows us what it is that makes a community of faith thrive. This will certainly be a book I go back to time and time again for wisdom and encouragement to move forward.

Justin Knoop
Unshakable Kingdom
youtube.com/@Unshakable_Kingdom

Jesus's standing instruction in the Great Commission is to go, make disciples, baptize them, and teach them to obey. Every believer is called to make disciples of the people around them. *Gospel Houses* will challenge and equip you to do just that. Through his years of diverse ministry experience and deep biblical understanding, Art Thomas provides a framework for fruitful ministry that is accessible to all believers. It is evident throughout the book that Art deeply loves the body of Christ and desires to empower believers to live out their God-given purpose to reach the lost and advance the kingdom of God on earth. You can become a disciple maker, and your house can be a gospel house.

Jesse Comrie
President, Global Renewal Inc.
Global-Renewal.org

Art Thomas's *Gospel Houses* brings you into his living room and lets you see and hear the unique work of God in Roots Church. Knowing Art and that living room well, reading the book was like visiting an old friend and being challenged and refreshed again by how the gospel has multiplied and grown. This is much more than a book about planting or multiplying churches; it will inspire, confront, and equip you. In *Gospel Houses*, Art depicts the life of Christ expressed in Roots Church and offers the simple truths that propel God's transforming work.

Jonathan Ammon
Author and teacher
Early participant in Roots Church

I am one of many living examples of people who have been transformed by Art's disciple-making approach, and today, I am living out the reality behind the theory of this book in my own house church. The teachings in this book have revolutionized the way I lead both in house church and in a quickly multiplying network of house churches.

In *Gospel Houses*, you'll learn how to make the same kinds of disciples Jesus made: rapidly multiplying, spiritually potent, and, most importantly, astonishingly committed to Jesus. This book isn't exactly about house churches, even though that's the strategy Art has chosen; it's really about the power of the Holy Spirit, obedience to Jesus, and the gospel of transformation. If you want to learn discipleship theory that has been thoroughly tested by real life and truly has the power to both rapidly and profoundly change lives, I highly recommend *Gospel Houses.*

Alex Perry
Spiritual Life Director
Roots Church—Metro Detroit, Michigan

Since the day I met Art, his main passion has been to unite people to Jesus Christ, allowing for their uniqueness to remain intact. Art has helped me greatly over the years to be united with Christ, and I'm sure *Gospel Houses* will do the same for you and all those who join you in your journey.

Dan Vander Velde
Church planter, friend, and mentor to Art Thomas

History will be defined not by the church growers but by the disciple makers. Art Thomas is not only a clear thinker and church strategist—he's a real disciple maker. Too many strategic church books have the wrong goal in mind: church growth. While a growing church is a wonderful thing, *why* and *how* it grows matters immensely. As many churches want to grow by being the best show in town, they sometimes end up growing at the expense of other churches in their area and often lose out on real community. They can even miss the mark of the Great Commission altogether: disciple making.

Art recognizes some of the shortcomings of modern church-growth strategy but doesn't write from that place. Instead, he intentionally focuses on seeing if a different approach could work. It has! This book isn't merely based on theory; it is rooted in the Scriptures and practical experience. Art practiced before he preached, and what you will discover in these pages has the potential to change your life and your church.

JonMark Baker
Evangelism and Discipleship Director
Roots Church—Metro Detroit, Michigan
JonMarkBaker.com

ACKNOWLEDGMENTS

This book would not exist if not for a few key people. First, of course, is Jesus. Since this is a Christian book, if I don't mention him right out of the gate, someone is bound to think I don't know my stuff. But for real, if not for Jesus, none of this would have happened in the first place. I owe him everything.

Next, of course, is my amazing wife, Robin. Her unwavering support and selfless love for other people makes her an invaluable partner in the gospel. Robin is the unsung hero of my ministry—spending quality time with people, hosting a church in our home every week, and making disciples of kids while their parents meet for more adult conversation. Robin is my best friend, and I wouldn't want to live this crazy adventure with anyone else.

Pastor Dan Vander Velde taught me to think outside the box about church. I share more of his story in this book. Likewise, Pastor Brooks McElhenny gave me the liberty to explore those outside-the-box ideas while serving in his church.

I'm also indebted to various authors whose books about small-group ministry and house churches have played a significant role in shaping my thinking and influencing my creativity. Of particular note are Joel Comiskey, Francis Chan, Bob Roberts Jr., James Rutz, Steve Murrell, Dave and Jon Ferguson, Rad Zdero, and George Barna. There were certainly many others, but these are the most relevant to this book.

James Loruss and Jonathan Ammon were my closest friends during the most experimental phases of our early house church network. Their late-night conversations and long ministry trips with me were foundational to the current movement and are bearing lasting fruit. Much of Chapter 9, especially pertaining to the roles of apostles and prophets, was born out of an extensive study we conducted together, and they deserve credit for many of the biblical observations.

Joe Loruss, Ron Dykes, JonMark Baker, and Alex and Gracie Perry, along with my wife and I, now compose the senior leadership team of Roots Church. These adventurers were crazy enough to go all in with me when we planted Roots Church, and they continue to serve our network of house churches with love, wisdom, insight, humility, and boldness. Their spouses and families are all priceless people whom I love deeply. This is the most amazing team I could imagine, and I'm grateful for each of you.

I also want to give a special mention to my friend Jason Hilliker. Early in the development of this book, I paused in my writing, second-guessing whether I should be writing a book that might be so challenging to the status quo in American Christianity. Then my phone rang. Jason said, "Art, I was praying for you. I see you sitting at your desk in front of your laptop, and you're trying to decide whether to do something God told you to do. He says, 'Do it.'" I praise God for my prophetic friends. Jason's timely word is a major reason this book exists.

Thank you to my many beta readers who dedicated time and attention to this manuscript when it was still raw. And special thanks belongs to my favorite editor, Lisa Thompson, who regularly makes me seem like a better writer than I am. Thanks for polishing this manuscript and making it shine for the masses. (Also, great work editing this paragraph.)

Lastly, I want to recognize the many participants in Roots Church. You're constantly pushing the envelope of what normal Christianity looks like, and I applaud you. This book is your story. You give my words credibility because you're living what these pages preach. As Paul wrote to the Corinthians, "You yourselves are our letter [of recommendation], written on our hearts, known and read by everyone. You show that you are a letter from Christ, the result of our ministry, written not with ink but with the Spirit of the living God, not on tablets of stone but on tablets of human hearts" (2 Corinthians 3:2–3).

CONTENTS

FOREWORD

BY JOEL COMISKEY

Most people leave their homes to go to church and then go back home to live. But that hasn't always been the case in church history.

The early church was a home-based movement that met from house to house (Acts 12:12; Romans 16:3–5; 1 Corinthians 16:19; Colossians 4:15; Philemon 1:2). Under the radar of the Roman Empire, God used the early house churches to evangelize, make disciples, and transform the world. They were so effective that Christianity eventually became the dominant religion.

Throughout church history, God has used the house church strategy to draw his followers back to a simpler church life and mission. In fact, since 1950, the global house-church movement has resulted in a spontaneous multiplication of churches that has proven to be one of the most significant influences of the modern-day church.

But what about house church networks in the US? This book shows us that house-to-house ministry is alive and well here too. Art Thomas has stepped out of the traditional program-based church to start a multiplying house-church network. Art represents the new breed of cutting-edge church planters fulfilling Christ's Great Commission through organic ministry.

God slowly birthed this strategy into Art's heart, even though he never intended to leave the conventional church. Art holds a high view of Christ's church; unlike some house-church advocates, he avoids bashing more traditional models.

This book offers an alternative model for the next generation of church planters who long for something simpler and reproducible. In the pages of this book, he shows you what he has done and how you can implement a similar model.

Art emphasizes the Spirit's work in planting new house churches, featuring two chapters on spiritual gifts and ministry roles. The book clearly emphasizes that God is the one who develops house-church leaders and inspires the members to do the work of the ministry.

In Art's model, each house church functions independently, but they are also interdependent in that they come together twice a month to celebrate. I loved Art's focus on disciple making. It's not really about house-church order or the house church itself; it's about knowing Jesus and making disciples of the Master.

God is doing something new today—just like he has worked throughout church history. In my study of small-group movements over the last two millennia, I found they all yearned to go back to the simplicity of primitive Christianity. Today's conventional church has become so complicated and expensive that many pastors yearn for a better, more biblical way to minister and *do church.* For many, this book will offer a path forward.

In *Gospel Houses,* you'll experience the passion and fire that stirred many of Christ's small-group movements throughout the last two thousand years.

Joel Comiskey, PhD
www.JoelComiskeyGroup.com

PREFACE

You can be more fruitful for Jesus than you ever dreamed possible, and all you need is a Bible, the Holy Spirit, and a place to meet.

It doesn't matter if you're part of a large established organized church or if you're the only Christian in your entire country. Your home can become a disciple factory where lives are transformed through the gospel.

Those of you who love your big church don't have to leave it. In fact, the lessons I'll teach you in this book will make you into a tremendous asset in helping your church fulfill Jesus's mission. I started my first three house churches while still attending larger, more conventional churches, and my pastors celebrated what God was doing as I made disciples in my home.

In about 2005, I read my first book about house churches. At the time, I was helping plant an Assemblies of God church in a rural community, leading the worship team and youth ministry. Meanwhile, I lived an hour away in the metropolitan area of Detroit, Michigan. Since the distance made it difficult to engage in daily relationships within the church I was planting, my girlfriend, Robin, and I decided to start a house church in our area with a Christian friend from my work.

I asked my pastor, Dan Vander Velde, what he thought. And thanks to his faith and emotional security, he gave me his resounding support, saying, "Of course, buddy! It's all kingdom!"

To make a long story short, as God continued to move at our rural church and grow its numbers, my little house church grew too. Robin's parents let us meet in their basement. Our main house-church meeting grew to an attendance of around twenty-five young adults. Some, like me, were already Christians who attended conventional churches, hailing from eleven different congregations in six denominations. For a few, this meeting was the only church they attended.

We met weekly for worship, fellowship, Bible study, communion, and prayer. God's Spirit moved in the meetings. We led new people to salvation, baptized them, and saw more genuine life transformation in a matter of months than I had witnessed in my entire life previous. We saw demons cast out, marriages strengthened, families restored, bodies healed, addictions overcome, financial miracles, accurate prophetic words, and more. It was like living immersed in the book of Acts.

Branching off that main meeting, we had a men's group, a women's group, and five Bible studies happening in workplaces during break times. At its height, we had more than forty people involved, about a quarter of whom were new converts.

In 2008, Robin and I were engaged, and I felt led to return to her church, which had sent out our rural church-planting team four years earlier. Within a few weeks, I was offered a job on staff at that church, but it came with a wise stipulation. My pastor, Brooks McElhenny, said, "I love what God is doing in that young adult thing you have going, but realistically, you're only going to be able to focus on one or the other. If you do both ministries, you'll be spread too thin."

After much prayer, I handed off the house church to someone who had been with us since the beginning. At the same time, two key families moved out of state, and several of the workplace Bible studies closed down, both of which significantly shrank the numbers. But the main group continued for several years, and lifelong friendships remain to this day.

The three most fruitful years of my ministry life (at least until that time) were followed by what felt like the three *least* fruitful years. Serving on staff at that large, conventional church, I think I might have scared more people away than I brought in. And since I was no longer attending college or working in a non-church career, I interacted with significantly fewer people who weren't already Christians. Worse still, the worldly people I did know were all adults, but I was supposed to be pastoring kids and teens, which meant I couldn't invite my adult friends to any sort of relational ministry context where I could personally follow up with them.

In short, I had a role that many might consider prestigious: serving as an assistant pastor at a healthy church with hundreds of members and a thriving youth group. But I was screaming inside. I felt trapped in an office-shaped box, buried under paperwork, event planning, and program management while the lost were drowning just outside my window.

To be fair to the Lord and to that church, it wasn't all that grim. I did make an impact on many people during that time and also learned more than I ever expected. My own life was changed for the better. It was definitely the Lord's plan for my life, and I'm incredibly grateful to Pastor Brooks, who set a fantastic example of leading with integrity and humility.

But this season of my life also painted a clear and stark contrast for me. I realized I wasn't the key to my earlier house church's success. Jesus was. If I had been the main attraction, then my youth group would have grown just as quickly. Instead, I successfully shrank the senior high youth group from about twenty students down to about three (two of whom were the senior pastor's daughters, who had to be there anyway).

In April 2011, based on clear direction from the Lord that was confirmed by my pastor, I launched into full-time traveling ministry. My gift to the next youth pastor was a youth group he couldn't possibly shrink any further, and he thrived in that role far better than I could have hoped.

Meanwhile, I had now been married for almost two years and had a newborn baby boy. At the same time, I continued to pastor that church's young adult group, just no longer in an official staff capacity. As soon as possible, I turned that young adult group into a house church.

Over the next couple of years, I traveled the world to preach the gospel, plant churches, and train Christians on the weekends. And on Thursday nights, fifteen to twenty young adults would pile into my double-wide to meet with Jesus together.

Soon that group evolved so that more than half didn't consider themselves part of the main church. A few were from other churches while others were new converts who liked our house church but didn't have any interest in attending a big meeting on a Sunday. With my pastor's blessing, I handed off the official young adult ministry to someone else. From then on, our house church became its own independent group and finally started to thrive like my first house church.

During the first five years, we saw many lives transformed in our living room. Miracles of healing were common. Accurate prophetic words flowed freely. Baptisms became normal again.

In 2015, we started a second house church, the leaders of which continued to attend my group while they reached their own friends in another city on a different night. In 2018, that group launched yet a third group. The Lord added to our numbers and met with us faithfully. I'll share more details of our story in chapter 1.

Fast-forward to 2023, at the time this book is being published. Our network of house churches operates under the collective name Roots Church. Miracles are commonplace. Salvations happen regularly, both on the streets and in our meetings. We locally have over three hundred people involved in fifteen house churches, and more churches are brewing.

Even during 2020, when the COVID-19 pandemic swept the world and local governments required people to stay home so as not to spread the virus, our local house-church network doubled. We then took our school of ministry online, and many other house churches have started abroad as a result.

This is not a movement built on me or my personality. Most of the people in our church don't even interact with me on a regular basis. Roots Church is a network of people seeking and encountering Jesus together, united in mission, and spreading God's kingdom through demonstrations of his love and power.

I write this book from this perspective. This isn't theory to me. It has been tested and tried over eighteen years in multiple homes with a variety of people. If it can work for the guy who shrank his youth group by ninety percent, it can work for you too.

I want to be clear about what this book is and what it is not. This book is specifically about how to make disciples in groups that meet in one's home. I'll discuss how to start, lead, grow, and multiply healthy, interactive, Spirit-filled, self-replicating house churches of five to twenty people. This book is about managing people, not programs. This isn't a detailed look at a prescribed organizational structure (though I'll mention a little of this in chapter 21). Rather, it is a practical guide to making disciples and cultivating an atmosphere for revival and spiritual growth.

This book could be useful to conventional churches who want to train home-group leaders, but understand that I'm writing primarily from a house-church perspective, and you may need to make some mental modifications as you read. You may possibly want to use the house church model for all the small groups in your organization, which will significantly transform the ways you reach people and make disciples, shifting the fulcrum of ministry from large to small and empowering the people of your church to step out in their gifts.

Basically, every Christian can grow into an elder who mentors newer believers in the faith. (See Hebrews 5:12.) We simply need help from the Holy Spirit, appropriate training, godly encouragement, and a willingness to go. I wrote this book to offer you the training and encouragement you need. The rest depends on your relationship with the Lord.

I believe God's next big move will happen primarily in living rooms, family rooms, and basements. The things I'm seeing in the Roots Church network are only a foretaste of what is coming. As you read this book, I don't want you to think that you need to move to Metro Detroit to experience what God is doing. Rather, I want you to see these stories becoming true in your own home. If you will partner with Jesus in his mission of making disciples, you will see the testimonies in this book firsthand. This isn't a story about me, my house church, or Roots Church. This is a story about you, united with Christ and empowered by his Spirit.

Some of the information in this book is neither necessary nor exclusive to house-church ministry, but my goal in writing is beyond merely informing you about house churches. I want to export a culture. Many have asked about the secret sauce that makes Roots Church the healthy, thriving family that it is. I don't believe it's any one ingredient. I have tried as much as possible to capture the many components of our culture, distill them, and offer easily replicated principles that you can apply in your own context. Beyond information, though, the most influential components are our people, so I have shared many stories throughout this book to help you catch the fire they are carrying.

As such, this book is longer than it would need to be if I were only teaching the essentials of house church ministry. Those essentials are indeed included, but I also desire to equip you with the broader scope of our culture and mentor you with my years of experiences in ministry.

There's a lot to learn about house churches over time, but it's simple to begin. If you have some friends, a Bible, the Holy Spirit, and a place to meet, you can join the global movement of house churches and see the book of Acts come to life in front of your eyes. My prayer is that this book will give you an eighteen-year head start so you can see lasting fruit even faster than I did.

A NOTE TO MY FRIENDS IN CONVENTIONAL CHURCHES:

I believe in you. Jesus is not finished with conventional churches. A variety of people will always come to faith in conventional churches because of the work you do and the way you do it. We're one big family, and we're on the same team.

I started a network of house churches, not because I don't believe in all the other churches in my region but because those churches are successfully reaching a narrow demographic of the population, and I wanted to make disciples among the people who would never set foot in one of their buildings.[1]

---

[1] When we started Roots Church, we learned that while 67 percent of adults in our region claimed to be some form of Christian, only 29 percent attended weekly religious services (of any religion). ("Religious Landscape Study," Pew Research Center, 2014, https://www.pewforum.org/religious-landscape-study/metro-area/detroit-metro-area/.) Conventional churches are successfully reaching less than one third of our population. Meanwhile, most professing Christians aren't interested in attending their meetings.

As I contrast house churches and conventional churches, it may feel like I'm casting stones. But my love for the body of Christ constrains me from being unnecessarily harsh with Jesus's bride. Occasionally, I'll be blunt for the sake of clarity. If what I say is true, then it's true regardless of whether it feels good. If you can forgive my obvious bias and search for biblical truth, you'll find principles that will make your churches more effective at fulfilling Jesus's commission to make disciples who make disciples.

If the principles in this book can help your church reach more people, then we've accomplished something great together. Perhaps your church will want to convert some or all of their small-group ministry into this model. Or perhaps your pastor will encourage you and others to organically make disciples in your homes through these principles. Either way, feel free to modify and experiment with these ideas in your own unique context.

I care very little about finding a perfect methodology. Such a pursuit is a bit of a fool's errand anyhow. The perfect methodology for reaching one group isn't necessarily perfect for reaching the next. And by the time we find such a thing and write our books, culture will have moved on anyway. I care much more about principles that can be adapted and implemented in a changing culture, and I hope to present that in the following pages.

We have a big mission to accomplish together. As long as we're all connected to the same head—Jesus—we'll have the sort of unity that makes the world take notice. Let's go!

INTRODUCTION

Andrea was living a lesbian lifestyle, but she was raised in a Christian home where the gospel was planted like good seed in her heart. Deep down, she knew something wasn't right, and those feelings eventually surfaced.

She called her high school friend, Emily, who she knew followed Jesus. "What should I do?" she asked. "I would go to a church, but I drive a truck all over the country and wouldn't be able to connect anywhere."

Emily Loruss is part of my house church network. Her husband, Joe, pastors one of our house churches and is part of our network's senior-leadership team. Accordingly, Emily knew that one of the two house churches I lead offered the opportunity to participate via Zoom video calls. She gave Andrea my number, and I gave her the instructions to join our meetings.

Andrea Zoomed in faithfully. As we discussed the gospel, her mind was transformed. She started thinking differently, and the Holy Spirit did a deep work in her life.

A few months later, Andrea was in our area for a doctor appointment, and she invited her sister, Carrie, to come with her and join our meeting in person. Carrie brought her kids. She had always wanted them to know God. She told them the Bible stories she grew up on and raised them with morals and prayer, but their family hadn't been to church in ten years.

The kids loved the meeting and begged to return. Carrie loved it too. They all wished Carrie's husband, Tim, would come too, but Tim and Carrie's marriage was on the rocks, and he wasn't interested.

The following week, Andrea was back on the road in her truck, joining via Zoom, and Carrie and her kids returned in person. At the end of the meeting, as people prayed for each other, Carrie's breathing grew heavy. She winced. Something was clearly not right, and she could tell.

My friend JonMark and I calmly invited her into my hallway, out of the way of the busy room with all the people praying. Carrie planted herself on the floor, rocking on her hands and knees while JonMark and I calmly sat next to her and commanded a demon to leave. Within minutes, Carrie was free and crying tears of joy. No one in the main room would have even known what happened if not for her testimony afterward. Carrie continued attending, her own mind renewed by the gospel and the love shown in our little church family.

This growing freedom was powerful for Carrie. With it came a certain amount of self-respect and emotional strength she didn't previously have. This time, when the problems in her marriage escalated and Tim chose to respond sinfully, Carrie made him leave for the kids' and her safety. She called me, asking if I could meet with him.

In addition to leading a house church network, I travel internationally as an itinerant minister. It just so happened that when Carrie called, I was on my way out of town for a speaking engagement. But thankfully, others in my church are also trained and equipped to minister effectively to others. I asked JonMark to reach out to Tim instead, which he did.

Tim and JonMark met for coffee soon after. As they waited in line, the Holy Spirit told JonMark some things about the cashier—things she needed prayer for that only God could know. He shared those thoughts with her (scaring her a bit because they were so accurate) and then prayed for her as Tim watched in astonishment.

The two men sat down with their food. JonMark listened to Tim's story and simply shared the gospel with him. By the end of their meal, Tim sat in tears in the busy restaurant and surrendered his life to Jesus.

I returned from my ministry trip to a house-church meeting and found Carrie and Tim sitting next to each other on our couch, holding hands. Their marriage had been restored. The gospel had brought healing to their family.

That was a year ago as of this writing. Soon after, their kids began prophesying powerful and accurate prophetic words over people and leading their friends to Jesus. Their whole family experienced God's healing, redemptive power.

Recently, Tim had to work during our house-church meeting, but he texted me, saying, "God told me someone there had a financial need. Can you ask who it is so we can help them out?" I asked, and to make a long story short, a man in our church had recently lost his job. He and his wife were unsure how they were going to pay their bills that month. We made the need known, and people pooled together over $750—just a little more than this couple needed. Tim and Carrie gave most of it.

Making Disciples in Homes

Tim and Carrie's story is just one of countless similar testimonies. In eighteen years of this lifestyle, I've witnessed miracle after miracle and changed life after changed life in my home. My wife and I are simple people. We don't have a curriculum to follow or a special discipleship track that we move people along. We just love God and love people, helping others understand and experience the gospel through the power of the Holy Spirit.

My house is a gospel house. Demons are cast out in my house. Marriages are restored in my house. Bodies are physically healed in my house. New believers are baptized in my house. Disciples are made in my house. Whole families encounter Jesus and learn to minister in spiritual gifts in my house.

When people come to my house, I expect them to leave different than they came. The gospel is "the power of God that brings salvation to everyone who believes" (Romans 1:16). Accordingly, if I saturate my home with purposeful application and declaration of that gospel, everyone who comes will experience the power and presence of God. Even my own family enjoys the rich benefits of living in a home saturated with gospel proclamation and practice.

In this book, I'm going to teach you how to do the same things. You, too, can partner with Jesus and see deliverance in your hallway, baptisms in your bathtub, mind renewal on your couch, and life transformation in your living room.

It's not complicated. It's simple Christianity.

And it's not a special ministry reserved for professional clergy. It's for every believer.

The best parts of Christianity were never meant to be limited to big church buildings. From the very beginning, they were practiced in homes. Today is no different. With a little bit of education, inspiration, and spiritual empowerment, you can do the same things I do and greater. Your house can be a gospel house.

GOSPEL HOUSES ~ Art Thomas

PART 1:

PRINCIPLES

CHAPTER 1:

TURNING HOMES INTO SANCTUARIES

Centuries ago, old church cathedrals were built to draw eyes to heaven. Today's church architecture is built to draw eyes to the stage. What if this present move of God literally changes the architecture of the church, removes the stage, and builds our gatherings in circles around the Lamb?

—Matt Lockett

How many people have you baptized in your bathtub? How many physical bodies have been miraculously healed in your living room? How many people's tears of repentance and transformation have seeped into your carpet? How many lives have exited your front door, completely different than when they entered?

When I first heard about what God could do in homes, something inside me sprang to life. The year was 2005, and I was serving as part of a church-planting team in the rural community of Fowlerville, Michigan. My pastor, Dan Vander Velde, encouraged our little team to think outside the box about the meaning of the word *church* so we could develop a truly unique ministry.

Our team spent a series of Sundays attending every church in town. Each week, we would discuss what we liked about each church and what they were doing well. Then Pastor Dan surprised us by saying something like, "Let's not do any of those things."

It wasn't that he fundamentally disagreed with anything those other churches were doing. It's that he knew those churches were all successfully reaching a specific demographic, and we didn't need to compete with them for the same fraction of the population. He challenged us to dream of a church that could somehow reach out to the people in our town who might never set foot in one of those established churches.

Much of what we did was similar to the churches in which I grew up. We had a worship team who played live music and led congregational singing, a weekly sermon, and a monthly after-church meal. But the real differences showed up in the culture of interactivity surrounding each part of our meeting.

When the worship team led congregational singing, we included an open microphone where anyone at any time could come up and read a Scripture, pray, or share what they felt God might be speaking prophetically for the people present. We had rows of chairs, but they were set up in a half-circle to make conversation easier. When Pastor Dan preached, he told everyone that we were welcome to interrupt his sermon with questions, biblical insights, or prophetic words that we received during the message. And when we gathered for our monthly meal, we spent considerable time speaking public encouragement and affirmation to those who celebrated birthdays that month.

We were constantly innovating. And in my search for new ideas, I happened across a few books about house churches that revolutionized the way I thought about my Christianity.

The Church Comes Home

Something was appealing about what I was reading. During the early days of our church plant in Fowlerville, Pastor Dan told us not to invite anyone. For the entire first year, we were committing to let God work on only us. Jesus told his disciples to remove the planks from their own eyes before dealing with the specks in others' eyes (Matthew 7:3–5), and that's exactly what we did.

For all of 2004, our little team of ten people (five of whom were my pastor's children) met week after week to study the Word, worship, pray, fellowship, and dream together in Pastor Dan's living room. It was the most transformative year of my life.

Soon our little church plant began to grow. New families joined us regularly, and we continued to reach out to those who either didn't fit the traditional churches in town or simply weren't interested in church as usual. So many wild, amazing testimonies came from that time. At one point, a new convert turned himself in to the police for past drug charges, and our church soon had more people attending a Bible study in the Livingston County Jail than we had in our Sunday meetings!

And while all that was thrilling, I sort of missed the simple conversational Sundays in my pastor's living room.

At the time, I was reading voraciously about unique expressions of church—especially house churches. That's when, in 2005, I read a book by George Barna titled *Revolution*; and for me, the book certainly lived up to its name.

Barna, founder of one of the most well-known Christian research groups, presented findings about Christians who were abandoning typical American churches and gathering in homes with other believers. And his research found that many of these people were not angry, wounded, or bitter. They were actually among the healthiest Christians out there.[2]

Barna posed a question that deeply troubled me: "If the local church is God's answer to our spiritual needs, then why are most churched Christians so spiritually immature and desperate?"[3] While many churches today are indeed healthy, many churched people somehow manage to attend our meetings week after week and remain dead in their sins. The same could be said of many house churches.

You might be surprised to learn that I'm not interested in presenting house churches as the solution to all our problems. I'm

---

[2] George Barna, *Revolution: Finding Vibrant Faith Beyond the Walls of the Sanctuary* (Carol Stream, Illinois: Tyndale House Publishers, Inc., 2005).
[3] Ibid., 30.

all for diversity in ministry. We need more churches, not fewer. But my experience has been that interactive Christianity consistently produces stronger Christians than mere sermons and teaching alone. Small-group gatherings, where the Spirit is free to move, are vital to Christian growth. In my context, we've decided to emphasize interactive house churches over large gatherings, and the results have been tremendous.

In some circles, *house church* is considered a bad word. The only house churches some pastors have interacted with were led by disgruntled former members who left their church in frustration and perhaps even took some other families with them. Groups born in bitterness have a tendency to be unhealthy and likely even damaging. Some have even evolved into cults. It's no wonder some pastors recoil at the mention of house churches. It's not necessarily that they're territorial or want all the people (and their money) for themselves; they probably care about people and want them involved in something that will truly help them grow spiritually.

But Barna's book seemed to go against the narrative. What he presented resonated in my soul. I felt like I was reading about myself. It shook me to the core, and I knew something more was available in the Christian life.

This led to reading another book, which led to another, then another—each more clearly articulating the concept of house churches. I learned that typical American churches are difficult to multiply, requiring stacks of money and crowds of talented people. But house churches could be replicated quickly, needing only a mature leader, a few spiritually hungry believers, and a home in which to meet.

I loved the church I was helping plant, so I didn't want to leave. But I also wanted the deeper, ongoing relationships that I saw in house churches (and had experienced during our first year in Fowlerville). Unfortunately, I lived and worked an hour away from my church, making such daily relationships logistically impossible. I needed something closer to home—something that included people who lived near me so that we could spend more time together than a weekly meeting.

I asked Pastor Dan if it would be all right if I started a house church with my girlfriend, Robin. And being the kingdom-minded shepherd he has always been, he gave me his resounding support.

Shortly after that, Robin and I had our first meeting in her parents' basement, joined by a Baptist coworker of mine.

Yeast Rises

As Robin, Tony, and I met, we discussed the meaning of "church" and why we do certain church things the way we do them. A few other friends joined us. We started taking communion together. We discussed the Bible. We prayed. We debated. We laughed, cried, and loved. We weren't a bunch of bitter, frustrated Christians who had left our old churches. We were all still fully engaged in other churches but loved what we were experiencing in our special meetings.

Soon, new converts started coming. Some we led to the Lord at college or at work. A few came to our group as lost people and quickly surrendered to Jesus. In short, as the kingdom of God spread within us, it also infiltrated our daily lives. Coworkers, classmates, friends, family, and neighbors started coming to Jesus. And we also continued to absorb Christians who still attended their conventional churches yet thought of us as their actual church family.

Within two years, we grew to a small network with about twenty-five people attending the main house church, plus a men's group, a women's group, and multiple Bible studies meeting during workplace break times. Over forty people were involved.

Jesus said the kingdom of heaven is like a little bit of yeast that works its way through a large batch of dough (Matthew 13:33). Our little house church quickly infiltrated our networks of relationships. People came to salvation. We baptized them in bathtubs, pools, ponds, and more. Lives were transformed. People were set free from addictions and life-controlling habits and attitudes. As the yeast of the kingdom worked its way deeper into our individual hearts, it also worked its way outward into our families and friendships.

Churches Are People; Not Places or Programs

As I mentioned in this book's preface, I eventually handed off that original house church to one of the participants and served a few years on staff at a more traditional church. All the satellite groups (the men's group, women's group, and all the Bible studies) stopped, and a couple of key families moved out of state. The network abruptly contracted back down to a single house church, but it continued for several years. Many of the relationships formed there continue to this day.

The two-and-a-half years I spent on staff at the large, conventional church were difficult for me. On one hand, I knew what it took to make disciples, and on the other hand, I felt my hands were tied when it came to doing it.

I was frustrated much of the time. I could successfully organize a large party where a hundred or so teens would join us and have loads of fun. Some might even respond to the short gospel message we included. But the next week, we'd be right back to the same mid-sized group of teens we had before the event. I only worked there part time, so all my working hours were eaten up by menial tasks—answering emails, documenting receipts, prepping sermons, creating graphics, editing video, attending meetings, and planning for the next big event that would produce the same stagnant results as the last one. I often peered out my office window, wondering why I was designing bulletin inserts while people were perishing.

I learned some valuable lessons during that season and grew tremendously in the Lord. But transitioning out of that staff role and back into hosting a house church was like a breath of fresh air. I felt like I was finally back to making disciples.

The English word "church" has an uncertain origin—perhaps from the Greek *kuriake* (meaning "of the Lord"), which made its way into the German *kirika* and, eventually, the Old English *cirice*. Some scholars think it may come from the Latin *circus,* meaning "circle"—because the early Christians apparently sat in a circle when they gathered. And this word made its way to the Anglo-Saxon *kirke,* which is presumably why many old church buildings in Scotland are called "kirks" (even though they may no longer be round).[4]

Whatever the case, the English word "church" is unrelated to the Greek word used in Scripture: *ekklēsia.* This word comes from two Greek roots and can be literally rendered as "called-out ones." It refers to an assemblage of people who can be identified together. The word was generally understood in the Greco-Roman world as a regular statutory assembly, but it could also be generically used to define any group of people gathered for a united purpose.[5]

In Acts 19, the word *ekklēsia* is used three times in reference to both (1) the confused, riotous mob who lashed out in response to the gospel's impact in Ephesus (vv. 32, 41) and (2) a legal assembly or court where formal charges could be made and settled

---

[4] Shayne Looper, "The Curious Origin of the Word 'Church,'" Register Guard, accessed March 13, 2020, https://www.registerguard.com/opinion/20200313/looper-column-curious-origin-of-word-church.

[5] "ἐκκλησία," Frederick W. Danker, *A Greek-English Lexicon of the New Testament and Other Early Christian Literature, Third Edition*, trans. William F. Arndt and F. Wilbur Gingrich, ed. Walter Bauer, (Chicago: University of Chicago Press, 2000), 303–4.

(v. 39). But in most of the New Testament, the word is used in reference to the united people of God, whether locally or globally.

What's clear is that the word *ekklēsia* cannot be used to refer to an isolated individual who claims to be a Christian but does not regularly gather with other believers. When people say the catchy slogan, "Don't go to church; be the church," some wrongly focus on the first phrase and think they're doing the second. There is no such thing as "being the church" that does not include purposefully gathering with other Christians.

At the same time, however, nothing in this definition—nor in the examples of New Testament churches—requires a building, programs, big events, sound systems, or much of anything else our culture often deems necessary for an official church. There's nothing wrong with such things; they simply aren't part of the definition. And that means multiplying churches is much simpler than many of us realize.

The Church Is an Organism

I'd like to introduce you to a laptop. This particular laptop is constantly doing bookkeeping for my businesses, writing computer programs that help my in-laws' business thrive, and more. This laptop is a regular fixture in my home and does a great deal of work for me and for others.

This laptop belongs to my wife, Robin. And the truth is, it doesn't technically do any of the things I just listed—Robin does. Robin is an amazing person even without her laptop, but she's able to do so much with her laptop that would be difficult if not impossible without it.

Sometimes, people introduce the church they attend like I just introduced my wife's laptop. But most churches as we think about them today are simply organizations—legal corporations that local Christians use to accomplish more than they could on their own.

I'm not married to a laptop; I'm married to the woman who uses it. And Jesus isn't married to any of the Christian organizations in your town. His bride is the church, which is comprised of people.

When it comes to the word *church*, there's a difference between the organism and organizations. The organism is the body of Christ—a living entity, comprised of multiple Christians, that is:

- unstoppable (Matthew 16:18)
- interdependent (Romans 12:5; 1 Corinthians 12:12–31)
- interactive (1 Corinthians 14:26)
- holy and set-apart (1 Corinthians 3:17; 1 Peter 2:5)
- non-rigid (John 3:8)
- the pillar of truth in the world (1 Timothy 3:15)
- a revelation of God's wisdom (Ephesians 3:10)
- the dwelling place of God (Ephesians 2:19–22)

An organization, on the other hand, is a structured institution—whether a legal corporation or otherwise—that coordinates the efforts of a group for various programs and activities.

We often call such organizations *churches* (and sometimes *parachurch ministries*), but these labels can be confusing because they don't adequately describe the word *church* as Jesus intended.

The best churches are organized organisms—living collections of believers from the body of Christ who purposefully unite to worship God, engage in relationship with one another, follow Jesus together, and make new disciples. This can happen with or without an official organization with articles of incorporation or other legal recognition, but it cannot happen without the Christians involved agreeing on the purpose of their regular meetings.

Like my wife's laptop, quality organizations make the organism more effective, not less. But not all organizations are the same. Church organizations (conventional and house church alike) operate in one of four ways: as cages, playpens, hamster wheels, or tools.

- **Cages**: Some organizations stifle the organism, pacifying Christians with dead rituals and a form of godliness that has no real power. Like glorified veal farms, Christians find themselves trapped there, their strength waning and their creativity stifled.
- **Playpens**: Some organizations draw artificial lines around the organism, allowing the body of Christ to engage in safe, enjoyable meetings but segmenting the Christians

off from the rest of the world and never encouraging them to do anything risky. Some of the most thriving congregations fit this category. They have life, fun, creativity, and vibrancy; but they grow mostly by welcoming other Christians who want to play with the same toys, not by winning the lost.

- **Hamster wheels**: Some organizations lock the organism in an endless cycle of fruitless activity and works, burning through money and wearing people out with events and programs that never actually accomplish anything of substance in people's lives. Such organizations often understand our mission and see the great needs in the community around them, but they think the solution is another program, another class, another event, another outreach, or another give-away. Yet no matter how much money they spend, they see few if any conversions.
- **Tools**: Some organizations serve as tools that make the organism more effective in its mission and purpose, leveraging strengths and synergizing action to affect a greater impact than if the organization didn't exist. These organizations are marked by new converts who quickly thrive in their relationships with God and his people. These organizations are often plagued with messy situations that need to be cleaned up, and they need constant fine-tuning to remain effective. But they are well worth the extra work to maintain.

The best organizations are tools in the hands of the organism, enabling the body of Christ to accomplish more for God's kingdom than they could do without a formal, institutional identity. Traditional churches are not bad as long as they fit the fourth category of organizational functionality—making the body of Christ more effective. The same goes for house churches.

I bless every healthy church that is effectively reaching the lost and multiplying God's kingdom. I have nothing against conventional forms of church. But I do boldly speak against the cages, playpens, and hamster wheels that have effectively neutered God's people. Such institutions ought to either repent or close their doors.

I believe I'm in the fourth type of organization. But I know not all house churches are. If you're currently in a house church that is a cage, playpen, or hamster wheel, perhaps this book will help you rethink the organization of your group. And if you're thriving in a large church that is an effective tool in the hands of Christ's body, keep doing what you're doing! We need you! We are all in this mission together, and we need all manner of useful tools engaged in making disciples who make disciples.

In August 2019, when my one house church had multiplied into a small, thriving network of four house churches, we decided to finally form a legal organization. One of our house churches remained independent while the other three joined efforts. We selected a leadership team, wrote our bylaws, appointed board members, built a website, and registered with the state of Michigan and the General Council of the Assemblies of God. Roots Church was born. We continued to operate as a network of house churches but now in a more formal capacity.

Clearly, I'm not against organizations. I'm not against church names, leadership, or even denominations. As long as these things are making the *ekklēsia* more effective rather than less, I celebrate them. We simply need to watch that our organizations remain effective tools in the hands of the organism.

A biblical church is a living entity comprised of multiple Christians who purposefully gather in a way that they can be identified together—uniting in vision, mission, and identity as a spiritual family. And that can happen anywhere, even in your home.

The Awakening

While house churches have been common expressions of Christianity in much of the world for centuries (especially in Asia), we are now seeing them spread throughout the modern, western world as well. What George Barna saw emerging in the early 2000s is now unfolding on a grand scale.

Many Christians in America finally took notice when the well-known author and preacher Francis Chan left his church of thousands in Simi Valley, California, in 2010. About a year later, Chan started a house church network in San Francisco, California. For a while, his work there was easy to ignore, but the publishing of his 2018 book *Letters to the Church* brought house churches back into popular dialogue. Some pastors I know began discussing how to integrate some of Chan's ideas into the small-group ministries at their large churches. Other pastors I know either debated the ideas in the book or flat-out rejected them.

Meanwhile, house churches and house-church networks have been cropping up all over the United States, mostly under the radar. Many are surprised to learn of already-thriving networks in their region that grew up without fanfare.

I don't believe God is finished with traditional churches. Some people will always be most effectively reached by these organizations. But now another form of church gathering is emerging in the West, and we would do well to understand it. I've personally found these house-church networks to be the most fruitful and rewarding form of ministry I've ever experienced.

Jesus is the one who will build his church (Matthew 16:18). Our role isn't to find the right strategy but to shepherd the local flock in such a way that they thrive and multiply as Jesus—the Chief Shepherd—entrusts more of his sheep to our care. The benefits of running house churches are not that it's the best organizational structure or that it attracts people better than other ministry models. The benefits of running house churches are that they are personal, interactive, and easy to replicate; any mature believers who feel led by the Spirit to start one can do so, and they are small enough that any unhealthy house churches will hurt only a few people, while the healthy ones will multiply to transform countless lives.

This movement is happening all over the world and may even be happening in your neighborhood. The question is whether it's happening in your home. And if it's not, I want to help train and equip you to plant, grow, and multiply a healthy, thriving, multiplying house church—not so you can simply say you started a church but so you can make disciples for Jesus.

How Many People Have You Baptized in Your Bathtub?

My bathroom has become a holy place. We've baptized more than twenty people in our bathtub over the last decade. Add to that the many we've baptized in swimming pools, lakes, rivers, and a few in the tarp-lined bed of a pickup truck, and suddenly, the nature of this awakening begins to take form.

Your bathroom can become a holy place. Your kitchen table can be a disciple-making machine. Your living room can be a sanctuary where people encounter the presence of God. You don't need to have a big house; you simply need to have a willing and obedient heart.

CHAPTER 2:

WHAT IS A CHURCH?

Imagine you find yourself stranded on a deserted island with nothing but a copy of the Bible. You have no experience with Christianity whatsoever, and all you know about the Church will come from your reading of the Bible. How would you imagine a church to function?

—Francis Chan

My missionary friend and I nonchalantly entered a high-rise apartment complex. More would be joining us, but everyone had to arrive in groups no larger than three and on a staggered schedule so as not to raise suspicion. I was in communist China, visiting an underground church, although the gathering, above the twentieth floor, was anything but underground. The meeting was secret, and the government could arrest everyone involved if we were found out. It didn't help that the host's apartment shared a wall with the home of a police officer.

When about twenty people had gathered, we began. One of the ladies was a new believer, but most of the participants were leaders of other house churches. Someone pulled out a small keyboard, and with the volume turned down on its little speaker, the people began to sing softly, trying to be heard by the Lord but not the neighbor.

I was told to preach softly. When I said something the people liked, they clapped with only the palms of their hands or fingertips, making the motion but avoiding any more sound than a soft tapping, sometimes not even touching their hands together.

Several people were healed in that meeting, but I think I may have been the most impacted. This was only one of the underground churches in China where I had the privilege of ministering, and it was life changing.

Some months before my journey to China, I preached in an American megachurch that had thousands of members. It was a Sunday night meeting reserved for small-group leaders in the church, and about three hundred people were present. The contrast with China couldn't be starker. They had the latest audio-visual equipment. Their stage was lit with more lights than the Chinese apartment had people. Everything was sleek, clean, and modern. The music during worship sounded like a professional concert. And Jesus showed up in that meeting too, healing many and strengthening the leaders.

I've helped plant more than ten churches in Uganda. Some meet in mud structures. Some have walls and roofs made of thin, corrugated sheet metal. One of our churches began in a small tent made of sticks, banana leaves, and several colorful dresses that the women donated for walls. Sometimes, when one of our churches first starts, they meet under a tree.

Back when I was ten, my adult brother, fifteen years my senior, attended an Antiochian Orthodox church. From time to time, I'd visit him for a weekend at his home in Ohio and attend church with him and his family on Sunday morning. I still remember the smell of the incense and marveling at the iconography that covered the windows, walls, and all the way up into the dome that sat atop the sanctuary. I remember the kindness and friendliness of the priest and the hauntingly beautiful drone of the chanted liturgy.

My brother's church was drastically different from the small Pentecostal church in which I was raised. I was used to a lot of singing and dancing—arms raised in worship while three or four ladies rattled tambourines on their hips. Between songs, some shouted out with tongues and interpretation or a prophetic word. Our pastor preached long sermons, punctuated by "amens" and "hallelujahs." There was an air of spontaneity, even though there was a regular pattern to every meeting. We had an unwritten liturgy all our own, and nearly any Pentecostal Christian would have understood it.

Years later, I read *The Heavenly Man* by Paul Hattaway.[6] There, I learned about persecuted Christians in China and how they were multiplying God's kingdom in homes, apartments, and even caves—now taking the gospel throughout the Muslim world in their back-to-Jerusalem movement.[7] This was the first time I ever heard about house churches, and it led me to many other texts. Little did I know, I would one day visit some of those secret churches, let alone lead a house church network in the United States.

I soon learned about persecuted Christians all over the world, in places like Iran, Nigeria, northern India, and more. Many gather in as small of a group as possible so as not to incur the wrath of an oppressive government or majority religion. In North Korea, sometimes people are executed simply for owning a Bible, so Christians have secret hiding places for their Bibles. They wait until dark, drawing the curtains and whispering the Scriptures to their families. They might whisper some songs, but only when they're "in a bold mood."[8]

Can all these Christian gatherings be considered real churches? What qualifies as a church? How do we know if the meetings we're attending are real churches?

---

6 Paul Hattaway, *The Heavenly Man: The Remarkable True Story of Chinese Christian Brother Yun* (Marietta, South Carolina: Monarch Books, 2002).

7 For more information, please visit https://BackToJerusalem.com.

8 "This Little Buried Old Bible is Her Most Treasured Possession of Kim Da-Bin," Open Doors, accessed July 14, 2021, https://www.opendoors.org.hk/en-US/news/latest/this-little-buried-old-bible-is-her-most-treasured-possession-of-kim-da-bin/.

What Does the Bible Say?

Some Scriptures are descriptive while others are prescriptive. In other words, some Scriptures tell you what happened (descriptive), and others tell you what ought to happen (prescriptive). The descriptive passages contain principles we ought to consider, though we're not necessarily required to do everything they did. But the prescriptive passages are necessary components in Christian meetings.

Sometimes we can misinterpret the Scriptures when we treat descriptive passages as though they're prescriptive. Just because someone did something a particular way doesn't mean it must always be done that way. However, these things are written for us for a reason, and principles can be unearthed as we study them.

Consider the following descriptive passage:

> They devoted themselves to the apostles' teaching and to fellowship, to the breaking of bread and to prayer. Everyone was filled with awe at the many wonders and signs performed by the apostles. All the believers were together and had everything in common. They sold property and possessions to give to anyone who had need. Every day they continued to meet together in the temple courts. They broke bread in their homes and ate together with glad and sincere hearts, praising God and enjoying the favor of all the people. And the Lord added to their number daily those who were being saved. (Acts 2:42–47)

Does this mean we must all sell our property and join a commune? Of course not. It's simply describing what the early Christians did at the time of Acts 2. We do, however, learn some principles that appear consistently outside of Acts 2.

- Dedication to sound doctrine—faithfulness to the Scriptures, which includes learning from spiritual elders
- Fellowship—authenticity, transparency, and friendship
- Breaking bread—sharing a meal or taking communion
- Prayer—dialoguing with God together
- Generosity—giving to each other and the larger mission
- Daily gathering—friendships that extend beyond meetings
- Meeting openly and in homes—expressing public and private faith
- Praise—celebrating God for who he is and what he has done
- Growth—Jesus adds people to healthy churches

We can all look at these principles and say, "Yes, that sounds like a healthy church."

Still another descriptive passage is found in Titus 1:5, where Paul writes, "The reason I left you in Crete was that you might put in order what was left unfinished and appoint elders in every town, as I directed you." Here we learn that those who oversee networks of small churches have a responsibility to identify and appoint qualified elders to oversee each small flock of Jesus's sheep. (As I'll explain in chapter 9, elders are also called pastors, which is a word that literally means "shepherds." See 1 Peter 5:1–4.) Network-level leadership from recognized ministers is important and healthy for growing churches to thrive.

We also have various prescriptive passages. For example, Paul writes, "What then shall we say, brothers and sisters? When you come together, each of you has a hymn, or a word of instruction, a revelation, a tongue or an interpretation. Everything must be done so that the church may be built up" (1 Corinthians 14:26). In this passage, we learn that church meetings are supposed to be highly interactive. Everyone has something to contribute to the meeting. Some actions on the list are spontaneous gifts of the Spirit (like tongues and interpretation), and others are planned or prepared (like hymns or instruction).

Yet another prescriptive passage is Hebrews 10:24–25, which says, "And let us consider how we may spur one another on toward love and good deeds, not giving up meeting together, as some are in the habit of doing, but encouraging one another—and all the more as you see the Day approaching." Clearly, action is expected from Christians. If someone's life has no action, everyone else has a responsibility to spur them on. Everyone has a responsibility to encourage everyone, which means we do not settle for one person encouraging from a stage while the flock sits silently. We all exercise our voices to build one another up.

Is Your Church a Church?

Looking at what the Bible says about churches, is your church a church? It doesn't really matter if it's an apartment in China, an ornate cathedral, a sleek megachurch, a Pentecostal party, or a handful of people in your living room. Is there devotion to sound doctrine, real fellowship, communion, prayer, generosity, friendships, evangelism, praise, righteous leadership, interactivity, spiritual gifts, encouragement, and action?

If so, we can look at the Scriptures and comfortably say, "Yes, this is a church." But if not, the Scriptures would imply that things need to change. Either we need to become a real church, or we need to go find one.

But be forewarned: The church is comprised of people, not buildings or programs. Such structures can hinder or aid the people in being the church, but they are not the church. Speaking against a church is speaking against people Jesus loves. Be careful that in your confrontation of that which hinders, you don't forget to love the people in the middle of it all.

Pastor Dan Mohler once told me a story of a woman who said, "I left that church because no one there was loving."

Dan answered, "I don't see how that's possible. *You* were there!"

In other words, often our indictments against our former churches are actually indictments against ourselves, because we were components of those churches. Before you leave a church, become a pacesetter there. Live the Spirit-filled life you wish everyone else was living. You'll either change the culture over time, or you'll be rejected and pushed out. And if you're rejected for loving well, making disciples, and living for Jesus and his kingdom, then don't choose bitterness. Instead, rejoice!

Remember, you joined that church for a reason. You likely saw something healthy. Regardless, while you were participating in that church, you grew enough to see what needed to change to make the congregation more in line with Jesus and his heart for us and the world.

Be careful not to beat up on Jesus's bride. Church organizations are generally full of people who are sincerely trying to follow the Lord and would change if they saw a better way of living. Be that example.

If you feel the need to approach church leaders with concerns, do so with gentleness and respect (1 Peter 3:15). As Paul taught Timothy, "Do not rebuke an older man harshly, but exhort him as if he were your father. Treat younger men as brothers, older women as mothers, and younger women as sisters, with absolute purity" (1 Timothy 5:1–2). When Scripture tells us to "honor one another above yourselves" (Romans 12:10), it doesn't say that the other Christians need to be honorable. This command is about your behavior, not theirs. Again, set the example. How you address problems is, in many ways, more important than the problem you're addressing.

Also watch that your concerns are merited on biblical grounds and not merely human tradition. When style preferences and methods become more important to us than people, we've lost the heart of the Lord. Jesus flipped tables in the court of the Gentiles in the temple because his Father's house was supposed to be a house of prayer for all nations. (See Mark 11:17.) Yes, he was upset that they had made the temple into a market, but his primary concern was for people and their access to God.

Today, we are the temple. (See 1 Corinthians 3:16.) Some of us have lost sight of what matters most. Perhaps Jesus needs to flip some tables in our hearts to bring us back to true worship.

The Church Is Bigger than You

In Scripture, we find the word *church* used both for a local congregation and the global collection of all Christians. Many times, Luke, Paul, and John used the plural word *churches*, indicating that each local congregation—at the time, essentially all meeting in homes—was a church in its own right. At the same time, Jesus talked about building "my church" (Matthew 16:18). Somehow, there are both churches and Jesus's one, singular global church.

The book of Ephesians gives us a wonderful look at Jesus's worldwide church. He is the head over everything for us (1:22). Through us, God's multifaceted wisdom is revealed to high-ranking angels and demons in the spiritual realm (3:10). And a healthy human marriage is a prophetic picture of Jesus and his church relating to each other (5:21–33).

Meanwhile, John addressed the book of Revelation to seven churches throughout Asia Minor, which today is basically the nation of Turkey. From what we know of history, these were all either house churches or networks of house churches within the various cities. In Revelation 2 and 3, Jesus had something different to say to each church, just as he still does. But the rest of John's vision was for the global church (and continues to speak to us today).

Whenever God speaks on a small scale, it's to connect us to what he is speaking on a grand scale. Jesus wants a unified bride. He ministers to individuals to help them integrate into churches, and he ministers to churches to integrate us into his global church.

As I'll show in chapter 9, apostles, prophets, evangelists, pastors, and teachers are necessary "until we all reach unity in the faith and in the knowledge of the Son of God and become mature, attaining to the whole measure of the fullness of Christ" (Ephesians 4:13). If we're not moving toward unity among all Christians, then something is broken.

But we must be careful with this line of thinking. Sometimes people seek unity with each other at the expense of seeking unity with Christ. They look horizontally—examining each other and deciding where to compromise for the sake of fellowship. But real unity happens vertically, when we look at Jesus and decide where to sacrifice to better reveal him to others.

My body can function because all the parts are receiving conscious and unconscious commands from my brain (head). If my legs tried to receive instruction from each other, I would have a terrible time trying to walk. If one leg tried to be exactly like the other, I would have to jump everywhere. But where do you suppose I would jump if my legs weren't receiving their commands from my head? I could end up anywhere!

The church is the body of Christ. This means that the true church is connected to him as our head. Some of his limbs have spasms now and then. Some of his members are lethargic or weak. But if the equipping ministers among us will do the work of training and equipping the saints, then "speaking the truth in love, we will grow to become in every respect the mature body of him who is the head, that is, Christ. From him the whole body, joined and held together by every supporting ligament, grows and builds itself up in love, as each part does its work" (Ephesians 4:15–16).

In my observation and experience, nothing brings unity like shared mission. I've led mission teams comprised of people from three or four denominations with theological differences, but we all became more like Jesus by the end of the trip. Those who were uncomfortable with miracles at the beginning of the trip were ministering healing by the end because they saw it in action and couldn't deny it. Those who were over-focused on miracles learned to love more fully because they saw people living out their faith in practical, non-flashy ways. And the various ministry gifts operating among us both showed us the sort of lifestyle that was available in Christ and helped facilitate conversations that led everyone toward a better understanding of what they saw. Shared mission brings unity because unity is less about an appearance of ecumenism and more about obedience to the same Jesus.

Gospel Houses and Unity

Why all this talk about unity in the global body of Christ? It's simple. One of the most common refrains I've heard against house churches is that they can sometimes be cult-like. Sometimes they're started by disgruntled Christians who carry wounds from past negative experiences in a previous church. Sometimes they're started by someone who has a lot of giftedness but poor or underdeveloped theology, and they just want an outlet to peddle their pet doctrines. And sometimes they're started by spiritual wolves who actually want to prey on people.

These three unhealthy types of house churches (and probably more) have one thing in common: None of them consider themselves part of the other churches in town. They see themselves with a certain sense of exclusivity and pride.

Real churches are extensions of Jesus's global church. They consider themselves part of the larger work God is doing in their region, not the *only* work. They look to Jesus as the head and celebrate every other ministry that is doing the same.

I'm not saying we must partner with every church in town. Some doctrines and practices are utterly disconnected from Jesus. We are under no obligation to see ourselves as being united with a Jehovah's Witness Kingdom Hall or a church with homosexual clergy, for example.

But when it comes to most churches, our differences in the finer points of doctrine become irrelevant if we're all aiming to obey the same Jesus—loving God and others. Unity is not based on our perfectly aligned doctrines. Unity is based on whether or not our eyes are on Jesus, beholding his glory, and being transformed more and more into his image and likeness (2 Corinthians 3:18).

So is your house church a church? Is it comprised of people who gather in love to worship, fellowship, pray, grow in sound doctrine, give generously, serve each other, encourage each other, practice spiritual gifts together, learn from Jesus together, develop friendships, receive communion, and obey Jesus, joining him in his mission? Do the people of your church see themselves as being on the same team as many other churches in your region? Together, are you looking to Jesus as the head, surrendering anything that doesn't look like him and regularly being conformed into his image? Is the Holy Spirit present and active in your meetings?

If yes, then it doesn't matter if you meet in an apartment, a cathedral, an auditorium, or under a tree. The people with whom you gather are a church that is part of Jesus's church. That's the sort of gathering that I regularly have in my home, and I pray this is either happening or about to happen in your home.

CHAPTER 3:

GOSPEL HOUSE DNA

Sure, there are advantages to meeting in homes: comfort, economy, warmth, infinite expandability, and more. For family warmth, there's no place like home. But what *is happening is way more important than* where *it's happening.*

—Jim Rutz

To the untrained eye, an apple seed and a pear seed can look essentially the same, but each one carries the unique DNA of a completely different plant. If you plant a pear seed, you can wish with all your heart that an apple tree will grow, but it will never happen. The DNA of the seed will replicate.

When I planted my first house church in 2005, I didn't really know what I was doing. I didn't yet understand such concepts as culture and vision. I simply knew I wanted something that looked like what I saw in the Bible.

That first house church was healthy in many ways. And it grew. But I didn't understand how to multiply it. I knew how to spread it—starting various satellite groups. But none of those satellite groups became house churches of their own. They were all Bible studies or affinity groups, where people gathered around a common interest. I had a network of groups but only one house church. The DNA of multiplication was not actually in the original house church.

Scientists have found ways to genetically engineer certain crops so that they are either seedless or else produce sterile seeds. It's not natural. One must do something unnatural or foreign to a plant to stop it from reproducing.

When I started that first house church, it was heavily influenced by the foreign culture of traditional church. Yes, my group was very different in many ways, but I still had a mindset of growth and expansion rather than a mindset of replication. This naturally affected the language I used, the goals I set, the vision I cast, the strategies I employed, and the results that emerged.

Over the years, various house-church leaders I've met have expressed similar struggles. They want to know how to multiply their current house church. But in many cases, it can't be done. Their house church doesn't have the DNA needed to replicate.

Not Just Another Small Group

There are many different types of small groups in western Christianity. Some of them have DNA for multiplication and others don't.

I want to be clear that this book is not against any of these types of groups. They all have their place. We simply need to be clear at the outset that if you're going to plant a house church, it must actually *be* a house church.

The following charts will help you think through what differentiates house churches from all the other forms of small-group ministry:

Bible Studies:	House Churches:
• Whether part of an organized church or just a meeting with friends or family, Bible studies generally unite for the sole purpose of studying the Scriptures and perhaps prayer for one another. • They typically follow an agreed-upon text or a book study that guides the discussion. • Generally, such meetings are facilitated by a designated leader, but some people may gather less formally and allow a curriculum of some sort to guide them. • Such meetings are sometimes marked with a start date and end date, generally dictated by the intended length of the study.	• House churches study the Bible, but unlike Bible studies, they do not follow a fixed curriculum or other book, they are not classes taught by a leader, and they invite insights, revelations, prophetic words, and other gifts of the Spirit from every person in the meeting.

Small-Group Ministry:	House Churches:
• Also known as life groups, community groups, etc. • Many church organizations have found that large Sunday gatherings are insufficient to foster meaningful relationships among people, so they implement a small-group ministry. • Small groups generally gather in homes but may possibly be facilitated in restaurants, coffee shops, office spaces, or classrooms at a church building. • The emphases of such meetings are generally fellowship, guided discussion, and prayer. • In most cases, a small-group leader is appointed to lead discussion and facilitate the schedule. • Discussion is generally guided—sometimes following a book or curriculum or perhaps following a list of discussion questions.	• House churches fellowship and pray like small groups, but their discussion time is not guided with fixed questions or talking points. • Most weeks, the house church pastor doesn't know what the topic of conversation will be at that meeting—only what he or she will briefly share. • According to 1 Corinthians 14:26, every believer in the meeting has something from the Spirit to contribute, and all of these things must be done. • The goal of the meeting is to identify what Jesus is communicating to the entire group through what everyone shares and then meaningfully respond to it.

Affinity Groups:	House Churches:
Some Bible studies or small groups are: • gender-specific (men's breakfast, women's ministry, etc.) • age-specific (youth group, senior citizens ministry, etc.) or • interest-specific (crafting group, hunting group, camping group, homeschool moms group, etc.) • These affinity-based groups can be great for inviting friends with shared interests or from shared walks of life, but they are rarely capable of reaching and making disciples of whole families (at least on their own).	• House churches may contain people who join because of shared interests (like affinity groups), but those shared interests are not the point of the group—in fact, those shared interests may never even come up in the house-church meeting. The only shared interests discussed are the Lord, his presence, his people, and his Word.

Cell Groups:	House Churches:
• Cell churches often look like typical churches, generally having a building or at least centering around a weekly large gathering. But such churches also have a robust and intentional small-group ministry that is highly organized. • The main church has a pastor, and his or her ministry is spread to cells—easily replicated small groups where people generally discuss material recommended by the main pastor. • Cell groups often follow an in-house curriculum, which may be built on the pastor's Sunday message or anything else the pastor recommends. • Some of the largest churches in the world follow this cell model. It tends to thrive best in cultures where people are used to following directions from strong leaders.	• House churches ideally network together (like cell churches) for greater organizational impact, but unlike cell groups, there is no lead pastor recommending the weekly topic of discussion. Instead, each house-church pastor exercises his or her own God-given wisdom in shepherding the sheep Jesus has entrusted to them.

Friend Groups:	House Churches:
• In a completely informal sense, friend groups indeed gather irregularly, simply to enjoy each other while also including a spiritual component to their time together. While they may not think of themselves as a small-group ministry, they do minister to each other in the context of a group that's small. • While components of church may indeed happen in such informal gatherings—perhaps a spontaneous time of singing together, discussion about the Bible, a spiritual gift or two, and even prayer or communion—the irregular schedule of such meetings and the fact that they are not intentional (and therefore might be nothing more than a hangout or game night) make them a poor substitute for a purposeful church meeting.	• While house churches are comprised of friends who hopefully spend time together outside of scheduled house-church meetings, they are more deliberate about pursuing God together than any ordinary friend group. House churches gather weekly with a dedicated focus on ministering to each other, learning from each other, praying for each other, and loving Jesus together.

House churches are regular, self-contained (though ideally networked), self-replicating gatherings of believers in homes where every believer is a minister and where a dedicated local pastor takes appropriate biblical responsibility for the spiritual well-being of the people in the group.

House churches are *regular* in that they meet at a scheduled time and place. Most follow the early church model of meeting weekly, which I find to be best, but others have been known to meet every other week or even monthly. I have yet to see a house church that only met monthly and still thrived. People need far more interaction with one another. In fact, one of our house churches meets three times a week! People are creatures of habit, and our schedules generally operate on a weekly rhythm, which means weekly meetings will always have the best momentum.

House churches are also *self-contained*. Each house church is a full expression of Christianity, which means if someone only ever attends house church and never a larger meeting, they are adequately obeying the biblical command to gather with other believers. In house church, we have communion, worship, prayer, fellowship, spiritual gifts, evangelistic outreaches, baptism, and biblical instruction. We live life together beyond a weekly meeting. We are not only friends in our gatherings but throughout the week.

And thirdly, house churches are *self-replicating*. Each house church is not merely a spoke attached to the hub of the group that spawned it. Each house church is a potential hub. Every healthy house church contains the capacity to raise up new leaders and start new house churches.

The Church Jesus Started

Jesus prioritized making disciples over hosting great meetings. He regularly gathered with people in homes, both for evangelism and discipleship. He also took disciples to the towns, the hillsides, and the streets, sometimes sending them out in pairs to preach the gospel and minister healing and deliverance.

By the time the disciples finally received the Holy Spirit, they knew exactly what to do. They met in homes. They preached in the temple courts and synagogues. They developed relationships, served each other, and ministered publicly with boldness. They prayed together, reached out to nearby communities, and ministered healing, working miracles, signs, and wonders in the streets.

The church Jesus started attracted people, but attraction wasn't their priority. In fact, they sometimes acted in ways that frightened people and made them not want to join their ranks (Acts 5:13). This church introduced people to our Lord through demonstrations of God's power and love, coupled with a clear proclamation of the gospel. This brought them to a crisis of decision. Those who couldn't deny the truth they encountered either surrendered to King Jesus and joined his family or else rejected him.

The cost of joining was high. A certain social stigma was involved with identifying as a follower of the Way. Following Jesus meant total surrender to this King and his kingdom. It sometimes meant the confiscation of property, the loss of family, and perhaps even torture, imprisonment, or death.

Too often, we try so hard to include everyone that Christians in our churches don't even know life transformation is available. They think the church is either full of hypocrites who wear masks or authentic people who are steeped in sin but are at least honest about it. Either way, they see church as little more than a collection of broken people who talk about holiness but can never experience it.

But in the church Jesus started, people—although not yet completely perfect—experienced real transformation and lived closely enough together that others could observe a changed life. Thus, a terrorist like Saul could experience a genuine conversion and become the apostle Paul, no longer identified as a persecutor but as a minister who emphasized love and unity among believers. Those who pretended to be believers but embraced lifestyles of willful sin and self-indulgence were either corrected or excommunicated. And those who pridefully lied to the Holy Spirit were supernaturally struck down in the face of truth.

The church Jesus started was both beautiful and terrifying. The cost of joining wasn't merely the potential for persecution but included a standard of living imposed by the gospel—a standard where genuine transformation is available to those who wholly trust God. Real holiness is a vital trait of Jesus's true church.

Establishing Culture on the Gospel

The word *gospel* means "good news." In Christian terms, the gospel is the good news about Jesus—specifically who he is, what he has done, and what he has made available in his kingdom.

Who is Jesus? He is God in the flesh, perfectly revealing the Father to us. What has he done? He came to earth as a human being, lived a sinless life, died a criminal's death in our place, and rose to life victorious over sin, death, and the grave—all in fulfillment of hundreds of years of prophecy. Today, he is seated in heaven at the right hand of Father God—the highest place of authority in existence. And what has he made available? Complete wholeness of both body and spirit but, most importantly, spiritual and relational union with God.

The gospel is the answer to everything.

Our union with Jesus in his death, resurrection, and victorious life at the right hand of the Father permeates everything I teach and do in my church. When a couple comes to me for marriage advice, we talk about the gospel. When someone asks for parenting tips, we talk about the gospel. When someone needs to process inner pain, resolve a relational mess, or recalibrate their priorities, we talk about the gospel.

The gospel isn't only a message of salvation. It's a message for thriving in all of life. As a house-church pastor, you'll encounter all manner of situations that you aren't taught to handle in Bible school. But if you have a solid grasp of the gospel, you will thoroughly be equipped to manage most of them.[9]

In my network of house churches, the gospel is our central theme. Our house churches don't multiply in response to some sort of secret power in our organizational model. Our house churches multiply because real people have been impacted by a real gospel that has transformed them into world-changers.

If you want to plant a house church, there's one thing you need to understand more than any method—it's a man, and his name is Jesus. And the more fully you believe his gospel and walk in union with him, the more easily you will start a church and the more effectively it will reproduce.

We could say so much about the gospel—enough to fill entire volumes of books. But at the core of everything I ever teach are these three simple truths:

First, we begin our union with Jesus by being united with him in his death. This doesn't require a literal, physical death. It simply requires that we so surrender to Jesus that we consider our old life to be dead. (See Romans 6:11.) Paul wrote, "I have been crucified with Christ and I no longer live, but Christ lives in me. The life I now live in the body, I live by faith in the

---

[9] Know your limits, though. Your role is to preach the gospel. Most of us, however, are not licensed counselors. Always refer people to Christian professional help when appropriate. Your gospel influence plus Christ-centered professional counseling will provide a powerful environment for the person's growth and transformation.

Son of God, who loved me and gave himself for me" (Galatians 2:20).

It's like signing your name to the bottom of a blank contract, handing it to Jesus, and saying, "Fill in whatever details you like, no matter what it costs me. You're worth any price. I surrender my definitions of morality, my ideas about who I am, and my hopes and dreams for my future. And I willingly embrace your definitions of morality, your ideas about who I am, and your hopes and dreams for our future. No matter how difficult it is for me, I know your way is better. I would rather live united with you than spend another moment apart from you."

When we confess our sin and surrender to Jesus, he doesn't merely cover or overlook our sins; he removes them entirely. He cleanses and purifies us from all unrighteousness. (See 1 John 1:9.) He sets us free from sin altogether. (See Romans 6:6–7.) If we ever slip up, Jesus will still speak in our defense. (See 1 John 2:2.) But we are no longer ruled by sin. (See Romans 6:6, 14.) We have become the righteousness of God in Christ Jesus. (See 2 Corinthians 5:21.)

Second, we receive new life from the Holy Spirit. Those who are united with Jesus in his death also receive his resurrection. (See Romans 6:5.) Even now, before the end-time resurrection of the dead that the Bible promises, we experience a down payment of resurrection life. Paul wrote that "the one who has fashioned us for this very purpose is God, who has given us the Spirit as a deposit, guaranteeing what is to come" (2 Corinthians 5:5).

In this way, the same "Spirit of him who raised Jesus from the dead" comes to dwell in us right now (Romans 8:11). He then transforms us to make us into new creations. The old life we used to live is gone, and we become entirely new people. (See 2 Corinthians 5:17.) Not only that, but this new self is "created to be like God in true righteousness and holiness" (Ephesians 4:24).

Third, we are transformed to be like Jesus as he presently is. First John 4:17 says, "This is how love is made complete among us so that we will have confidence on the day of judgment: In this world we are like Jesus." The New King James Version renders the last phrase, "As he is, so are we in this world." It's as he *is*, not merely as he *was*. Jesus is right now risen and victorious, seated at the right hand of the Father, and we are his body. (See 1 Corinthians 12:27.)

For this reason, Paul writes, "And God raised us up with Christ and seated us with him in the heavenly realms in Christ Jesus" (Ephesians 2:6). Inasmuch as we are in Christ and he is in us, we are where he is, and he is where we are. We walk in his authority, expressing his love, and generally participating in his divine nature. (See 2 Peter 1:3–4.)

The Gospel-Centered House Church

When we apply the above message in a house-church setting, those who believe the message experience dramatic change. When a couple comes to me for advice about a conflict in their marriage, my role is simply to identify the influence of sin and selfishness that we can together bring to the cross and then ask the Holy Spirit to breathe the new life and nature of Jesus into the two of them.[10] When a person complains to me about their work situation, we talk about what death to self and the life of Christ looks like in that environment. When people need a miracle, we who are dead to sin and alive in Christ address the situation in union with Jesus—whether ministering healing, compassion, generosity, encouragement, or whatever he wants to do.

The gospel truly is the answer to everything. When people live it, they become light in darkness, imposing the righteousness, peace, and Spirit-filled joy of God's kingdom upon the chaos of this world. Living it requires understanding it. And for this reason, the gospel must be the central theme of every single house-church meeting.

When your house church talks about forgiveness, for example, the application, surprisingly, is not to forgive. We can't forgive on our own. (See John 15:5.) Rather, the application is to die to our old, unforgiving selves and let Jesus express his perfect forgiveness through us. Likewise, when your house church talks about evangelism, the application is not to get out and preach more. The application is to die to our old, timid selves and let the love, power, and words of Jesus flow through us in our daily interactions. It's never about trying harder in the strength of our

---

[10] This is not to be understood at the expense of seeing a licensed Christian marriage counselor. My role might include referring people to more professional help. But I always start with the gospel, and typically, this is enough to bring the couple back to relational health.

flesh. It's always about dying to self and letting Jesus live through us.

The gospel—lived and proclaimed in the power of the Holy Spirit—is the only environment in which Christians can thrive as God intended. When the gospel takes root in your heart, you will live and proclaim it with conviction, and this will lead to the formation of new disciples and the ongoing transformation of older ones.

Jesus taught, "Others, like seed sown on good soil, hear the word, accept it, and produce a crop—some thirty, some sixty, some a hundred times what was sown" (Mark 4:20). The gospel is a seed that multiplies. It is the DNA of the body of Christ, telling each new cell about its identity and function. If you want to plant a house church, start by making real disciples who have accepted the message of the gospel.

Good Meetings Aren't Enough

The greatest danger to any house church movement is people who know how to start home groups but don't know how to make disciples. What they start may look like house churches, but without purposeful disciple making, it's not at all what Jesus established. It's like they're trying to grow an apple tree from a pear seed.

Ed Stetzer and Warren Bird wrote *Viral Churches* in 2010 as a study of churches that multiply. They gave a chapter of honorable mention to house churches but were rather critical overall. Amid their criticism, they made some important observations that were true, at least in 2010, and (I believe) are still relevant today. Among them,

> To date . . . the North American house church movement has largely been a reform movement, drawing mostly from existing believers who want something "better" than and "different" from what they currently have. Of course, "better" and "different" are highly relative terms. With only a few exceptions house church participants seem to be more excited about the "house" (the fellowship part) than the "church" (making and congregationalizing new disciples). They tend to gather more because of a desire to go deeper on some issue, whether it's Calvinism, charismatic practice, participative worship, or something else, but rarely is that issue a passion for evangelistic reproduction. Too many house churches lack a heart or track record for outreach beyond the existing fold of disenchanted Christians.[11]

Stetzer and Bird have a point. One of the most common hindrances to disciple making is nice church meetings where everyone falls so deeply in love with their small, personal group and the ways they do things that they don't want to mess up their

---

[11] Ed Stetzer and Warren Bird, *Viral Churches: Helping Church Planters Become Movement Makers* (Hoboken, New Jersey: Jossey-Bass, 2010), 123–4.

routine with an influx of new Christians. Worse yet, they probably don't even think about how new Christians might mess things up. They're too distracted with their wonderful meetings. This happens in churches of all sizes, not only house churches; but it seems especially common among independent home groups where two or three families can fall into a warm, tidy, loving routine.

The Right DNA

As already stated, the DNA of the body of Christ is the gospel message. All healthy churches—not only house churches—operate on this fundamental message. The gospel fuels healthy growth and multiplication. Any gathering of people lacking the gospel is not a church.

Just as human DNA is distinct for all humans yet also has variations from one human to the next, every church—large and small—has gospel DNA, and yet there are variations from one church to the next. In a human cell, DNA is made up of a combination of amino acids that link up to tell the cell what to do. Similarly, the DNA of a church is made up of a unique combination of people who link up to define that church.

When thinking of the DNA of house churches, think **D**isciple makers **N**etworked in an **A**rea. Healthy house churches are comprised of disciples who meet and work together to reach lost people in a defined region.

First, let's look at Disciple makers. House church participants must see themselves as disciples who are either already disciple makers or being formed into disciple makers. Jesus invited his first disciples, saying, "Follow me, and I will make you fishers of men" (Matthew 4:19 NKJV). They didn't start out as fishers of men, but Jesus formed them into such as they followed him.

This principle is brilliantly articulated by Jim Putman in his book *DiscipleShift.* I highly recommend this book to any church, large or small, seeking to train people to make disciples who make disciples. Putman notes three things at work in this verse: (1) "Follow me . . .," which means we no longer live for ourselves but take our cues from Jesus; (2) ". . . and I will make you . . .," which means Jesus will not leave us the same but transform us; and (3) ". . . fishers of men," which means we ought to expect to become disciple makers and take obedient action in our new lives. [12]

Every person in your house church either knows how to reach lost people or needs to learn. And they are either actively doing it or not. Nag them like a mother of newlyweds who wants a grandchild! Those who are ready to multiply ought to multiply!

When Christians become secure in their identities in Christ—not only understanding the gospel but working it into the fabric of their lives—we are ready to lead others in their discovery of Christ. Make your house church a gospel-centered gathering where Jesus transforms people more and more into his image and sends them out in his name to make disciples.

---

[12] Jim Putman and Bobby Harrington with Robert E. Coleman. *DiscipleShift: Five Steps that Help Your Church to Make Disciples Who Make Disciples* (Grand Rapids: Zondervan, 2013) Kindle Edition, p. 46.

Next, these disciple makers are Networked. This network starts among the individuals in the house church and extends to other house churches and even the rest of the body of Christ.

Relationships matter. A great deal of leading a house church is helping improve relationships among people. Sometimes, you might help a married couple through a rough patch. Other times, you might help a mother reconcile with her daughter. Or perhaps a couple of people in the house church are irritated with each other, and you have the privilege of restoring their friendship.

Disciples of Jesus are identified by their love for one another. (See John 13:35.) That means if someone in your house church refuses to love the rest of the people in your house church, they're not a disciple of Jesus.

In the same way, consider how the people of your house church talk about other churches. If you see brokenness, bitterness, anger, and resentment, call it out for what it is. The web of relationships between us and all other Christians matters. We don't necessarily have to work together with or even stand alongside every other Christian in our city, but we do need to have the Lord's affection for them.

Furthermore, a synergistic strength emerges when house churches network together with a united purpose. When I only ever led one house church, we spent years with an attendance hovering between fifteen and twenty-five people. We slowly started a couple of other churches, but these, too, were only loosely connected. Then, when we officially organized as a network with a leadership team, a school of ministry, and shared outreaches and events, the move of the Spirit and the burst of growth were dramatic. Purposeful networking introduces new parts of the body of Christ, revealing new aspects of Jesus from which everyone can benefit. House churches multiply faster and healthier when a strong network is in place keeping everyone focused on Jesus, his Spirit, and his mission.

And finally, these disciple makers are networked in an Area. Think of your neighborhood, apartment building, condo, or rural community as a piece of God's mission field where you are responsible to work. If you're pastoring a house church, see yourself as a pastor of people in that locale.

Some of my house churches include people from other cities, states, and even countries who join us via video-conferencing software. But what they experience long-distance through the lens of a camera will always fall short of what we experience as we gather in person—sharing food together, giving real handshakes and hugs, laying hands on one another in prayer, comforting each other with a pat on the shoulder, and living closely enough to each other that we can serve each other when someone is sick, experiencing tragedy, or grieving loss. Furthermore, it's difficult for someone who lives many hours away to join us in reaching out to our local city. We value their spiritual gifts and biblical insights, but we encourage them to start their own house churches in their local regions.

House churches are more than Bible studies, small groups, affinity groups, cell groups, or friend groups. House churches contain elements of all those things, but their DNA is different. House churches are missional communities of Christ-followers who love God, each other, and their communities. House churches receive their DNA from Jesus.

CHAPTER 4: UNDERSTANDING HOUSE CHURCH

Planting a house church, or movement of house churches, is all about loving people into the kingdom. The beauty is the simplicity. It's about reaching out to non-believers, gathering them in, and continuing the process with another house church.

—Joel Comiskey

It's Monday night. The door opens. It's Mike and his wife, Pam. Just like she does every week, Pam brought baked goods—this time, brownies. My seven-year-old, Jeremiah, scurries toward her white-chocolate-covered marshmallows and asks Robin if it's all right. JonMark and Kara are here with their three-year-old son, Evan. They've been living with us for the last several months while they save for a house.

Jeremy just showed up. He's a waiter who doesn't own a car, but people in the group pay for his Uber or Lyft ride each week, so he isn't financially burdened by the trip. Two more couples enter the door: Mary and Hannu, followed by Ron and Belinda. And right on their heels is my niece, Catherine, and her two young boys. Next is Lavinia. And Alex and his wife, Natalie, who co-lead another house church, decided to join us tonight too.

The house is abuzz with people. Some are eating the lasagna we just pulled out of the oven while others are munching on Pam's brownies and homemade caramels. Some are making small talk about the day. Others are following up on what we prayed about last week. One person just asked another if they've been having any pain in their shoulder. After a brief prayer, the person is healed and has restored mobility. Two of the men are raiding my refrigerator for a Sprite and an A&W Root Beer.

"Okay, everyone!" I shout with a smile, "Come on into the living room so we can get started!" One person darts into the guest bathroom while everyone else finds a spot on a piece of furniture or a dining room chair we brought into the room. I sit down on a piano bench, making sure my guests all have the most comfortable seats in the room. Robin takes the kids downstairs for an interactive meeting of their own.[13] Our friend exits the bathroom just in time.

"Father," I pray, "Thanks for being here tonight. Thank you for bringing us together to love each other and encounter you. Jesus, I ask you to bring us deeper into your presence and help us know you more. Speak to us and through us as we seek you

---

[13] I'll share more about what our kids do during house-church meetings in chapter 16.

together. Help us to see you more clearly tonight so we can become more like you. Amen."

"All right!" I grin as we all open our eyes. "What is God speaking to you for tonight?"

For the next ninety minutes, the conversation bounces around, hovering on one topic and then the next. Some people come with insights they received while reading the Scriptures during the week. Others might have received a vision or prophetic word. Someone else sings a song that's on their heart. One person bears their heart about a struggle they're having with a family member. We pause to pray, and the conversation proceeds. When the topic becomes a little too cerebral, someone asks, "Okay, but realistically, how do you do that?" People start offering practical ideas. In the course of conversation, someone remembers a lengthy passage of relevant Scripture, and we read it, pausing from time to time and allowing the words to bolster or correct the conversation we've been having. Or if an hour has passed without an in-depth reading of Scripture, we shift gears and open to the next part of whichever book of the Bible we've been studying for the past few months. Often, the passage connects to our general discussion.

With about a half hour left, it has become obvious that one or two common themes have been woven through every topic we've discussed tonight. This time, it's forgiveness. I step into our open kitchen and grab some fresh bread that I bought today and start pouring grape juice into small paper Dixie cups. The conversation turns to the beauty of what Jesus accomplished for us and the example he set when he forgave those who were actively crucifying him. We pass the bread and thank him for his body, which was broken so that we could together become one whole body in him. Then we eat the bread together.

After passing the cups around as well, I thank him for how completely he forgave each of us. And I thank him that his blood not only covers our sins but also the sins of the people who wronged us. No other sacrifice is necessary. "To wish that the person who wronged you would pay for what they did is to look at Jesus on the cross and say, 'The price you paid is inadequate.'"

I assure everyone that real forgiveness isn't just difficult—it's impossible. Jesus said we could do nothing apart from him. (See John 15:5.) The only way to truly forgive is to die to your own flesh and let Jesus forgive through you. We pray through forgiveness toward the people who wronged us. We speak blessing over them in the name of Jesus. Then we thank Jesus for the blood that sets us free from our own sin and the sins of others. And finally, we drink the cup together.

I rotate around on my bench and turn on my electric piano. Then we all sing together until our two-hour house-church meeting has ended.

As soon as we're officially finished, a few leave right away so they can wake up early the next day for work. Others help clean up the room where the kids were playing. Still others sit around and chat for the next few hours—about nonsense, politics, entertainment, deep matters of the soul, etc.

This is my house church. Or rather, it is one of my house churches. Another gathering of about twenty different people will happen in my home tomorrow night. Meanwhile, another house church connected to our network met tonight in a nearby city. And another will meet tomorrow while my second church meets. I've never been to either of those house churches, but they are growing, thriving, and encountering Jesus in the same ways we are. Still other house churches in our network will meet on different nights this week—all in homes, and all over the course of a couple of hours. Half of these house churches sprang up in the last year.

House Churches Are Unconventional

If you've spent any time in a traditional church, you probably noticed how different the meeting I just described is from a traditional church. First, you may have noticed the conversational format. There was no formal sermon. Each person shared as the Holy Spirit led. We studied the Bible and applied it to our lives in a powerful and meaningful way. But there was no curriculum, no formal liturgy, and no agenda except to learn from Jesus.

I tell the people in my house churches that there is no such thing as a disciple of Art Thomas. There are only disciples of Jesus. Sometimes he teaches you through me, and sometimes he teaches me through you. Everyone has a voice—whether they've been following Jesus for fifty years or fifteen seconds. We're all learners, and he teaches us through each other as we gather around his written Word and share how we're experiencing him.

Accordingly, each such meeting becomes a powerful piece of the puzzle in making disciples. Everyone who participates in the meeting—even the newest believer—finds the meeting itself to be a practical outlet for obeying Jesus's commission. Through our interactive conversation and the exercise of spiritual gifts, we all become vessels through whom Jesus disciples us together.

The application during the last half hour of each meeting varies. Some weeks, we break into smaller groups and pray for each other. Some weeks, we go around the circle. Each person receives a turn for personal ministry while various others speak words of encouragement or prophetic impressions from the Lord. Other weeks, we have a prayer meeting, minister healing, take communion together, worship the Lord in song, or engage in some combination of the above. Our goal is to identify what Jesus is teaching us (collectively), typically by sharing what he has been speaking to each of us (individually) throughout the week, plus what he reveals in the moment. Then we respond the best we know how.

Most American church meetings tend to involve a tiny fraction of people ministering the Word from a stage (generally the pastor and sometimes a select few others who might lead worship, pray, or read a Scripture during their appointed time slots) while the rest of the people listen passively. In some Pentecostal or charismatic churches, a small handful of others may occasionally burst into a prophetic word or tongues with an interpretation, usually between songs as people worship. Some churches include

Sunday School teachers (though this appears to be a dying breed), and a few others work in children's ministry. But an unfortunate adage continues to be lamented by many pastors: Only 10 percent of the people end up doing 90 percent of the work. Only a small fraction come to church, asking God what he wants them to share or do when they arrive.

There's a place for such meetings. Large gatherings are a great outlet for corporate musical worship and quality teaching ministry. They're an excellent venue for vision-casting, disseminating prophetic words, and welcoming ministry from guest speakers. In our house-church network, we gather in a large meeting twice each month plus a monthly prayer meeting. We love these meetings, but we remain primarily committed to the small, interactive gatherings that happen in our homes. In fact, only about one third of the people in our network generally attend our big meetings. It's simply not the priority.

House Churches Are Unique

Conventional small groups (or cell groups or life groups or whatever you want to call them) in American churches sometimes suffer from the same limitations as big meetings. Often, one teacher or discussion leader teaches via a curriculum, book, or perhaps a list of questions distributed by the pastor. The conversation is determined or led by the set book, topic, or questions—not by what the Lord is uniquely speaking to the people.

In a house church, there is an elder (a mature believer who takes healthy responsibility for the spiritual growth of the people entrusted to them), but every believer is a minister. (See 1 Corinthians 14:26.) Room is made for everyone's spiritual gifts to operate as the Spirit leads. The Scriptures are still taught by a qualified leader but never at the expense of Jesus expressing himself through most of the people present.

Even as a pastor myself, I believe that what Jesus wants to say to my church is far more important than what I want to say. What I've heard from him is only a fraction of his words. We "know in part and prophesy in part." (See 1 Corinthians 13:9.) I regularly tell my church family that what God has spoken to them is more important to me than what he has spoken to me. Why? Because I already know what he has spoken to me. I want to experience all of him that I can. Yes, I believe God spoke to me, but I believe he spoke to them too. And for this reason, I keep my own teaching as clear, concise, and compact as possible, often only unpacking a topic further if people are asking questions or engaging on the subject. Otherwise, my short teaching remains only one of several things the Lord speaks to us in the meeting.

House churches are a complete church experience. In house churches, we have communion, worship, prayer, fellowship, spiritual gifts, evangelistic outreaches, baptism, and biblical instruction. We live life together beyond a weekly meeting. We are not just friends in our gatherings but throughout the week. People in our house churches think of their specific small gathering as "my church" while the occasional larger gatherings are nice but optional.

House Churches Are Ancient

House churches are the context in which the New Testament was written. It's how the church began, first, meeting all together in one house (Acts 2:1–2) and then in many houses (Acts 2:46). Church buildings as we might think of them didn't become common until a few centuries later. That doesn't make such buildings wrong, but it also doesn't mean house churches are outdated or ineffective. In fact, many Scriptures don't even make practical sense when read in the context of a large church gathering.

For example, many pastors encourage their congregations to come together on Sunday using the words of Hebrews 10:24–25, which says, "And let us consider how we may spur one another on toward love and good deeds, not giving up meeting together, as some are in the habit of doing, but encouraging one another—and all the more as you see the Day approaching." But how is a room full of eighty people supposed to do that in practical terms? The writer of Hebrews didn't invite everyone together to hear one person spur them on toward love and good deeds or to be encouraged by the preacher. Rather, the admonition is to do that for each other. That means everyone is supposed to encourage everyone else. And that's not logistically possible in such a large gathering, let alone the many churches far larger than eighty.

I have nothing against larger, more conventional churches. In fact, I praise God for all the people they're able to reach and the ministries they can host. Our network of house churches holds large meetings as well. But we are also clear that our big meetings are just a garnish on the main course of church. An effective church meeting is a gathering of people that is small enough to do what the Bible says must be done.

Yet another example is 1 Corinthians 14:26, which says, "What then shall we say, brothers and sisters? When you come together, each of you has a hymn, or a word of instruction, a revelation, a tongue or an interpretation. Everything must be done so that the church may be built up." I've never seen a big gathering of people where every single person could logistically express their gifts in a way that every other person benefitted. The closest I've seen is congregations breaking into smaller clusters at the end of a message to pray for each other. But consider what this is: small groups (minus the long-term intimacy). Paul's words to the Corinthian believers make sense in a house church of five to twenty people; but the bigger a meeting grows, the less actionable they become.

Over and over, we see New Testament churches gathering in homes:

- The first church gathering was in a house (Acts 1:13).
- The outpouring on Pentecost happened in a house (Acts 2:1–4).

- The believers met not only in the temple courts but also in homes (Acts 2:46).
- The apostles taught from house to house (Acts 5:42).
- Saul went looking for Christians by searching houses (Acts 8:3).
- The Spirit first poured out upon Gentiles at Cornelius's house (Acts 10:24–48).
- The believers gathered at Mark's mother's house to pray for Peter's release from prison (Acts 12:12).
- A church met regularly in Lydia's house (Acts 16:40).
- Paul taught both publicly and from house to house (Acts 20:20).
- A church met regularly at Priscilla and Aquila's house (Romans 16:3–5; 1 Corinthians 16:9).
- A church met regularly at Nympha's house (Colossians 4:15).
- A church met regularly in Philemon's home (Philemon 1:2).

Early Christian house churches didn't necessarily operate exactly the same as the ones in my network. For one thing, they didn't have the same access to Bibles that we do today. And the varied cultures, technology, and environments surely create some differences as well. But when the church gathers in small, interactive groups from house to house, we are far closer to the original design than when we *only* meet in large groups to passively watch a minority of people minister on stage.

House Churches Are Easy

This is the simplest form of ministry I've ever done. The hardest part is cleaning my house before people come over. The only preparation I need to do is my own devotional time with the Lord. I don't need to plan an order of service. I don't need to prepare or practice a set of worship songs. And I don't need to have a three-point sermon full of clever anecdotes or profound statements. I simply need to hang out with my friends and look for what Jesus is doing and saying among us.

By simplifying church meetings down to the bare bones like this, we make them easy to multiply. It's difficult to replicate a megachurch. You need millions of dollars, a massive staff, and a huge building. The smaller the gathering, the fewer resources are needed to sustain it, and the easier it is to replicate. Simple house churches don't need talented musicians, fancy buildings, quality equipment, snazzy websites, or gifted preachers. They simply need a Bible, the Holy Spirit, a spiritually healthy leader, and a place to meet.

House Churches Are Messy

There is one downside to house churches: they're messy. Sometimes people are offended by each other. Sometimes conflicts arise. Sometimes people say and do weird things when they realize they have a group of people who will pay attention to them. A certain amount of risk is involved in relinquishing control, opening the floor for discussion, and letting everyone minister.

We'll talk more about these messes in chapter 14. For now, simply know this: The messiest floors are in homes where children are thriving. Don't be afraid of the messes—they're a sign of life.

CHAPTER 5:
MAKING DISCIPLES WHO MAKE DISCIPLES

If you make disciples, you always get the church.
But if you make a church, you rarely get disciples.
—Mike Breen

Now that I've sung the praises of house churches, it's time to shock you: I don't really care about house churches.

Jesus didn't send us to plant churches. He sent us to make disciples. Churches are the logical outcome of making disciples.

If we set out to plant churches, then we'll succeed. But we'll probably only be shuffling sheep from one sheep pen to another. If we make disciples, however, then we will need to plant churches so they can gather and grow. Disciple making comes first.

Imagine being one of the disciples who witnessed Jesus's ascension. A few weeks earlier, the Rabbi you've been following was brutally crucified and killed. Then, three days later, he rose from the dead. For the last forty days, your Messiah has been appearing physically to you and others, teaching you about God's kingdom and what to expect next.

Now you're gathered with your friends on a mountain. Some of you are worshipping Jesus while others, strangely, are still doubting. "Then Jesus came to them and said, 'All authority in heaven and on earth has been given to me. Therefore go and make disciples of all nations, baptizing them in the name of the Father and of the Son and of the Holy Spirit, and teaching them to obey everything I have commanded you. And surely I am with you always, to the very end of the age'" (Matthew 28:18–20).

We call this the Great Commission. Imagine the weight the disciples must have felt on those words. They're supposed to carry this gospel into all nations, make disciples, baptize them in water, then teach those disciples to obey everything Jesus had commanded them—which includes the command that was just given, to go make disciples. The Great Commission is a self-replicating command to make disciples who make disciples who make disciples, and so on.

When a friend of mine was about to leave as a missionary to China, he said two things that have remained with me. First, he said that we often think God's will is the path of least resistance, and we can know his will for our lives by relaxing and trusting God to open the right doors and close the wrong ones. "But," my friend pointed out, "if that were true, then I wouldn't be going where I'm going. Sometimes God's will is the most difficult path, where all the doors seem shut." And the second thing he said was this: "We call it the Great Commission, but that's a bit of a misnomer. By calling it the Great Commission, we might think we can busy ourselves with a bunch of lesser commissions and never really get around to that great one. But it's the Only Commission."

Jesus gave many commands, but he only gave one commission: Make disciples who make disciples.

The Lifestyle that Makes Disciples

My dad is retired now, but he was once one of the top Ford salesmen in the United States. People kept coming back to him and referring others to him because he was so honest, kind, and selfless. He would often pray with people at his desk and share testimonies, even though he worked on commission and time was precious.

Suppose at that time, you and I attended a party, and my dad came along with me. I approach you with my dad at my side and say, "Hi! Have I ever told you about my dad? He's a great guy and an honest car salesman. If you ever need a new or used car, let me know, and I'll bring you to his dealership where someone else will tell you more about him and possibly even introduce you."

Wouldn't it be easier to simply introduce you to my dad? He's right there with me.

Christians generally know we're supposed to share our faith, but far too many think they accomplish this merely by inviting people to church services and events where someone else can preach the gospel and possibly introduce people to Jesus. Many Christians don't feel qualified or equipped to make disciples, so they relegate themselves to inviting people to church meetings.

But Revelation 12:11 doesn't say that we will overcome Satan by inviting people to church meetings. It says we overcome him by "the blood of the Lamb, and the word of our testimony," and by not loving our lives so much that we try to avoid the consequences of proclaiming that message—even death.

The lifestyle that makes disciples is one of boldly shining the light of Jesus, sharing the testimony of what Jesus's blood has accomplished in your life, and loving even the most unlovable with genuine affection. In this lifestyle, your old life is considered dead, and now, by your trust in him, the Holy Spirit expresses the new life of Jesus through you. (See Romans 6:11 and Galatians 2:20.) The lifestyle that makes disciples is unashamed of Jesus and unafraid of the consequences of talking about him with clarity.

This is how I led people to Jesus in college and in my workplace. This is how I continue to live in front of neighbors, family members, and friends. Other Christians want to emulate this sort of lifestyle, so they start to come to you for advice on Christian living. Before you know it, your house becomes a gospel house, and people want to meet with you to learn to follow Jesus the same way you do. Your job is simply to remain consistent, pointing people to Jesus and showing them how to humbly love others, honoring them above yourself. Add a regularly scheduled, weekly meeting to this, and before you know it, you've got a church where disciples are growing and thriving.

See? It's not about starting a church. It's about making disciples. And it starts with a lifestyle of introducing people to Jesus.

Relationships with Purpose

We encourage everyone in our church to build relationships with lost people for the sake of winning them to faith in Jesus. This is not about mere conversion, although we do celebrate the opportunity to pray with someone to begin a relationship with the Lord. Rather, it's about helping establish the person in a thriving, long-term relationship with Jesus and his people.

Purposeful relationship is authentic. We don't pretend to be unsaved until the person likes us. From the very beginning, people know who you are and who you represent. Not much time passes before it becomes apparent that you desire for that person to experience the same hope you have received. You tell them. Purposeful relationships lead people to a crisis of decision in which people either want to draw closer to Jesus or avoid you at all costs.

Purposeful relationships are not passive. Any relationship you have in which you merely live a good life and hope someone notices and asks about it is passive, not purposeful. Our mission is far too important to entrust to happenstance. Intentionality is necessary.

Of equal importance with intentionality is proximity. Ask yourself, "Am I in proximity to those I hope to reach with the gospel?" Many of us need to make a drastic change to the rhythms of our lives in order to put ourselves in proximity with those who need Jesus.[14]

Huge efforts to change your lifestyle are rarely sustainable. Drastic change requires small, intentional changes made consistently over time. Those changes could look simply like finding excuses to talk to your neighbors. Bring them cookies, just knock on the door and introduce yourself, invite them to join you for dinner, etc. Don't wait for a neon sign from heaven or for your church to become perfect before you start living missionally in your daily life. If you do it, others in your church will too.

Deliberate relationships make disciples. And only deliberate people develop deliberate relationships. Be purposeful. Lovingly and prayerfully target people with help from the Holy Spirit, and shine the light of Jesus and his gospel into their lives in meaningful ways.

Some Christians think of disciple making as a slow warming-up to Jesus—bringing people into deeper and deeper experience with Christianity and church life until they start to see themselves as believers. While this sounds noble, it is at odds with Jesus's ministry and the example in the book of Acts.

---

[14] I want to credit JonMark Baker, part of our senior leadership team in the Roots Church network, for the language used to make this point.

We do not make disciples through bait and switch—offering easy entry and then slowly inviting people to greater levels of commitment. We make disciples by offering an all-or-nothing commitment to the lordship of Jesus Christ. Scripture discusses this as new birth or becoming a new creation or death and resurrection. In short, it is a binary option whereby someone either chooses to follow Jesus or not. There is no half-condition between dead and alive.

People in the community of faith claim to follow Jesus and are therefore accountable for their confession. Whatever we do in a disciple-making relationship needs to come with a clearly articulated gospel message—one in which the person understands the cost of following Jesus and can make a clear decision between either following him or remaining dead in their sins.

Disciple making doesn't happen by accident.

Your Role as a Disciple Maker

In our next chapter, I'll make the case that disciple making is a group activity. You're not responsible to do this all alone. Nevertheless, every Christian has an individual role to play.

Every believer is responsible to follow the Holy Spirit in presenting and representing Jesus in everything they say and do. This includes sharing your testimony, praying for people, ministering healing, explaining the gospel, and generously loving people in practical ways.

As an evangelistic people, we do these things even when there isn't an opportunity for long-term discipleship. We express Jesus as a lifestyle while actively looking for opportunities to build relationships and invest in people's lives. Whenever those relationships can be built, we take the initiative in mentoring new believers. We look for the area of need in the person's life—their potential, their identity in Christ, and their work for the Lord—and we speak life into them with encouragement and wisdom. We spend meaningful time with them, encouraging them to observe our ways of life and our walks with the Lord.

And now that you've introduced the person to Jesus, it's time to invite these new believers (or pre-believers) to an interactive house-church meeting so they can experience more of Jesus through his people than you could reveal on your own.

Admittedly, the above looks great on paper but can feel daunting to the average Christian. It doesn't need to, however. The Lord promises that the Holy Spirit will help us.

Furthermore, we can simplify all this by remembering that we as individuals are not solely responsible to perfectly express the fullness of Jesus nor are we even expected to personally teach everything there is to know about following Jesus. None of us—even seasoned, educated ministers—are qualified for either of those tasks. "For we know in part and we prophesy in part" (1 Corinthians 13:9).

In a courtroom, a witness's duty is to present what they have personally witnessed. The witness doesn't need to convince the jury or judge of anything. The witness simply needs to testify. If the attorneys do their jobs right and if the witnesses truthfully convey their testimonies to the best of their abilities (even if those testimonies are limited or even imprecise), the truth will be settled by those seeking to determine it.

In other words, your greatest and simplest responsibility is to share what you have witnessed. For the brand-new believer, this may be nothing more than your own personal testimony. For the mature believer, this includes your best understanding of the Scriptures, experiences with the Lord, revelations you've received, what you've learned while following Jesus, and so forth.

If every believer regularly and boldly shares whatever parts of their testimonies are relevant in any given situation, a compelling case will emerge for those who are perishing—a case that the Holy Spirit will argue in people's hearts as the Father draws them to Jesus. New disciples will be made, and Jesus's church will multiply.

CHAPTER 6:

MAKING DISCIPLES IS A TEAM SPORT

Paul says in 1 Corinthians 14:26 that everyone has something to bring to the table. The setting really does matter for this, and creating an environment where people can be trained and discipled into action is the key to seeing the church expand in greater measure.

—Justin Knoop

Dan grew up in a Christian home. His parents were part of a Dutch Reformed church where their theology held that Dan was saved simply because his parents were saved. But Dan's lifestyle as a teenager was anything but Christian.

Despite her church's doctrine, Dan's mother prayed fervently—and asked others to pray fervently—for her Danny's salvation. She knew his life was literally hellbent for destruction, and only a miracle could turn the situation around.

When Dan was about thirteen years old, his dog ran away, and Dan raced off to look for him. But his parents were worried and called their pastor to help look. Pastor Vander Hoven eventually found him and his dog, and, while treating him to a bite to eat, said, "Dan, you need Jesus." But Dan didn't go for it.

Over and over through Dan's teen and early young adult years, Pastor Vander Hoven continued to reach out. He was there to help Dan when he got arrested. He counseled Dan after a drunk driving rollover. Little by little, he continued showing Dan the love of Jesus. But Dan kept refusing his help.

Meanwhile, a bunch of people kept inviting Dan to a local Bible study. Eventually, he decided to go simply to shut them all up.

Dan was a tough guy. He fancied himself a rebel, riding a motorcycle and wearing a stereotypical leather biker jacket. But when he walked in the front door, a scrawny redheaded freckle-faced guy named Earl was leading the meeting in a buttoned-up shirt. Dan wanted to run. What could this total nerd offer him?

Earl opened up his Bible and began to read from the first chapter of Ephesians, and suddenly, Dan's heart was gripped. Somehow, the Holy Spirit moved Dan into a crisis of faith as he heard the Scriptures read aloud. Dan was undone.

After the meeting, Earl asked Dan what he liked to do for fun. Dan mentioned playing softball with friends, so Earl invited Dan to join him at the nearby ballpark to pitch some balls and hang out.

As it turned out, Earl was great at softball. He had turned down playing for a couple of AAA softball leagues, but he played on Dan's team just to spend time with him. For about three or four years, as Dan and Earl met up to throw softballs, Earl talked to him about Jesus and ministered to him. It turned Dan's whole life around.

Soon, Dan went off to Bible college. He was excited to learn more about God, but his first class terrified him: English. Dan didn't know how to write well and had terrible grammar. In high school, Dan had flunked English, and now this intimidating class stood between him and his calling to ministry.

Soon, into the classroom walked an elderly woman who stood about six feet tall. She stepped to the front of the class, stretched out her long, skinny arms, and began to sing an old hymn titled "This is My Father's World." Dan suddenly realized this would be an English class like none other.

After class, Dan confessed to his teacher, Nellie Vander Ark, that he was terrified of English and had flunked the subject in high school. But Mrs. Vander Ark told Dan that if he would meet with her after class regularly, he would ace the course.

Week after week, Dan met with Mrs. Vander Ark. She would encourage him and speak life into him. She would sometimes tailor-fit assignments just for Dan. For example, when the rest of the class was writing an essay, Nellie asked Dan to write a devotional for her. When he turned it in, she read it in front of him and said, "Wow." Dan later said that when Nellie Vander Ark said "wow," he felt like God the Father himself said "wow." He credits her with giving him the courage to excel in academics and continue asking tough questions.

Another faculty member at the college—a man who had been a missionary in Pakistan and a few other places—took Dan under his wing. He'd sit with Dan in his office and answer questions and tell stories.

Dan met his wife Sarita there, and they soon became missionaries to Sierra Leon in west Africa. Once there, Dan and Sarita were baptized in the Holy Spirit and spoke in tongues. Their denomination, which rejected the Pentecostal experience, no longer had room for them.

Dan and Sarita returned to the United States and joined the Assemblies of God. They served as itinerant evangelists in Rhode Island for a while before returning to Dan's home in western Michigan, where he served for a time as an elder at a church that experienced a tremendous revival in the 1990s. After that, Dan moved across the state to serve on staff at a thriving church in Northville, Michigan.

And that's where I met pastor Dan.

I am who I am today because of his influence. Many times, pastor Dan Vander Velde sat with me in his office at the church, sometimes for an hour or more, talking about spiritual things that no one else would talk to me about. We often discussed the theoretical realm of what "ought to be" and what "could be" in church. And when the Holy Spirit called pastors Dan and Sarita to plant a church, the Lord told me about it before they announced it, and I felt led to join them. And as I've already shown, that decision ultimately led to my rethinking of the word *church* and eventually the birth of a healthy, growing house-church network.

Spiritual Lineage

I can tell you stories of people whom I have poured my life into—people I've mentored—who are now serving in ministry both locally and around the world. But their stories of transformation started with my story of transformation. And my story started with Dan Vander Velde's story (and others like him: Mike Byrum, Shane Fritz, Ed Link, my parents, and others). When disciples are made well, they make disciples who make disciples.

Notice, though, that in both Dan's story and my own, multiple voices ministered to us. That's because there's no such thing as a disciple of Dan Vander Velde or Art Thomas. There are only disciples of Jesus.

When Jesus commissioned his disciples to make disciples, he commissioned them collectively, and they fulfilled the mission collectively. Yes, people must respond personally to that commission because there is no "we" without "me." But my yes joins your yes so that together we can partner with Jesus to accomplish his mission.

When I was in a college anthropology class, I met a classmate named Jeff. He was dabbling in Buddhism at the time. Following each class, we had long conversations about faith and the spiritual world. I tried several times to lead him to Jesus, but he kept saying he wasn't ready.

After a month or more of these discussions, Jeff told me he had started attending a Wednesday night class at a nearby church. After a few questions, I was thrilled to discover that, of all things, the class Jeff was attending was one taught by Pastor Dan.

A month or two passed, and Mel Gibson's movie *The Passion of the Christ* was released in theaters. I invited Jeff to watch it with me and afterward went home and led him to Jesus in my living room.

I had just started my first house church, and Jeff started attending regularly. He eventually met his wife there. In time, he earned his degree in pastoral ministry and started serving at a church plant in a nearby city. I'm blessed to be part of Jeff's story, but I didn't make him a disciple by myself. Pastors Dan, Shane, Jason, and others poured into him too. Jeff is a disciple of Jesus.

To be part of someone's spiritual lineage doesn't require that you invest all your time and attention into that one person. You're not their savior—Jesus is. You're not their teacher—Jesus is.

If Paul's teaching is true that each of us is a unique part of Christ's body, then we cannot become territorial with his disciples. In other words, I cannot monopolize a person's time as though I have all the answers. I only know in part and prophesy in part. (See 1 Corinthians 13:9.) The best thing I can do for one of Jesus's disciples is introduce them to other people who will reveal him more fully than I could alone. Then, as we minister together, Jesus is more clearly seen.

Yes, I am indebted to Dan, Shane, Ed, my parents, and others for their mentorship in my life. But these were all vessels Jesus used to teach and train me as *his* disciple. My spiritual lineage may have many names and faces attached to it, but if diagrammed on paper, it would look less like a widely branched family tree and more like a stick with a straight line between Jesus and me. Jesus revealed himself in diverse ways through multiple people who, in turn, each learned from Jesus through multiple others.

> For when one says, "I follow Paul," and another, "I follow Apollos," are you not mere human beings?
>
> What, after all, is Apollos? And what is Paul? Only servants, through whom you came to believe—as the Lord has assigned to each his task. I planted the seed, Apollos watered it, but God has been making it grow. So neither the one who plants nor the one who waters is anything, but only God, who makes things grow. The one who plants and the one who waters have one purpose, and they will each be rewarded according to their own labor. For we are co-workers in God's service; you are God's field, God's building. (1 Corinthians 3:4–9)

If every Christian would embrace their role as "co-workers in God's service," we would care less about how much we have individually discipled a particular person and more about following the Holy Spirit to do whatever he wants us to do at any given moment.

Disciple Factories

This is yet another reason why I am so passionate about house churches. When a new believer enters an interactive, relational environment where everyone is revealing their own unique expressions of Jesus, he or she is immersed in the strongest possible environment for transformation and growth.

My house didn't truly become a gospel house until I started regularly gathering other Christians there. That's when the fuller picture of Jesus emerged.

Healthy house churches are disciple-making factories. Sure, some in a house church will invest more time in someone than others, but we all reveal Jesus to them as we gather.

Kayla was invited to our house church by another young woman (also named Kayla). She came with a lot of emotional hurts, fear, confusion, depression, and so forth. But she was proactive about her spiritual growth, reaching out to people in our house church—especially Robin, another woman named Astrid, the other Kayla who invited her, and me. Meanwhile, she benefitted from conversations and advice people gave in our weekly house-church meetings. We baptized Kayla in our bathtub only two years ago at the time of this writing, and today, she is spiritually gifted, sharing her faith with friends, and growing in ways she never thought possible.

Not everyone in our house church has been a mentor to Kayla, but everyone has revealed Jesus to her in some way. And Kayla has grown faster and stronger than many Christians ever do because she has been immersed in an environment where Jesus is regularly revealed to her through multiple people, ensuring a more complete picture of what he is saying and doing.

Jesus told his first followers that if they follow him, he will make them fishers of men. That means that to follow Jesus is to allow him to transform you into someone who brings new people to him. It also means that if we're revealing Jesus well, he is going to make the people around us into fishers of men too.

As stated earlier, when Jesus commissioned his disciples, he commissioned them collectively. What did he commission them to do? First, they were to "go and make disciples," then baptize them, then "[teach] them to obey everything I have commanded you" (Matthew 28:19–20). Jesus's commands to the twelve are therefore commands to us. One of those commands was the one he just gave: Go and make disciples!

In the church Jesus started, a group of disciples fishes for people and ministers to them in such a way that they, too, become disciple makers and people-fishers. This requires every believer in a church revealing Jesus in whatever ways the Holy Spirit leads. Spiritual gifts, then, are machines in the disciple-making factory by which Jesus creates new disciples through us.

Spiritual Gifts Are Disciple-Making Machines

Paul said that when we express spiritual gifts in our gatherings, we are actively being unique expressions of Jesus's body. (See 1 Corinthians 12.)

> For by the grace given me I say to every one of you: Do not think of yourself more highly than you ought, but rather think of yourself with sober judgment, in accordance with the faith God has distributed to each of you. For just as each of us has one body with many members, and these members do not all have the same function, so in Christ we, though many, form one body, and each member belongs to all the others. We have different gifts, according to the grace given to each of us. If your gift is prophesying, then prophesy in accordance with your faith; if it is serving, then serve; if it is teaching, then teach; if it is to encourage, then give encouragement; if it is giving, then give generously; if it is to lead, do it diligently; if it is to show mercy, do it cheerfully. (Romans 12:3–8)

As individuals, we should each faithfully and passionately express whatever gifts God gives us, meanwhile, trusting that others in our spiritual family are gifted by the Spirit to reveal other aspects of Jesus's work. I should not assume that I am adequate to make disciples by myself. I'm not. I am not strong enough, smart enough, spiritual enough, insightful enough, or *whatever* enough.

But neither is any other believer. The clearest picture of Jesus emerges as we each reveal the measure of him that the Holy Spirit has invested in us.

We'll talk more about spiritual gifts in chapter 7. The issue at hand is that the more believers who can partner with the Holy Spirit to reveal Jesus in a meeting, the more effective we will be at helping Jesus transform new believers into high-quality disciples who make disciples. We must see disciple making as a team sport if we're going to fulfill the commission Jesus gave us.

Paul planted and Apollos watered, but God caused the seed to grow. My friend Dan's mother prayed fervently for her son's salvation. Pastor Vander Hoven pursued Dan even when Dan was running his hardest from the Lord. Earl led a Bible study, played softball, and chatted with Dan. Nellie Vander Ark taught Dan English and greatly encouraged him. And others fulfilled the role the Lord called them to. But God caused that seed to grow. Jesus transformed Dan into a disciple maker, eventually making him one of the most influential people in my own spiritual development.

Who has God placed in your path? What relationships do you already have where the example of your life and the integrity of your speech bear influence? If you can't think of any, then a little more time in the disciple-making factory of a house church will shape you into the type of person whom others want to follow. But if you can think of such people, tell them about Jesus and invite them to your house church so they can more fully encounter him through everyone. You don't need to have all the answers. You simply need to offer the piece of Jesus you carry and introduce your friend to the rest of him through the church.

Pastors and Leaders Still Matter

Jesus has given some people to the church as shepherds. (See Ephesians 4:11.) And one of the gifts the Holy Spirit gives is leadership. (See Romans 12:8.) Yes, disciple making is a team sport; but the best teams have quality coaches.

Many people start house churches because they've been hurt by church leaders in the past, and they want a church without leaders. Little do they know that they are leading, whether they like it or not.

If you're starting a house church, expect to lead it. You may not feel qualified, but I have learned that Jesus does all the heavy lifting as we simply point people to him and focus on proclaiming the gospel. Let me be clear: Even if you are actively trying not to lead, if you are gathering Christians in your home, you will be responsible to give an account for the ways in which you watched over Jesus's people. (More on this in chapter 11.)

Church leadership isn't a bad thing. But bad leadership is a bad thing. Good church leadership is valuable and necessary.

> Have confidence in your leaders and submit to their authority, because they keep watch over you as those who must give an account. Do this so that their work will be a

> joy, not a burden, for that would be of no benefit to you. (Hebrews 13:17)

Every person in a house church has a role to play, and someone must fulfill the responsibility of leader. The good news, as I mentioned before, is that God gives a special grace to accomplish this ministry if you'll ask for it. Leadership is a spiritual gift, and we would do well to eagerly desire all the gifts.

CHAPTER 7:

FREEDOM FOR BODIES AND SOULS

The gospel is "good news," not "good history," because when it is preached, it happens.

—Reinhard Bonnke

The pickup truck rolled over and over. As shattered glass and gravel pelted my aging parents, my mom prayed, "See you in a minute, Lord!" Both my parents thought this was the end.

Driving through the open plains of Kansas, a burst of wind threw their truck and travel trailer off the road. The trailer broke free from the hitch and burst open, flinging all their belongings onto the highway median. This force launched their truck into a spin, rolling it four complete times until it landed on its wheels. A muscular truck driver who witnessed the accident successfully opened the crumpled doors of the vehicle as flames burst from the hood.

My dad is an amateur photographer and takes pictures of just about everything. In my family, if you're not dead, it's an event. While a nurse, who stopped on her way to work, tended to Mom, Dad filled up his camera with images of the aftermath.

After a brief visit to the emergency room for minor injuries and gathering what belongings they could into a rental car, Mom and Dad decided not to let the accident ruin their vacation. They continued their trip, staying in hotels.

When they finally returned home to Michigan, Dad showed me photos of the demolished trailer, the scattered debris, the truck in flames, and even the moment the truck's gas tank exploded in a column of fire. They were blessed to be alive. Dad has shared his testimony in several churches, showing the pictures and seeing many people stream to the altar, drawing closer to the Lord.

Several years after the accident, my dad's only physical reminder of the crash was a tiny piece of glass that had migrated behind his left eye. Most of the time, it didn't bother him. But every day, when he took his shower, something about the heat and steam irritated that eye so that it became red and painful for a short time.

My parents retired to Tennessee and drove to visit us in Michigan once or twice a year in their motorhome. But on the morning of one of their trips to visit us, Dad's eye never calmed down after his shower. My mom had to drive most of the nine hours. They arrived just in time for our house-church meeting and came inside, exhausted.

"Before you start the meeting," Dad announced, "I need you to pray for me." He told us about the glass, expecting me to go over and pray for him. But I didn't. Instead, I asked, "Who wants to do this one?"

A couple of guys jumped up and laid their hands on my dad. With gentleness and a smile, they commanded the glass to come out of his eye in the name of Jesus. "Any change?"

Nothing happened. Dad's eye was still irritated.

But I had taught these men to persevere for healing and not settle for the first result. We had seen far too many people healed after the second or third prayer to stop just yet. They laid their hands on him a second time.

"Wait! Wait!" my dad protested. "If we do this now, we'll never start the meeting. Let's just have the meeting, and you can pray for me more afterward."

The guys backed down, and we opened in prayer.

About halfway through the house-church meeting, the Holy Spirit told my dad, "Go into the bathroom. I'm about to perform surgery on your eye. It's going to hurt for a moment, but don't worry."

Dad went to the bathroom. A searing pain then started behind his left eye and moved up over the top. Then, he blinked a couple of times, and a little cube of glass fell into his cupped hand. Dad's eye was completely healed that day, and he hasn't had a problem since.

And it all happened in my home when Jesus's body touched him in faith.

The Body of Christ

How we relate to one another matters. A body has trouble functioning when limbs and organs aren't attached. In the same way, together, we are the body of Christ. According to 1 Corinthians 6:15, "Your bodies are members of Christ himself." That means "the body of Christ" isn't just a beautiful metaphor. We are actually physical extensions of Jesus in the world. Or at least we're supposed to be.

Jesus had a perfect track record when it came to healing ministry,[15] and so did the newborn church. (See Acts 5:16.) But today we see varying degrees of results in different churches, ranging from zero healings to lots of healings. But I'm not yet aware of anywhere that consistently demonstrates one hundred percent results like Jesus did. It seems we're still learning to be like Jesus in this way.

---

[15] See Matthew 4:24; 8:16–17; 9:35; 12:15; 14:35–36; Mark 6:56; Luke 4:40; 6:18–19; and Acts 10:38. From these nine verses and others, we learn that Jesus healed every single person who came to him, called out to him, reached out and touched him, or had someone else come on their behalf, plus some whom he took the initiative to approach. Only in Jesus's hometown do we see that he could only work a few miracles due to the people's lack of faith in him, but this probably had less to do with Jesus trying and failing to minister and more to do with the fact that many wouldn't have even approached him. (See Matthew 13:54–58.) Not to mention the fact that they tried to throw him off a cliff, which doesn't leave a lot of time for healing ministry. (See Luke 4:16–30.) Nevertheless, Jesus apparently healed everyone on whom he laid his hands. (See Mark 6:1–6.)

As the equipping ministers among us bring us into greater unity with Jesus and each other, and as we love one another and step out in the gifts and ministries to which the Lord is calling us, "we will grow to become in every respect the mature body of him who is the head, that is, Christ. From him the whole body, joined and held together by every supporting ligament, grows and builds itself up in love, as each part does its work" (Ephesians 4:15–16).

Could it be that the reason we don't yet see 100 percent results in healing ministry is because we need to better walk in love and unity among ourselves?

Paul seemed to think so. He confronted the Corinthian church for their cliques and factions. (See 1 Corinthians 11:17–18.) Accordingly, he noted that when they consumed the bread and cup of communion, "it is not the Lord's Supper you eat" (1 Corinthians 11:20). Then he said that many were weak and sick among them, and others had died, because they failed to discern the body of Christ. (See 1 Corinthians 11:29–30.) God disciplines a fractured church.

Are we discerning Jesus in each other? Are we practicing authentic fellowship? Are we walking in the ministries to which God has called us? Is our little home group united in love with Jesus's global church, especially churches in our local region?

Or are we isolated, bitter, suspicious, and prideful?

How we relate to one another is directly related to whether we are truly being the body of Christ. And the more we grow up into "the mature body of him who is the Head," the more we can expect to see the miraculous.

And it's not about being perfect; it's about being on the journey toward perfection. James connected healing to confession of sins, which means our openness and authenticity with one another is part of the culture that sees healing. (See James 5:16.) As Hebrews 10:14 puts it, "For by one sacrifice he has made perfect forever those who are being made holy." As long as we're in process, we're perfect. It's not about whether "I" qualify; it's about whether "we" are relating well to the Lord and each other.

The Gospel of Peace

When Paul taught about the armor of God, he said we need to have our feet "fitted with the readiness that comes from the gospel of peace" (Ephesians 6:15). The Greek word for *peace* is not limited to peaceful feelings or personal wellbeing. It's also "a state of concord" and "harmony" between governments and personal relationships, plus personal health and welfare; and it's a defining characteristic of God's kingdom.[16] Paul likely drew his language from Isaiah 52:7.[17]

> How beautiful on the mountains
>
> are the feet of those who bring good news,

---

[16] "εἰρήνη," Danker, *A Greek-English Lexicon*, 287–8.

[17] Craig S. Keener, *The IVP Bible Background Commentary: New Testament, Second Edition,* "Divine Armor," (Downers Grove, Illinois: InterVarsity Press, 1993, 2014), 554.

who proclaim peace,
who bring good tidings,
who proclaim salvation,
who say to Zion,
"Your God reigns!"

The Hebrew word used for "peace" here is *shalom*—a word that carries the same range of meaning as the Greek word Paul used and points toward complete wholeness (personally, relationally, and, ultimately, globally).[18] God's righteousness produces this overflowing, world-altering peace. (See Isaiah 32:17.) It's an expression of God's kingdom, which consists of "righteousness, peace, and joy in the Holy Spirit" (Romans 14:17).

In short, the message we proclaim is that the answer to sin and all its effects is what Jesus accomplished for us. The good news is that his work rights every wrong—whether spiritually within us, physically in our bodies, or even socially, economically, governmentally, etc. As his kingdom breaks into the world, his righteousness changes brokenness into wholeness. This is the message Jesus proclaimed.

"The Spirit of the Lord is on me,
because he has anointed me
to proclaim good news to the poor.

---

18 "Lexicon :: Strong's H7965 – šālôm," Blue Letter Bible, accessed April 19, 2023, https://www.blueletterbible.org/lexicon/h7965/kjv/wlc/0-1/.

> He has sent me to proclaim freedom for the prisoners
> and recovery of sight for the blind,
> to set the oppressed free,
> to proclaim the year of the Lord's favor."
>
> (Luke 4:18–19)

The gospel Jesus gave us is good news about a heavenly kingdom. (See Matthew 24:14.) And all the wonderful aspects of that kingdom are possible because of what he accomplished in his life, death, resurrection, and ascension to the right hand of the Father.

When this message is proclaimed and applied among a family of believers, we become an outpost of God's glory in the earth. Just as we see in Jesus's ministry and that of the early church, when broken people want freedom, they come to us to find it. The gospel applies God's rule and authority to transform lives, heal bodies, mend relationships, restore families, provide for the needy, and drive out demons. It truly is good news.

Healing Is Part of the Atonement

The word *atonement* refers to the work Jesus accomplished, reconciling us to God. There is no question that this work applies to our spiritual salvation, but some Christians question whether it has anything to do with physical healing.

Yes, the prophet did say that "by his wounds we are healed" (Isaiah 53:5). But some careful students of God's Word have pointed out that when Peter—an apostle writing Scripture under the inspiration of the Holy Spirit—quoted this verse, he did so in the context of being healed from sin.

> When they hurled their insults at him, he did not retaliate; when he suffered, he made no threats. Instead, he entrusted himself to him who judges justly. "He himself bore our sins" in his body on the cross, so that we might die to sins and live for righteousness; "by his wounds you have been healed." For "you were like sheep going astray," but now you have returned to the Shepherd and Overseer of your souls. (1 Peter 2:23–25)

What these brothers and sisters miss, however, is that another apostle quoted Isaiah 53 while writing Scripture under the inspiration of the Holy Spirit: Matthew. And the context could not be clearer. "When evening came, many who were demon-possessed were brought to him, and he drove out the spirits with a word and healed all the sick. This was to fulfill what was spoken through the prophet Isaiah: 'He took up our infirmities and bore our diseases'" (Matthew 8:16–17).

Isaiah 53 is a prophetic word all about the atonement. The challenge here is that Matthew 8 happened nineteen chapters before Jesus went to the cross—at least a year before the first drop of his blood was shed for our salvation.

But there's an easy response. Perhaps the atonement is not limited to the events of the cross and the empty grave. Perhaps the atonement begins with "the Lamb who was slain from the creation of the world" (Revelation 13:8). Perhaps the atonement was inaugurated when "the Word became flesh and made his dwelling among us" (John 1:14). Perhaps the atonement is best understood as the entirety of Jesus's existence—the one who "ever lives" to bring relationship between us and God (Hebrews 7:25).

All that Jesus was and is brings God and us together, eliminating sin and conquering its effects. "The reason the Son of God appeared was to destroy the devil's work" (1 John 3:8). In Jesus, we find the kingdom. And "the kingdom of God is not a matter of talk but of power" (1 Corinthians 4:20).

The Pastoral Temptation

I've served the body of Christ as both a local pastor and a traveling minister. As a traveling minister, I've preached in hundreds of churches in about twenty countries. Most of the time, I'm invited to teach on healing ministry, and then I have the people of the church minister to each other and report the miracles. I've had the joy of witnessing thousands of miracles performed through ordinary Christians around the world—most of whom have never even seen a healing miracle before.

It's easy to have a renewed mind when you witness this almost every week. The Word of God is proven true again and again. And while I certainly was aware of those who were not healed in my meetings, I didn't have to think about them because each week, I was moving on to a different city and seeing more miracles.

But as a local pastor, I not only see miracles regularly in my church, I also see, every week, the people who still are not healed. And that can play with my head.

Proverbs 13:12 says, "Hope deferred makes the heart sick, but a longing fulfilled is a tree of life." In other words, when the thing we hope for—in this case, a healing—is delayed, our hearts can become sick. And if we're not careful, our disenchantment can twist our theology. Before we know it, we're offering excuses and explanations for a lack of healing. We may even chalk it up to a mystery. But if we're honest, we don't like the idea that our prayers haven't yet brought visible results, so we hide behind spiritual-sounding answers and words of comfort. All this is the unbelief of a sickened heart.

The temptation for pastors is to cater to the status quo. We might contend for healing in short sprints, but then we settle into a ministry of comfort and platitudes that allow sicknesses in our churches to continue unchecked.

We need our minds renewed. Consider the kingdom we represent. Consider the message we carry. Consider the Jesus whose body we comprise.

More is available, and we ought to aim for it.

Down-to-Earth Healing Ministry

Miracles don't happen through thinking the right thoughts, feeling the right feelings, or saying the right words. I used to strive to make miracles happen—trying to jump through all the hoops I thought God required of me—but I never saw results. But when I stopped struggling in my own strength, rested, and trusted Jesus's finished work at the cross, I saw my first miracle.

Today, I minister healing with my eyes open and a smile on my face. I rest in my heart, knowing I can't do a thing to make God want to heal the person more than he already does. I simply make the opportunity for him to act, then I trust that he wants the miracle to happen even more than I do.

Your authority is not based on the volume or tone of your voice; it's based on the fact that you are seated with Christ in the heavenly realms. (See Ephesians 2:6.) You don't have to shout or bark orders at the person. You can minister with gentleness and compassion. In fact, words aren't even required. Many times, Jesus ministered healing with only a touch, and Mark 16:17–18 tells us that one of the signs that accompany believers is that we will place our hands on sick people and see them healed. It's simple.

People experience God's healing power in many ways—whether through a Christian laying on hands, through a word of authority, after forgiving someone, during angelic encounters, while reading the Scriptures, while worshipping, while in a room full of Spirit-filled believers, and more. We don't have to only experience God moving in one particular way.

The Gospels are full of stories where Jesus performed miracles in diverse ways. Perhaps he put mud in a blind man's eyes, rebuked a fever, drove out a demon, spoke to a body part, touched the person, let them touch him, or told them to do something that would only be possible if they were healed. God is not limited to only one delivery method for his miracles.

With that said, during Jesus's ministry, people sometimes begged Jesus to let them touch the edge of his cloak so they could be healed. (See Matthew 14:36 and Mark 6:56.) We don't see Jesus telling them that God wants to heal them another way. They seemed to choose the method, and Jesus worked the miracle. Apparently, God, in his love, is less concerned with how we are healed and more concerned that we're healed at all.

For this reason, we don't need to overcomplicate healing ministry. As Christians, our default expectation ought to be that simple faith will accomplish the miracle. If we're constantly troubleshooting with people and questioning what method will unlock their healing, then our faith is likely more in the method than in the man, Christ Jesus. We've misunderstood and misrepresented God's heart, as though he is more concerned with right *behavior* than right *believing*. (See Galatians 3:1–5.)

When we know God, he will sometimes tell us to minister in a particular way. But in my experience, most of the time, I don't hear any particular guidance in my spirit. Most of the time, I rely on simple trust and the fact that Jesus wants the person healed even more than I do.

This is a healthy culture for a house church. No one needs to strive for their own healing or anyone else's. The breakthrough we're looking for has nothing to do with proving ourselves to God. The only secret key to seeing healing miracles is that there is no secret key. Jesus is the healer, and we are his body. Healing is logical.

So unless the Holy Spirit is giving you specific directions about how to minister, simply lay hands on people. If you want, speak a simple word of authority in the name of Jesus. Then, if possible, see if the person can safely test out their condition and find out if the miracle happened.

If you feel led to minister in a particular way, the proof will be in the pudding, as they say. Either the person will be healed or not. I once told a woman to remove her hat, and when she did, her neck was healed. If her neck hadn't been healed when she took off the hat, I would have humbly apologized and let her know that I thought I was hearing from God but apparently missed it. People are not guinea pigs. We don't experiment with them and then blame them when our experiments fail. Love honors others.

Keep healing ministry simple.

Down-to-Earth Deliverance Ministry

Our house-church meeting was about to begin when there was a knock at the door. Usually people just walk in, so I figured maybe it was a visitor.

It turns out, it was a neighbor from down the street whom I had never met. One of the young men in our house church had accidentally parked a little in front of her driveway, and she couldn't back out her car.

While my friend moved his car, I chatted a little with her. Mary was an older woman with a quirky personality who had been living with her boyfriend for about ten years.

Based on an impression I felt from the Holy Spirit, I asked her if she had pain in her right shoulder. Seemingly unfazed by my knowledge of her life, she answered, "All the time. I was shot in my shoulder when I was carjacked a couple of years ago."

I listened to her story and followed up by asking if I could pray for her. Mary answered, "Of course! You know, I believe in miracles."

I placed my hand on her shoulder and commanded the pain to leave in the name of Jesus. Mary moved her arm to test it and said, "Well, that's funny. It's not hurting at all!" Then she turned and looked at our house full of people and asked, "So what are you guys all doing here?"

Mary became a regular attendee of our house church. A couple of months later, she said, "I think God told me I need to move out of my boyfriend's house because we're not married, and he doesn't want to get married."

I replied, "That sounds like Jesus to me. Let me know if we can do anything to help you out."

After that, weeks passed without seeing Mary. I couldn't reach her on the phone or at home. I wondered if she actually went through with leaving or if she was avoiding us.

Weeks later, after a house-church meeting, half the people had left, and the rest were lingering and chatting. Then, Mary knocked on the storm door. I flagged her inside, and she stepped onto our landing.

Her face was glazed over, and she reeked of alcohol.

"How are you doing, Mary?" I asked from the couch.

Mary answered with a string of disjointed, random words, her gaze darting all over the room. I couldn't tell if it was the alcohol or if she had suffered a stroke.

"Can I pray for you, Mary?"

Mary's eyes locked onto mine. A deep, guttural voice answered back, "*No!*"

Still resting in my heart and now knowing exactly what was going on, I smiled. "Well, I'm going to pray for you. Father, thank you for your love for Mary. Thank you for drawing her here so she can be free. In the name of Jesus, I command all impure spirits to leave her now. Amen."

Mary breathed a loud sigh, perked up, and said in completely coherent speech, "Thank you! It seems you're the only one who can get them to leave. How do you think that happened?"

I approached Mary to chat more privately with her.

"Well, Mary, for one thing, I can see you're drunk. Do you think that might have something to do with it?"

"Maybe. But I've been drunk before and didn't have this problem."

"Also, the last time I saw you, you told me that God had instructed you to move out of your boyfriend's house. Did you follow through on obeying the Lord?"

Mary became angry. She began to yell and curse at me. And within moments, her language returned to incoherent, random, disjointed words.

"I'm sorry you're choosing darkness over light, Mary. I'm going to have to ask you to leave now."

I wish that story had a happier ending. About four years later, her boyfriend died of a sickness, and she started to get her life on track, but my wife and I moved and lost track of her after that. The last I saw her, she was attending church, so I pray she found the help she needed.

Nevertheless, this story perfectly illustrates the sort of things you can expect in a gospel house. The sick and demonized will come to you. And you don't have to make a big show out of ministering to them. It's just part of ordinary life.

You may have noticed that I didn't have a big, loud argument with the demons. There was no flailing around on the ground (although I've seen that happen). I didn't even need to find out the names of the demons or anything like that. I simply told them to leave with the authority of the only name that matters.

I don't let demons make exhibits of people or use them as puppets. I don't give them an audience for their lies. I don't let them shame people in front of others. (It's one thing if the *person* confesses sin, but I don't need the demons to do the confessing.) I've seen hundreds of people delivered this way. Like healing ministry, many have overcomplicated the matter. Are there ever exceptions when ministry is less straightforward? Sure. But I never want to make the exception the rule. Follow the Holy Spirit. But again, keep it simple.

Keep the Main Thing the Main Thing

People often ask me, "What happens if I minister to someone, but they don't get healed or set free?"

I believe that's the wrong question. What happens if you minister to someone, but they don't get loved?

Scripture tells us that "if I have a faith that can move mountains, but do not have love, I am nothing" (1 Corinthians 13:2). In the apostle Paul's mind, if the miracle happens but I don't love, I've failed.

Along these lines, in Matthew 25:31–46, Jesus shared a metaphor about the final judgment, comparing it to separating sheep from goats. To the sheep, the King said, "Come, you who are blessed by my Father; take your inheritance, the kingdom prepared for you since the creation of the world. For I was hungry and you gave me something to eat, I was thirsty and you gave me something to drink, I was a stranger and you invited me in, I needed clothes and you clothed me, I was sick and you looked after me, I was in prison and you came to visit me" (vv. 34–36).

The sheep asked him, "Wait … we never saw you. What are you talking about?"

To which the king answered, "Truly I tell you, whatever you did for one of the least of these brothers and sisters of mine, you did for me" (v. 40).

What I find fascinating is that Jesus did not say, "I was sick and you healed me." He said, "I was sick and you looked after me." When we stand before the King in the final judgment, we won't have to answer for whether we ever worked a miracle, but we will have to answer for whether we loved.

If you make your priority the healing or the deliverance, then the person will probably be damaged along the way. But if you make the priority love for the person, then Jesus himself will thank you at the final judgment, regardless of whether the miracle happens.

Love as you minister. Behave honorably toward the person. Some have joked about being "prayer hostages"—being unable to escape the group of praying Christians who surround them. But love doesn't take prayer hostages. Love does not abuse or take advantage. Love is more concerned with the person receiving ministry than with the minister's own reputation.

In our church, the first thing we do is show love and compassion to the person. That might look like listening to their story, finding them a chair to sit in, or taking them to a place where they won't be a spectacle. The second thing we do is minister. If the healing or deliverance happens, we keep loving. We don't turn off love for those who are whole and free. And if the healing or deliverance doesn't happen, we keep loving. We do the hard work of caring for the sick—the very thing Jesus will thank us for at the judgment.

Finally, we continue loving people through tragedy. If the miracle never happens and a person dies, we are present for their family in the weeks and months afterward. We give them room to grieve and make ourselves available to listen and sometimes help process emotions and theological questions. "Love is patient" (1 Corinthians 13:4). We take our time with people and don't rush them into a place of pretending they're okay.

We encourage people to bank on God's justice. If Jesus paid with his own blood for a person to be free and whole, then he deserves to receive those things. If the miracle doesn't happen, that's unjust. Jesus is worthy. Thankfully, Scripture demonstrates that God loves to overcompensate for injustice. Satan brought all manner of sickness and destruction to Job, but God blessed Job with double of everything that was taken, plus 140 years of long life to enjoy it. (See Job 42:10–17.) Proverbs 6:31 says that if a thief is caught stealing, he must repay seven times what he took. God spoke through the prophet Joel, "I will repay you for the years the locusts have eaten" (Joel 2:25). This means that not only does the famine end, but now people will reap more than they can consume until the debt is paid off. And of course, Jesus is the prime example: one innocent, spotless Lamb of God died a criminal's death and paid the price for all humanity's sin. God loves to overcompensate for injustice.

So if the miracle you've been believing for hasn't happened yet, be encouraged. God's justice will prevail, and the blessing will be even bigger when it comes than if it had been received immediately. And if you lost someone to a tragedy, call out to the God who loves you. He will hear your faith and see that restitution is made. Jesus is worthy.

Aim High

All this is part of having a gospel house. Healings, miracles, and deliverances are to be expected because these are all part of the gospel. They are all expressions of God's kingdom, which has authority in your home.

The presence of a contingency plan doesn't mean we settle for second best. The fact that we know how to love people when they aren't healed doesn't mean we take our foot off the accelerator when it comes to healing. Healing and deliverance are part and parcel of the gospel of salvation and ought to be treated as such. We would never hold back part of the message, so why would we hinder part of the application?

Jesus is worthy to receive everything for which he paid. This is why we do everything we do in a gospel house. It's why we make disciples for him. It's why we help those in need. It's why we minister to the sick and demonized. It's why we gather for fellowship and worship.

So always love, but don't settle for a powerless Christianity. Even if it's the thousandth time you're ministering to the same person for the same issue, minister as though it's the very first. Expect a miracle every time. (Otherwise, why are you bothering to minister in the first place?) Jesus is worthy.

CHAPTER 8:

SPIRITUAL GIFTS IN THE HOME

Today, more than ever, we need to get back to the small group as the primary place to exercise spiritual gifts. It is the most natural context for worship and prayer together. It is the best place to find encouragement and accountability as we grow in our relationship with Christ. It is also the most spontaneous and biblical place for the discovery of our spiritual gifts.

—Joel Comiskey

Mercedes choked back tears throughout her entire first meeting at my house. The love she felt from everyone was amplified by the Jesus revealed in our conversation. Every person who spoke in the meeting seemed to speak directly to her.

At the end of our meeting, we broke into smaller groups to pray for one another. JonMark felt like he had a word for her throughout the entire meeting, so he made his way over to her to deliver it.

"When you walked in the door, the Lord showed me you have a broken heart. The Lord says he is going to heal you. I feel like you suffered a significant loss recently, like in the last couple years. He showed me you are concerned for your three children, and he wants you to know they are going to be fine. It's almost as if you have been injected with poison that's going through your whole body. The Lord's going to heal you. And you have felt that a calling on your life has been pushed back time and time again, but the Lord says it will happen. You are a writer. The Lord says you are going to write again. You also have a prophetic gifting that you feel has been dormant, and the Lord is going to stir that up again."

Mercedes' eyes welled with tears.

JonMark continued, "Were the things I said accurate? Or did anything in there not make sense?"

Mercedes replied, "No, it was accurate, except the thing about having three kids. I used to have three kids, but my youngest passed away about a year and a half ago."

Clearly, this was the "significant loss" Mercedes had experienced, but the Lord knew her son was still alive, and she would see him again. JonMark and others prayed for Mercedes. The Holy Spirit captivated her attention that night, and she hasn't turned her gaze.

Over the following weeks, Mercedes cried throughout most of our meetings. Little by little, her heart healed. She grieved in a healthy way. Her heart was transformed by the gospel. She started prophesying more frequently and would go out of her way to help others. Mercedes became a powerful example of love, faith, perseverance, and strength in the face of tragedy. And her prophetic gifting has proven to strengthen, encourage, and correct us, drawing us all closer to Jesus.

About six months later, a young mother in our church named Roxy, who had miscarried her second child, Zion, a year earlier, was pregnant again. At only fourteen weeks gestation, her water broke. Our church prayed for Roxy and her baby, and we felt an assurance that the little one would be okay. A few times, Mercedes helped Roxy with her older daughter so she could rest. Miraculously and against all expectations of the doctors, Roxy carried her baby all the way to full term and gave birth to a healthy little girl. As I write this, Amaryah is just over one month old.

Another couple came a few months ago with their kids. They had been attending a Protestant church that didn't teach or practice spiritual gifts. But both of them knew enough of the Scriptures to know that something more was available in Christianity. They found our network's website and asked to attend.

On one of their first weeks with us, a couple of ladies—Lisa and Kim—prayed with the wife after the meeting. Soon, Lisa came to me and said, "I think we need help with this one. Can you come over?"

I joined their little group. The woman explained that she really wanted the ladies to pray for her but also really *didn't* want them to pray for her. With wide, concerned eyes, she explained that it was as if she had two minds inside her—one that really wanted God and the other that just wanted to run.

I smiled and assured her, "Okay. That's not crazy. You're safe, and we're here for you. Is it okay if I pray?"

She nodded her head and grabbed my hand on one side and one of the ladies' hands on the other.

I calmly and gently offered a simple prayer. "Father, thank you for your love. Thank you for being here and keeping my friend safe. And I command that unclean spirit to leave right now in Jesus's name."

The woman's grip tightened on our hands to an almost unbearable level. It was like she was riding a rollercoaster. She began to yell for her husband, asking him to come and make the sensation stop. "It hurts! Help!"

I stayed calm and focused. "You're safe."

"I need to stop! You need to let me go!"

"No one is holding you—you're holding us. You're safe," I calmly continued. "But I'm also not going to leave you in this condition. Just trust us. It will be over very soon."

Her husband watched with concern, but he trusted us and prayed for his wife with another man in our church.

Within a minute or two, the woman felt a sudden release. The intense fear and pain were gone.

"That's it?" she asked with a hesitant smile.

I chuckled. "Basically, yeah! There's probably more to pray about—like identifying how the enemy gained access so we can close that door for the future. And there's a difference between being delivered and being mature, so there's always room to grow. But you're free now."

Over the next few days and weeks, we prayed through a lot of issues, especially forgiveness toward people in her past.

Like Mercedes, she would come most weeks, feeling as if she wanted to cry through the entire meeting. Everyone seemed to be talking directly to her throughout the conversation. And, also like Mercedes, little by little, her heart healed and her mind was renewed.

Stories like these are commonplace in our house churches. No doubt, God is truly among us. Because every believer is free to exercise spiritual gifts, new people are often shocked to find themselves encountering the tangible power and love of God throughout our meetings. In a gospel house, the Scriptures are literally fulfilled. "But if an unbeliever or an inquirer comes in while everyone is prophesying, they are convicted of sin and are brought under judgment by all, as the secrets of their hearts are laid bare. So they will fall down and worship God, exclaiming, 'God is really among you!'" (1 Corinthians 14:24–25).

What Are Spiritual Gifts?

A lot of books about spiritual gifts are available. I've read many of them. And I dislike most of them. Some treat spiritual gifts like personality traits, identifying people with natural tendencies in one area or another and calling them gifted. Others limit what God can do by focusing entirely on one biblical list or another. Still others put so much emphasis on identifying someone's singular gift that they inadvertently discourage people from eagerly desiring other gifts, as the Scriptures command. (See 1 Corinthians 14:1.)

Another challenge is that most books about spiritual gifts try to explain how those gifts operate in a modern, conventional church meeting. But this is a foreign environment to the New Testament. The biblical passages about spiritual gifts were written to house churches. Therefore, the instructions given make the most sense in a small-group environment.[19]

Spiritual gifts have been a major area of study for me for more than two decades. One day, I may write an entire book on the subject. For now, though, I'll simply offer the most important things I've learned, which will help you turn your house into a gospel house.

First, the Bible includes multiple lists of spiritual gifts. (See Romans 12:6–8; 1 Corinthians 12:7–10; and 1 Peter 4:10–11.) Some teachings treat these lists as completely different subjects, as though they're not talking about the same thing. But a careful study of each list will show common gifts, common language, and common subject matter. For example, whenever Paul talks about spiritual gifts, he connects it to a teaching about how we are all

---

[19] My favorite book on this subject, which successfully contextualizes spiritual gifts within small group meetings, is *The Spirit-Filled Small Group* by Joel Comiskey. If you want to explore this subject further, I recommend starting there.

unique members of the body of Christ.[20] The gift lists in Scripture are not meant to be exhaustive; they're meant to give a selection of examples.[21]

So what are spiritual gifts? They're anything the Holy Spirit empowers a Christian to do beyond natural human ability. Furthermore, and perhaps more importantly, spiritual gifts are expressions of Jesus. As mentioned, Paul connects the expression of gifts to being the body of Christ, also noting that they are "for the common good" (1 Corinthians 12:7). And Jesus described how the Holy Spirit operates, saying that the Spirit takes from what belongs to Jesus and makes it known to us (John 16:13–15). Thus, spiritual gifts are expressions of Jesus, displayed through a believer by the Holy Spirit's power for the common good.

---

[20] First Corinthians 12:1–11 is about spiritual gifts while vv. 12–31 are about being the body of Christ. Similarly, Romans 12:4–5 is about being the body of Christ while vv. 6–8 are about spiritual gifts. Even the equipping ministries mentioned in Ephesians 4:11 are followed by a teaching about how we are all parts of one body in vv. 15–16. We'll discuss these unique gifts in the following chapter.

[21] We generally like the idea of exhaustive lists for teaching purposes, but sometimes lists are limited in scope. If you were asked to list animals found in a zoo, chances are you might name a selection of exotic animals—lions, tigers, elephants, giraffes, apes, zebras, polar bears, and penguins—and feel content with your list, even though you could name hundreds or thousands of other animals. Meanwhile, another person might list an entirely different selection, with only a few overlaps—lions, panda bears, kangaroos, elephants, monkeys, cheetahs, antelopes, and ostriches. Neither list is incorrect, only limited. The one or two words shared between the lists remind us we're talking about the same subject. So it is with the biblical lists of spiritual gifts, all of which include prophecy in some form. No gift list is exhaustive, and they ought not be treated as such.

In my search of Scripture, I've identified more than thirty supernatural activities that fit that definition—actions the Holy Spirit has empowered believers to do beyond natural human ability, as they reveal Jesus in ministry to others. And some gifts might not even be mentioned in Scripture.

Knowing a list of gifts is less important than understanding spiritual gifts in general, as evidenced by the fact that no biblical list is exhaustive. So for the purposes of this chapter, I'll share the principles that will help turn your house into a gospel house, and I'll let you discover the list through your own study of the Word.

Gifts Are Not Natural

The Greek word for "grace" is *charis*.[22] In most Scripture, this word indicates the favor of God that provides supernatural benefits to us. Grace is God's active favor on our lives that empowers us to live in a way that would be impossible without his direct activity.

A related word is *charisma*—which is a gift freely and graciously given—and its plural, *charismata*.[23] This is the word used in reference to spiritual gifts.[24] Such gifts are called the work of the

---

22 "χάρισ," Danker, *A Greek-English Lexicon*, 1079.

23 "χάρισμα," Danker, *A Greek-English Lexicon*, 1081.

24 I am aware of teachings that suggest there is a difference between "spiritual gifts" and "manifestations of the Holy Spirit," but this is an unhelpful distinction and not proper biblical interpretation. Yes, 1 Corinthians 12:1 uses the Greek word *pneumatikos* (spiritual things) where the translators rendered "spiritual gifts." But in verses 4 and 31, Paul uses the word *charisma*, which is the word for "gift." All spiritual gifts are manifestations of the Spirit, and 1 Corinthians 12 does not list different or unique gifts.

Spirit (1 Corinthians 12:6, 11), and the manifestation of the Spirit (1 Corinthians 12:7). In these moments, the Holy Spirit makes himself known, working through a believer to powerfully serve others (1 Corinthians 12:5, 7). Spiritual gifts are expressions of God's grace. As 1 Peter 4:10 says, "Each of you should use whatever gift you have received to serve others, as faithful stewards of God's grace in its various forms."

When we operate in spiritual gifts, we are stewarding God's grace. We are responsible to administer the grace we have received, distributing it to others. As Jesus said in Matthew 10:8, "Freely you have received; freely give." Around AD 125–200, an unknown early Christian (identified as "Mathetes," which is the Greek word for "disciple"[25]) wrote in reference to spiritual gifts, "Grace, widely spread, increases in the saints. It furnishes understanding, reveals mysteries, announces times, and rejoices over the faithful."[26]

Spiritual gifts are the distribution of God's supernatural grace, in varied forms, as determined by the Holy Spirit. They are expressions of Jesus—not merely human traits.

Some gifts mentioned in Paul's letters appear to be virtues that other Scriptures require of all Christians, such as faith, hospitality, service, mercy, generosity, and so forth. (See Romans 12:6–8.) Nevertheless, Paul indicates that not every Christian operates in every spiritual gift at all times. (See 1 Corinthians

---

[25] "μαθητής," Danker, *A Greek-English Lexicon*, 609.

[26] "Letter to Diognetus," in *Ante-Nicene Fathers Volume 1*, ed. Alexander Roberts and James Donaldson, (Carol Stream, Illinois: Hendrickson Publishers, 2004), 29.

12:29–30.) Shall we conclude that not every Christian is supposed to serve, give, or be hospitable? This would seem to contradict other Scriptures.

One of the gifts mentioned is faith. If you don't have faith, you can't be saved. (See Ephesians 2:8; John 3:36; 1 Peter 1:9.) Shall we conclude that only some Christians have faith and are saved? Or shall we conclude that every Christian has received this spiritual gift from the Holy Spirit? Or is there perhaps another explanation?

There is a difference between the virtues that are gradually developed in us—those that grow over time through character formation—and virtues or abilities that are supernaturally bestowed on us by the power of the Holy Spirit. Those grace-gifts bestowed by the Holy Spirit are expressions of Jesus.

So in the case of faith, there's the *measure* of faith we all grow in, and then there's the perfect, Jesus-level *gift* of faith that the Spirit distributes as he determines.

Most of the time, I operate on the measure of faith I've been given. I go "from faith to faith" (Romans 1:17 NKJV). But sometimes, the Holy Spirit determines that the level of faith I've grown into isn't sufficient to help me past the situation I'm facing. So by grace, he takes Jesus's faith, makes it known to me, and suddenly, I operate at a supernatural level of faith that would otherwise be unnatural for me. This is a gift of faith.

The same goes for all the other gifts. There's natural service, which happens in our own strength as we honor others above ourselves. And then there's a gift of service, which happens "with the strength God provides" (1 Peter 4:11). Everyone is expected to serve, but sometimes, Jesus personally serves through someone as the Holy Spirit drops a special expression of grace on that person.

Some gifts mentioned are signs that Jesus said would accompany everyone who believes, such as speaking in tongues, healing the sick, and working miracles. (See Mark 16:17–18 and John 14:12.) How do we reconcile this with the gifts that Paul indicates are demonstrated only in some?

There is arguably a difference between the signs that we all grow in through our walk with Christ (which are generally imperfect or limited in our expression of them) and the gifts whereby the Holy Spirit empowers us to go beyond our personal growth level and operate at the level of Jesus.

For example, I see a lot of people physically healed, but the results are hit-and-miss. The sporadic results I see are a far cry from the 100 percent we see in Jesus's life and ministry. But I have been in a few meetings around the world where every person I laid hands on was healed. I have been in other meetings where 100 percent of eye conditions were healed through my hands (while other illnesses were hit-and-miss). But I ministered to someone with eye problems a week later and saw nothing (and neither did they). In these cases of Jesus-level results, I don't believe I was operating in the *sign* of healing that is for "those who believe." Rather, I believe the Holy Spirit gave me one of the *gifts* of healing that revealed Jesus.

Spiritual gifts take us beyond our human abilities or the signs that are for all believers. They are expressions of Jesus, operating by grace through the power of the Holy Spirit.

Spiritual Gifts and Gospel Houses

What makes a house a gospel house is the active presence of Jesus. I can't transform anyone's heart. If someone comes over and only meets me, then nothing profound will happen. But if a person comes into my house and encounters Jesus, then everything changes.

This is why spiritual gifts are so important. They're the means by which we all express unique aspects of Jesus to each other.

It's like the classic parable of the blind men describing an elephant. One felt the trunk and said, "An elephant is like a mighty snake." Another felt the leg and said, "An elephant is like a towering tree." Another felt the body and said, "An elephant is like a formidable wall." Still another felt the tail and said, "An elephant is like a paint brush!"

As each man explained the piece of the elephant he experienced, a fuller picture emerged for all. And with enough descriptions from enough people, eventually, a clear concept would take shape.

Full participation is vital to a healthy church meeting. As Paul wrote, "What then shall we say, brothers and sisters? When you come together, each of you has a hymn, or a word of instruction, a revelation, a tongue or an interpretation. Everything must be done so that the church may be built up" (1 Corinthians 14:26).

A house-church meeting is not a one-person show. It is an interactive conversation in which Jesus is the primary focus, and the Holy Spirit reveals him through his people. You do not need to be the answer to everyone's problems. Jesus is the answer, and he lives in more people than just you.

Sometimes, God will speak through one person and then act through another. For example, he might give a word of knowledge for healing through one and then administer the healing through another. Sometimes, he will give a prophetic word about blessing someone financially, then those with gifts of giving will generously step out as the first vessels to distribute that blessing.

Since spiritual gifts are so vital to a thriving gospel house, talk about the gifts regularly. As Paul wrote, "Now about the gifts of the Spirit, brothers and sisters, I do not want you to be uninformed" (1 Corinthians 12:1). When gifts are normally discussed as part of church culture, people will start to desire them for themselves. When gifts are treated as normal expressions of Christianity, they are expected and become common.

A great way to do this is to celebrate the expression of others' gifts. Paul showed us how this is done: "I always thank my God for you because of his grace given you in Christ Jesus. For in him you have been enriched in every way—with all kinds of speech and with all knowledge—God thus confirming our testimony about Christ among you. Therefore you do not lack any spiritual gift as you eagerly wait for our Lord Jesus Christ to be revealed" (1 Corinthians 1:4–7).

Even though the Corinthian church was in terrible disarray, Paul still celebrated their use of the gifts. When we celebrate the use of gifts (and even the attempt to use them), people feel encouraged to step out in them more fully.

If you're a leader, don't expect the people in your house church to be more on-fire than you are. Certainly, people can be, but your job is to lead. Set the tone. Be the first to share testimonies when no one else will. Be faithful to step out and attempt spiritual gifts. And encourage others to step out.

In addition, invite people into the process of ministering gifts. Ask questions like, "Is anyone hearing something from the Lord for everyone right now?" Then wait a bit. Or when someone needs healing, ask who feels led to minister to the person or perhaps assign someone as the Spirit leads. From time to time, it's good to ask at the end of a meeting, "Does anyone else have something they feel is for everyone tonight, but you weren't sure how to fit it into the conversation?"

Give people grace if they mess up or get it wrong. The more freedom there is to make mistakes, the freer people will feel to step out into something new. This doesn't mean you shrug off mistakes or pretend they didn't happen. Scripture tells us to pass judgment on prophetic utterances. (See 1 Corinthians 14:29.)

We can address such missteps with mercy and love. One might say, "Thanks for stepping out with that message. Scripture commands us to pass judgment about whatever is prophesied. That's because it's possible to miss the mark in our delivery. Is anyone discerning something about that prophecy? Or does anyone know of Scripture that would support or refute it?"

Let people discuss it. If you need to correct someone for coming out with guns blazing rather than gentleness and love, this, too, will be a great learning experience for everyone.

This is one reason why it's important to have a clear, designated leader in a house church meeting. It provides a certain level of safety to the group, which helps people rest in their hearts, knowing someone has their back and will protect them if someone starts attacking.

If you will facilitate a meeting where everyone has room to express their unique gifts as the Holy Spirit determines, where prophecies are judged, and where the gospel is regularly articulated, then Jesus will be seen and experienced. People will cry through your meetings as their minds are renewed and their hearts are transformed. Sinners and newcomers will fall on their knees and declare, "God is truly among you!" Your house will be a gospel house.

CHAPTER 9:

TRAINERS AND EQUIPPERS

Ephesians 4:11 speaks of a group of people who are for the body; they are God's gifts to the church, supplying Christ for the building up of the body . . . . How do [the apostles, prophets, evangelists, shepherds, and teachers] serve the body? They must be those who have gone through special training under the Lord's hand and have been specially molded through the environment ordered by the Spirit; they have a history of knowing Christ. They are tried and tested and instructed by Christ, and they are qualified to transmit spiritual values. They have a secret history in tribulation, and the cross has wrought the things that they minister to the Body into them.

—Watchman Nee

Many churches operate like cruise ships. A minority of the people onboard work tirelessly to serve the many passengers. Most people on a cruise ship are consumers. They chose this cruise line expecting a certain experience that the crew aims to provide. And if the quality of the experience drops over time, then those consumers will simply choose a different cruise line for their next vacation. What you win people with you win them to, and far too many churches are after consumers, always trying to make bigger and better programs and productions to keep the people coming back.

The church Jesus started, however, is more like a battleship. Every person has a role to play. The captain is Jesus. Everyone else is a member of the crew. And within that crew are a few specialized and necessary service roles—like the chief engineer, who oversees all the mechanical operations and maintenance; or the chief steward, who makes sure meals are prepared for everyone; and so on. These special officers serve their crewmates, exercising a certain amount of authority within their designated departments while also sacrificing for the sake of others, making the entire crew more effective in their respective assignments.

The analogy isn't perfect, but hopefully you get the idea. Every Christian is a minister. Every crewmate on the ship is valuable and needed for the ship to run smoothly. Likewise, every part of Jesus's body has a distinct function and purpose in the church. But Jesus has also given certain people to the church to serve the body in a variety of specialized ways, making everyone more effective in our shared commission.

> So Christ himself gave the apostles, the prophets, the evangelists, the pastors and teachers, to equip his people for works of service, so that the body of Christ may be built up until we all reach unity in the faith and in the

> knowledge of the Son of God and become mature, attaining to the whole measure of the fullness of Christ.
>
> Then we will no longer be infants, tossed back and forth by the waves, and blown here and there by every wind of teaching and by the cunning and craftiness of people in their deceitful scheming. Instead, speaking the truth in love, we will grow to become in every respect the mature body of him who is the head, that is, Christ. From him the whole body, joined and held together by every supporting ligament, grows and builds itself up in love, as each part does its work. (Ephesians 4:11–16)

These ministers—the apostles, prophets, evangelists, pastors, and teachers—have an expiration date attached. They're here to train and equip their fellow Christians "until … " Until what? "Until we all reach unity in the faith and in the knowledge of the Son of God and become mature, attaining to the whole measure of the fullness of Christ" (Ephesians 4:13).

Has this happened yet? Have Christians everywhere reached unity of the faith? Do we all know Jesus the same way? Have we become mature? Are we revealing Jesus in his fullness?

The obvious answer to all these questions is no, and therefore, we can conclude that such ministers are still walking among us, given to the church for the purpose here stated.

Every believer is a minister, and some ministers are specially graced by God to equip other believers for more effective ministry.

Equipping a Gospel House

Judy, Roman, Sunni, JonMark, Kim, Lisa, and others in our house-church network share Jesus almost everywhere they go. They're so passionate about evangelism, they make other Christians uncomfortable. They encourage others to share their faith and teach them how to minister in the same way—perhaps receiving and delivering words of knowledge or prophecies, or approaching strangers to offer physical healing. Our entire network is more evangelistic because these people serve as engines for evangelism among us. Many have joined our house churches because of them.

Alex, Greg, Amy, Sueli, and others are deep thinkers who are gifted in articulating the Scriptures. They ask great questions that help people think critically and understand the Bible. They distill hours of study into accessible, life-giving principles that bring clarity and new life to others. Our entire network is more biblically literate and able to express truth to others because of their ministry among us.

Joe, Roxy, Mercedes, Jason, and others so passionately pursue God's presence and listen so intently to his voice that they challenge the status quo for everyone else. They hear from God before anyone else. They foretell what God is about to do, and within months, we see God fulfill his word. They encourage everyone toward worship, repentance, and holiness—reminding us all that more is available in our relationships with the Lord. Their very presence makes our entire network more spiritually vibrant.

Gracie, David, Robin, and others have keen insight into human relationships and demonstrate an abnormal level of care for people in need. They self-sacrifice regularly to help others thrive in life—spiritually, emotionally, relationally, etc. They constantly remind the rest of us to consider others in our decisions and actions. They provide wise counsel and loving rebukes. We have many pastors in our network who oversee house churches, but these select ministers are gifted in ways that invite even our pastors to become more pastoral. They carry a special grace from God to equip others in love, care, honor, and service to one another.

Many of these same people and others also demonstrate a more apostolic grace on their lives. They are engines of multiplication and expansion of God's kingdom among us. Our house-church network is multiplying, and the people of our network are healthier overall because of the grace they carry to self-sacrifice for the rest of the body. Some, who cannot be named for security reasons, have gone to foreign mission fields while others have remained locally.

A single gospel house may not have such a broad selection of ministers, but in time, God will bring them. This is one of the benefits of networking with other churches—not only house churches. The body of Christ is much bigger than your small group.

If you want your house church to thrive and multiply, the people within it will need to be trained and equipped into maturity, and God has designed his church in such a way that no minister can do this alone. Therefore, your role in leading a gospel house is to identify such ministers—both within and without—and welcome their gifts in your meetings. It is necessary, then, that you understand these roles and how they function.

Functions, Not Positions

Biblically and practically speaking, these special roles seem to be more functions than offices. In other words, the names of these roles describe what people do, not who they are. Identity is found in Christ, not in gifting. As noted, Ephesians 4:13 uses the word "until," indicating that these ministries are not eternal roles. Those who find their identity in their ministry will be disappointed one day when everything is made perfect and such ministries cease.

The Bible also seems to indicate that a person can operate in one role and then step into to a different role. For example, Paul and Barnabas were numbered among the "prophets and teachers" in Acts 13:1. Then, in the next couple verses, the two men were set apart "for the work to which [God had] called them," and they were "sent out," a term connected with apostolic ministry. Notice they were set apart for work, not a position or title. For this reason, I don't think of these ministries as positions or titles in a hierarchy but instead as functions that serve the body of Christ.

The main work of such ministers is to bring the body of Christ into unity and maturity. Since verse 14 says that "we will no longer be infants … ," we can extrapolate that these ministries do influence individuals with the goal of moving them toward unity. Equipping ministers help bring individuals into healthier fellowship with other believers. Infants are individuals, but we will "grow to become in every respect the mature body of him who is the head, that is, Christ." Maturity only happens together.

In other words, immaturity looks like individuality, and maturity looks like unity and interconnectedness. Those who serve in equipping roles are not lone-wolf ministers, no matter how gifted they may be. They are living examples of unity, love, and faithfulness in our community.

The equipping minister's role is not to be the center of attention or a stage persona with many followers. Rather, it is to make others into more effective ministers. It is a ministry of service and humility, raising up others and sending them out to shine even more brightly than they already do.

Every Believer Is a Minister

Every believer is to share the gospel (Mark 16:15–18). Every believer is prophetic (Acts 2:17–18; 1 Corinthians 14:31). Every believer is to mature into the role of teaching others (Hebrews 5:12; Colossians 3:16). Every believer is sent out to make disciples (Matthew 28:18–20).

What, then, is the difference between the fivefold ministry (the popularized term for the five special equipping minister roles discussed in Ephesians 4:11) and the work to which every believer is called?

As with other gifts of the Spirit, the difference seems to be whether there is a special grace from the Holy Spirit upon a person's life that enables them to express an aspect of Jesus beyond their human ability. For example, there is a difference between those Jesus has given to the church "to be . . . evangelists" (Ephesians 4:11) and merely doing "the work of an evangelist" (2 Timothy 4:5).

Those with special grace from the Lord are trailblazers—demonstrating lifestyles that challenge and inspire others. For instance, Paul was gifted as an apostle, but he still expected non-apostles to follow his example (1 Corinthians 11:1; Philippians 3:17). A fivefold minister is a frontline worker in the kingdom who ministers beyond natural, human ability with strength from the Lord, serving as a pacesetter for the church and training others to do the same. "[Jesus] is the one we proclaim, admonishing and teaching everyone with all wisdom, so that we may present everyone fully mature in Christ. To this end I strenuously contend with all the energy Christ so powerfully works in me" (Colossians 1:28–29).

For this reason, fivefold ministers are unique expressions of Jesus to the church. Jesus was and is all five roles, and he does them perfectly.[27] Any of us may be called upon by the Holy Spirit to minister in a particular way in the strength of Christ, serving his people beyond the limits of our own human ability.

Apostles

There's a difference between the twelve, who Jesus uniquely appointed to establish the church, and apostles, who the Scriptures indicate numbered more than the twelve.[28] The twelve served a unique leadership role in establishing the first church. They were people who had physically been with Jesus from the beginning of his ministry and were eyewitnesses of his crucifixion and resurrection (Mark 3:14; Acts 1:21–22).

The word *apostle* simply means "sent one" and is sometimes used in ancient Greek literature for messengers.[29] Jesus didn't invent the word. The culture of those times originally used the word for naval expeditions (and possibly their commanders) and later for certain ambassadors and delegates who carried administrative responsibilities.[30]

---

[27] Jesus is revealed in Scripture as an Apostle (Hebrews 3:1), a Prophet (Matthew 13:57; 21:11; Luke 24:20; John 4:19, 44; 6:14), an Evangelist (Mark 1:14–15), a Pastor (1 Peter 2:25; 5:4; Hebrews 13:20; Mark 14:27; Isaiah 40:11; John 10:11, 14–15), and a Teacher (Luke 20:21; John 3:2; 13:13–14).

[28] For example, Barnabas and Paul (Acts 14:14), Andronicus and Junia (Romans 16:7), Silas and Timothy (1 Thessalonians 1:1 and 2:6), and Apollos (Acts 4:6–9).

[29] "ἀπόστολος." Danker, *A Greek-English Lexicon*, 122.

[30] Ibid.

In the church, an apostle is one who has been commissioned to go and raise up disciples with demonstrations of the Spirit's power and with authority (Matthew 10:1–8; 28:16–20). They do so through a dedication to prayer and the ministry of the Word (Acts 6:2–4), accompanied by miracles, signs, and wonders (Acts 5:12; 2 Corinthians 12:12). This may sometimes include foretelling the future and warning of specific trials to come (Jude 1:17–19).

Apostles speak with authority about doctrine and Christian practices (Acts 15:1–2)—not because they are bold about their own ideas but because they have encountered Jesus Christ, and they see such things in him (Galatians 1:12). Their encounters with the Lord have granted them insight into the mystery of Christ and his unified body (Ephesians 3:4–6). In fact, one cannot truly serve as an apostle without personally witnessing Jesus, whether in person (like the twelve) or by special revelation (like Paul) (1 Corinthians 9:1; Acts 1:21–22; 4:13).

Apostles carry the message of Christ on their hearts. They preach Jesus (Colossians 1:28). To the apostle, merely preaching "about" Christ is unsatisfying. If Jesus is not made manifest to and through the hearers, the apostle would rather not waste their time (Galatians 4:19).

Apostles are servants. First, they are servants of Christ, entrusted with the secret things of God (1 Corinthians 4:1). But second, they are servants of all—the lowest of the lowly (1 Corinthians 4:9–13). Apostles affirm and release others into their God-given ministries as the Holy Spirit leads (Acts 6:6). Their ministry is ultimately proven only by meaningful fruit in other people's lives (1 Corinthians 9:2; 2 Corinthians 3:3). And they do all this with the expectation of persecution and possibly even martyrdom (Luke 11:49).

Prophets

A prophet is one whose chief concern is right relationship with God—first their own and then the rest of the church. He or she labors in the strength of the Spirit, crying out to man to be restored to God (Zechariah 1:4) and crying out to God for the preservation of life and the staying of judgment (Genesis 20:7). But when God decrees judgment, prophets will nevertheless speak forth his words (1 Kings 20:36). Or they will offer warning meant to convince people to choose obedience to the Lord (2 Kings 17:13). The greatest of all Old Testament prophets, John the Baptist, has no recorded miracles attributed to his ministry but rather is known for proclaiming repentance and baptism (Luke 3:1–20; 7:24–28).

For this reason, prophets are often not well received and are sometimes even hated for the words they proclaim (1 Kings 19:10). They are often ignored by people who know them well (Matthew 13:57; Mark 6:4; Luke 4:24; John 4:44). They can expect persecution and possibly even martyrdom (Luke 11:49; Acts 7:52).

Calling oneself a prophet does not make them a prophet (Revelation 2:20). Titles are nothing; fruit is everything (Matthew 7:15–20). Even signs and wonders are insufficient evidence of the

Lord's hand upon a prophet (Deuteronomy 13:1–5). God speaks harshly against anyone who presumes to speak words in his name that he has not spoken (Deuteronomy 18:20; Jeremiah 23:16–32; Ezekiel 13).

The prophet's message is whatever God is saying, and they receive this message in any of the myriad ways God speaks (Numbers 12:6–8; Hebrews 1:1). Together with apostles, they have been given insight into the mystery of Christ (Ephesians 3:4–6) and have been sent by Jesus to confront the religious spirit among his people (Matthew 23:34; Luke 11:49). They are pacesetters and leaders in praise and worship (Exodus 15:20–21). Driven by God's heart to restore right relationship, prophets point the way to God when others can't find it.

A prophet speaks the very words of God with boldness and humility to give blessing, direction, insight, correction, or anything else the Lord needs to convey in the moment (Deuteronomy 18:18). But even when there is no specific word from the Lord, they so share God's heart for reconciliation that they still testify about Jesus and preach forgiveness of sin (Acts 10:43). Because the prophet speaks for God, those who do not respond to the Lord's word are answerable to the Lord for their disobedience (Deuteronomy 18:19).

Prophets deal in secrets (Jeremiah 23:24). They see what people do in secret and hear what is whispered behind closed doors (2 Kings 5:26 and 6:12). They are sometimes welcomed into the heavenly council where God plans his strategies (1 Kings 22:19–

23). They perceive God's intentions and make them known to people (2 Kings 2:3). In fact, God doesn't do anything without first communicating it to his prophets (Amos 3:7). For this reason, they can receive insight into future events (Acts 11:27–28; 21:10–14). But they don't share everything they hear (Daniel 8:26; 2 Corinthians 12:2, 4; Revelation 10:4) and may only disclose truth in parables (Hosea 12:10).

Prophets deal in truth. They speak truth into the midst of lies so that light may shatter the darkness and bring forth life (Jeremiah 1:6–10). They can discern the spiritual origin of statements and confirm whether those statements are truly from God (1 Corinthians 14:37). They even discern and identify what spirit is at work in a person's life (2 Kings 2:15). They prove the true God against false gods (1 Kings 16:18–40) and call false prophets to task (Ezekiel 13:2). Prophets have an anointing from God to identify and affirm callings on other people's lives, even before those people are ready to walk in their callings (1 Samuel 16:1–13; 1 Kings 1:45; etc.).

Prophets give wise advice (1 Kings 22:7). They can even give direction, according to God's instruction (1 Samuel 22:5). They speak life into death and plant good seed, bringing strength and encouragement to the hearts of all those to whom the Lord sends them (Acts 15:32).

A prophet is one who comes before the presence of God and has a fire set in their heart that will burn until that message is shared in its entirety (Jeremiah 20:9). The word they speak is an expression of that very fire, smashing falsehood and shattering darkness (Jeremiah 23:29). Then they return to the Lord's council until the torch falls again from his mouth and reignites them.

Evangelists

The word *evangelist* refers to one who proclaims good news.[31] Their feet are considered "beautiful" because, unlike those who merely share Jesus within known relationships and everyday life, evangelists deliberately travel to others for the purpose of sharing the message of the gospel (Isaiah 52:7).

An evangelist is one who easily makes known the mystery of the gospel and successfully conveys the message of Christ with power to a dying generation. As they speak and act, an authority from the Lord is present to lift the blinders off the eyes of those who cannot see truth (2 Corinthians 4:4).

An evangelist carries a heart of incense—the fragrance of Christ—that they have received from the Lord himself (2 Corinthians 2:15–16). As they go, they have an ability to share that incense with others in such a way that those people, too, become the fragrance of Christ (2 Corinthians 2:14).

Philip was one of the seven mentioned in Acts 6:5, chosen to distribute food to widows in the church. He was also an evangelist (Acts 21:8) and was full of the Holy Spirit and wisdom (Acts 6:3). Philip exercised a gift of signs and wonders so that people paid

---

31 "εὐαγγελιστής." Danker, *A Greek-English Lexicon*, 403.

attention to what he said (Acts 8:4–8). As an evangelist, he proclaimed the good news of Jesus Christ. Evil spirits were cast out of people, and many paralyzed and crippled people were healed. The result, as one would expect from someone who proclaims good news, was that there was "great joy in that city" (Acts 8:8).

An evangelist passionately wields the light of Christ with joy and reverence. They speak forth truth in love—meeting people where they are and drawing them to Christ, just as the Father is already drawing them (John 6:44–45).

Philip the evangelist picked up where the Holy Spirit left off and "told [the Ethiopian eunuch] the good news about Jesus" (Acts 8:35). Philip also baptized the man before being swept away by the Holy Spirit and transported to another town (Acts 8:36–40).

We learn two things from this. First, it is interesting to note that apparently, God didn't deem it necessary for Philip to stay with the new convert and disciple him. Evangelists play a unique role in the disciple-making process. As specialists in introducing people to Jesus, they generally devote their time to proclaiming and demonstrating good news and then entrust the rest of the process to the Holy Spirit and other believers (Acts 8:14–17).

Second, Philip didn't also preach to and baptize the eunuch's entourage who were traveling with him. That privilege belonged to the eunuch. Church history indicates that "this man was also sent into the regions of Ethiopia, to preach what he had himself believed."[32] Through the evangelist, God granted a man who couldn't bear physical children an opportunity to spiritually father a nation. Evangelists set up others for success, giving them a clear message that can be shared easily.

Since Ephesians 4:12 says that the evangelist's ministry is to "prepare God's people for works of service," their role apparently includes declaring the gospel to the church and setting an example in evangelism for other Christians to follow—equipping them as they go. Sometimes this happens deliberately through intentional teaching, and sometimes it happens naturally through time spent with the evangelist as they minister.

Pastors

Pastor is another word for "shepherd." While the word "pastor" only shows up once in most English Bibles, the concept of "shepherding" (and related words) can be found in many places. For this reason, our understanding of biblical pastors is directly linked to how the Scriptures discuss shepherds.

In the Old Testament, God foretold a future day when the ark of the covenant would no longer be needed. In that day, God promised he would raise up shepherds after his own heart who would "lead you with knowledge and understanding" (Jeremiah 3:14–18). While this prophetic word has not yet been fulfilled for

---

32 Irenaeus, "Against Heresies," in *Ante-Nicene Fathers, Volume 1,* ed. Alexander Roberts and James Donaldson (Hendrickson Publishers, 2004), 433.

the people of national Israel, its fulfillment has now begun among the spiritual children of Abraham: the church.

Today, under the new covenant, God has indeed raised up humble servants who watch after the spiritual wellbeing of the sheep the Lord has entrusted to them. Peter linked this concept of "shepherding" to the role of "elders" in the church, ultimately pointing to the Chief Shepherd, Jesus.

> To the elders among you, I appeal as a fellow elder and a witness of Christ's sufferings who also will share in the glory to be revealed: Be shepherds of God's flock that is under your care, watching over them—not because you must, but because you are willing, as God wants you to be; not pursuing dishonest gain, but eager to serve; not lording it over those entrusted to you, but being examples to the flock. And when the Chief Shepherd appears, you will receive the crown of glory that will never fade away. (1 Peter 5:1–4)

A literal shepherd leads the sheep in his care to food and water so that they can be healthy and multiply. Similarly, a pastor is gifted by God to lead and can effectively gather people, teach them, and coach them to help them develop and multiply. Shepherds aim to create an optimal environment where sheep thrive. In the church, this looks like gathering the people, teaching truth, facilitating healthy relationships, and guarding the sheep against predators and other dangers.

Pastors are sensitive to the needs of the flock and see practical ways of meeting those needs. They are effective in guiding people into the presence of God to feast and grow (Psalm 23).

In one place, Jesus saw the people "like sheep without a shepherd" and "had compassion on them" (Mark 6:34). In a similar situation, this compassion was said to be born out of the realization that the people were "harassed and helpless" (Matthew 9:36). Shepherding, then, often comes with a heart of compassion that longs to gather people together for the sake of their own spiritual health and safety. In response to what Jesus perceived in the people, Jesus "began teaching them many things" (Mark 6:34). Sometimes pastoral compassion looks like feeding people truth that changes the way they think.

In John 10:1–18, Jesus spoke at length about the role of a pastor. He said that a true shepherd will only lead his sheep in by the gate (John 10:2); and Jesus is that gate (John 10:7). Therefore, anyone who tries to convince people that they can participate in the kingdom of God or enter heaven by any other way than Jesus (via death to self and life in him) is a false pastor who should not be followed.

Biblical pastors live self-sacrificially for the sake of the people who have been entrusted to them (John 10:11; Ezekiel 34:1–3). This doesn't mean that they must do so without any form of remuneration or honor (1 Timothy 5:17). It does, however, mean that they do not lord over people or take advantage of them for dishonest gain (1 Peter 5:2–3).

Shepherds have a responsibility to strengthen the weak, heal the sick, bind up the injured, search for the lost, and bring back the strays (Ezekiel 34:4). And all those shepherds who do not take the role seriously, living selfishly, will be held directly accountable for the condition of the flock that was under their charge (Ezekiel 34:10).

Shepherding is terrifying work, but it becomes easy when we realize that Jesus is the Chief Shepherd (1 Peter 5:4) and the Good Shepherd (John 10:11). And he has promised to shepherd his own people (Ezekiel 34:11–16). Therefore, the best shepherds in the church are dead shepherds—those who have died to their own self-effort and instead let Jesus shepherd through them by faith (Galatians 2:20).

Teachers

Teachers train others in both information and revelation, helping people understand the words and ways of the Lord. They present both fresh revelation and accumulated knowledge, blending teachings about God's law with insights about the kingdom of heaven, just as Christ did (Matthew 13:52). Some of this teaching happens with words, but some happens through action.

Jesus gave us an interesting example of teaching with action:

> On reaching Jerusalem, Jesus entered the temple courts and began driving out those who were buying and selling there. He overturned the tables of the money changers and the benches of those selling doves, and would not allow anyone to carry merchandise through the temple courts. And as he taught them, he said, "Is it not written: 'My house will be called a house of prayer for all nations'? But you have made it 'a den of robbers.'" (Mark 11:15–17)

Notice verse 17. "And as he taught them, he said . . . " In this passage, it appears that the "teaching" was the flipping of tables and benches, driving out those who were buying and selling there. And that teaching, it so happens, was also accompanied by words that made sense of Jesus's actions.

The Jewish teachers—the rabbis—taught through more than words. They taught through life-on-life modeling. Words helped learners understand what they witnessed. Likewise, biblical teachers are examples of Christian living. They identify teachable moments and engage with words and actions that help people learn effectively.

Teachers, therefore, are not necessarily seasoned orators who captivate people with their words. Teachers are simply those who are gifted by the Holy Spirit to effectively teach others by any means available to them.

Teachers are sent by Christ to correct and confront the religious spirit among God's people (Matthew 23:34). They teach with authority from personal experience rather than spouting theory, rhetoric, or hearsay (Mark 1:22). Their teaching leads to encounters with God's power (John 3:2).

Teachers replicate themselves in the lives of those who learn from them (Luke 6:40). For this reason, they are held to greater scrutiny by man and firmer judgment by God (James 3:1). Therefore, teachers need to guard their own lives and doctrine closely, persevering in the godly examples they set and the message they proclaim (1 Timothy 4:11–16).

How These Ministries Operate in a Network

You may recall that I distinguished in chapter 1 between the organism and the organization. A lot of confusing teaching about fivefold ministry tries to squeeze these ministries into a hierarchical organizational structure when they are actually functions of the organism.

In our house church network, we recognize these ministries exist without needing to create hierarchical positions for them. With that said, we also want to leverage our resources through healthy organization. So in Roots Church, we have an equipping team that consists of (1) fivefold ministers, (2) mature believers who have become teachers and trainers (Hebrews 5:12), and (3) trustworthy, reliable people who are competent to pass along teaching to others (2 Timothy 2:2). These are not staff positions as much as they are responsibilities within our network.

When one of our house churches needs teaching or training in a particular area, we see which member of our equipping team is gifted to bring breakthrough for that church. Then we connect them for one or more meetings until the breakthrough happens.

I don't know what function God has invited you to express. Perhaps as you read the descriptions above, you saw yourself in one of those ministries. Or perhaps you're not an equipping minister on the Ephesians 4 list, but you're still a mature believer who is competent to teach and train others. No matter what part of the body of Christ you are, you are still a disciple who makes disciples alongside the rest of us. We all have roles to play.

Your ministry giftings and callings will influence your emphasis in how you make disciples. I know prophets, apostles, teachers, and evangelists who pastor house churches in our network. As one might expect, the house church led by the prophet sees a lot of supernatural activity. The house church led by an evangelist is constantly emphasizing evangelism. The house church led by the teacher is strong in biblical literacy as people wrestle with important questions. And the house church led by an apostle has multiplied more than any other house church in our network. None of these four are necessarily graced or called as pastors in the equipping sense, but they are all elders who shepherd God's flock. They are pastors in the practical sense, while also serving our network in their broader capacities.

Meanwhile, we also have a house church that's pastored by a true Ephesians 4 pastor. The church is healthy, lives are being changed for the better, and people with significant struggles find refuge for their souls in the love, encouragement, and community there. That pastor trains and equips others in our network to be more effective at pastoring. But he continually needs evangelists to equip him to lead people to salvation, apostles to equip him to multiply his church, and so on.

No matter your function in the body of Christ, you are a disciple who makes disciples. And if you invite people into your home for such ministry, your house will become a gospel house. The rest of your ministry callings will emerge as you serve God's people. If you're faithful with the small work of making disciples, God will be able to trust you with any other work to which he has called you. Don't worry about which type of minister you are; simply be a son or daughter of God. In time, God will connect you to people who are called and graced in these five different ways, and together, you'll witness God's work, building a thriving church.

Becoming Like Jesus

We're all sent. We all hear God. We're all expected to share the gospel, care for one another, and teach others what the Lord has taught us. Why, then, do we need all these special ministers?

Fivefold ministers are pacesetters, walking in a special grace for their unique expressions of Jesus's ministry. Through their activity and words, they challenge, train, and equip the church to become more like Jesus in those ways.

Some teachings about fivefold ministry treat these roles like a personality test: "You're really confrontational, so you're a prophet," or "You're really sweet and caring, so you're a pastor," and so on. But the aim of fivefold ministry is to equip the saints and grow us all toward maturity until we all learn to reveal "the whole measure of the fullness of Christ."

Accordingly, the goal is not to figure out our fivefold role and then lean into it at the expense of other ways we can reveal Christ. The goal is to become like Christ in all ways while faithfully and consistently walking in whatever grace we've received to reveal him in specific ways.

If God reveals your role to you, great. Embrace it and walk in it. But no matter what, seek out training and equipping from all five ministries so you can become more like Jesus in everything. And if you're not sure of your role, simply aim to be like Jesus, and see if a specific grace emerges in your life.

PART 2:

SHEPHERDING

CHAPTER 10:

FORMING A HOUSE CHURCH

Here the people are the resources, Jesus is the program, fellowship is the reason, multiplication is the outcome, and discipling the neighborhood is the goal.
—Wolfgang Simson

In my house-church network, we tell people that we're not interested in multiplying house churches. We're interested in making disciples. So far, house churches have proven to be the most effective way to make disciples in our context. And if we make disciples well, those house churches will multiply.

With that said, the transition from the moment of making a new disciple to starting your first house church is not at all intuitive. It takes a little bit of strategy, some clear communication, and a lot of intentionality.

From Zero to Church

At the time of this writing, the Tesla automotive company is developing a car that they claim will accelerate from zero to sixty miles per hour in just under two seconds.[33] This is expected to be the fastest accelerating production car in the world when it hits the market.

Meanwhile, the 1963 Farmall tractor I used to drive on my father-in-law's farm had a top-speed of about twenty-five miles per hour, and it took a good thirty seconds or so to reach it. Setting aside the obvious difference in the purposes of each vehicle, one major limitation is that it takes a great deal of time to manually press in the clutch on the tractor, select a new gear, and carefully ease off the clutch to achieve the next level of speed.

The fastest accelerating cars have automatic transmissions. Similarly, the fastest way to establish a church is to start with automatic disciples—people who have already surrendered to Jesus and matured in him for some time.

A lot of church planting is done this way. Large churches might send a hundred or more people to open a new campus in another community. The people in the community think it's an instant success.

But if we measure success in new converts, some such churches might not be successful at all. In 2001, as church growth books and conferences were popularized, one study found that

---

[33] "Home Page," Tesla, accessed July 2, 2021, https://www.tesla.com/roadster.

institutional churches in the United States spent an average of $1,551,466 per baptism.[34] It is far too easy to be distracted with the work of erecting church buildings, acquiring technology, hiring staff, and running programs while completely missing the point.

The same is true of house churches. My observation is that far too many house churches have existed for more than a year without ever baptizing even one new convert. Is this because baptisms are not a priority? Or is this because everyone who comes is already a believer? Either way, something needs to change.

When I was preparing to launch Roots Church, my pastor at the time, Brooks McElhenny, told me, "You can ask anyone you want from our church to join you. I trust the Lord to fill the empty seats." I prayed fervently about who to ask. Hundreds of people attended the church, and I was friends with many of them, after serving on staff there for a few years and attending there for more than a decade. But in the end, I only invited two families and two individuals who were already attending one of our four house churches. I could have invited so many more, but I would have been asking people to completely change their understanding of the word "church" by leaving a traditional Sunday gathering in a huge building for small, interactive meetings in homes. If I was going to establish a new culture, I needed to start with people who weren't completely sold on the old culture.

---

[34] David Barrett and Todd Johnson, *World Christian Trends, Volume 1* (Littleton, Colorado: William Carey Library, 2001), 841.

My point is this: Automatic disciples may be the fastest way to start a church, but it's also the fastest way to establish a culture of inviting the already saved, rather than making new disciples. The already saved have cultural baggage—ideas about church that make sense in big gatherings but not in homes. They often think in terms of attraction—trying to design meetings and meeting spaces that will draw the greatest number of people. But this tends to mostly attract Christians, merely shuffling sheep from one flock to another. If you really want to start a house church, don't start it with a bunch of churched Christians unless they really, truly understand the wildly different reasons we gather in homes.

Tractors may accelerate slower than sports cars, but they're much better at bringing in a harvest. And like a tractor, effective house-church planting will typically require shifting some gears.

First Gear: Prayerfully Connect with Another Disciple Maker

In Luke, Jesus sent out seventy-two of his followers to preach the gospel and heal the sick in the towns where he was soon to minister. (See Luke 10:1–24.) Hidden in his instructions to them are principles that can help you start your first house church.

Jesus sent his disciples out two-by-two, which means he didn't expect anyone to do this ministry alone (v. 1). It's wonderful to have a burning desire to make disciples. You may even be gifted enough, skilled enough, or experienced enough to share your faith and lead someone to Jesus. But when it comes to establishing a house church, you're going to want that partner in ministry.

What if you don't have such a person? Jesus gave another instruction: "Ask the Lord of the harvest, therefore, to send out workers into his harvest field" (v. 2). The Lord of the harvest—the Master of the field—wants you to be successful. If you really want to plant a house church, ask him for a co-laborer, and he will gladly bring one.

Naturally, if you're married, you might think your spouse would be the perfect partner for the task at hand. By all means, include your spouse. But when I recommend teaming up with someone to help you start a house church, it's important for it to be someone outside your own household. In fact, you may even want to partner with another couple so there are four of you.

There's a simple reason for this instruction. It's difficult to introduce people to kingdom culture alone. As long as you're by yourself, a new believer will think that what they see in your life is just your personality. Or if it's just you and your spouse, they might see your lifestyle as a shared decision based more on family values than kingdom ones. But if you're joined by another believer from another home whose life also exhibits traits of transformation, the new disciple will be instantly immersed in a culture where those traits are seen as normal. Together, you will reveal Jesus more effectively than you ever could alone.

Talk to the Lord of the harvest. Ask him for a fellow laborer. Ask fervently. It won't be long before you're connected to the right person.

Once you have your ministry partner, make sure you both share an understanding of the task at hand. Jesus spent verses 4 through 12 explaining how the disciples should travel, what to expect, and how to respond whether they are accepted or rejected. A clear vision of the mission helps the two of you know exactly what to do at any given moment. Perhaps have your teammate read this book with you so they see just what you're aiming for.

Second Gear: Fearless Adventure in Dangerous Territory

Immediately after instructing his disciples to pray for laborers, Jesus commanded them, "Go! I am sending you out like lambs among wolves" (v. 3). Jesus didn't even give them an opportunity to pray the prayer he told them to pray. Don't spend too much time in first gear. Get out there and do ministry as soon as possible—even before you feel like you're ready.

I'm terrible about entering swimming pools. I don't like the transition from dry and comfortable to cold and wet. My wife and kids laugh and make fun of me as I stand on the first step and slowly enter the pool inch by inch, making all manner of yelps and hollers. The rest of my family jumped in without reservation and quickly adjusted to the new environment. But not me. In fact, I hate the transition so much, you're more likely to find me sitting outside the pool than swimming in it. If you stand on the side of the pool waiting to feel ready, you'll never be ready. You can slowly ease yourself into it, but you'll take forever to get started. You probably just need someone to push you in.

Jesus sent his disciples into an environment far more terrifying than a swimming pool. He sent them "like lambs among wolves." He led them to make themselves vulnerable as they ministered among lost and broken people.

I once joined a team of believers as we walked the streets of a slum in Rio de Janeiro, Brazil. We were deliberately searching for a drug lord who had agreed to meet with us. The gangs in this place were heavily armed and had recently used a 50-calibre gun to shoot down a police helicopter. Not long before our visit, the gangs opened fire on a tourist's car for not following the protocol of rolling down the windows and turning on hazard lights.

As we walked through the favellas, we were repeatedly met by gang members and drug dealers, asking us what we were doing in their community. Some had AK-47 rifles. Others had handguns. People on our team shared the gospel and prayed for them. Together, we led about twenty or more to Jesus. The wolves were heavily armed and opened fire on anyone who looked like a threat. But because we came like lambs, we were received.[35]

I had a similar experience ministering to an armed gang in the slums of Port au Prince, Haiti. And in the hull of a large boat, I've

---

[35] To watch hidden camera footage of this dangerous ministry, check out my two-part film, *Voice of God,* which is available at www.SupernaturalTruth.com.

preached to more than one hundred unruly passengers (including some drunk voodoo practitioners) who were moments away from rioting. I've preached in secret churches in China. I've had African Muslims come with gasoline to burn down the stage I was preaching on—while I was preaching on it! I've preached in Ugandan villages where other believers had been beaten for their faith and even led a witchdoctor's wife to salvation. There's nothing "safe" about our mission. But Jesus sent us.

Ask the Lord where he wants you and your teammate to plant a church. Does he want it in your neighborhood? Their neighborhood? Or does he want you to go into a different place and establish a church there? Prayerfully plan meaningful ways to reach out, and start doing it. Jesus gave his disciples a simple method. "Heal the sick who are there and tell them, 'The kingdom of God has come near to you'" (v. 9). Bring the love and power of Jesus to that community and see what happens.

My friend Jonathan Ammon felt led to minister in a small city tucked away in a corner of Detroit, Michigan, called Hamtramck. Founded by Polish immigrants, the two-square-mile Hamtramck is now primarily comprised of Bengali and Yemeni Muslims. It's the first city in the United States where the Muslim "call to prayer" is broadcast on loudspeakers five times a day. Jonathan moved into a small house there. Using Google Maps, he strategically mapped a path and knocked on every single door in the city, recording those who were receptive and those who were not. Over the course of about five years, many people were healed, many were saved, and

Jonathan started many Bible studies in various homes, eventually helping to start a church with a number of other disciple-making friends in the area.

You don't have to do it just like Jonathan. You just have to do it. Maybe knocking on doors isn't your thing. Maybe chatting with people in a park is. Or maybe you don't like talking to strangers. Then go to coworkers or neighbors. Be prayerfully strategic, then go for it. Don't waste time dipping your toes in the water and waiting until you feel ready to take the next step. That feeling will never come. Just jump in and start swimming.

Third Gear: Find a Person of Peace

The disciples had been sent out like lambs among wolves. They didn't have money, food, extra clothes, or a place to stay. They had to depend entirely upon the hospitality of strangers. And in first-century Jewish culture, such hospitality to strangers was expected. The disciples would show up unarmed and vulnerable, needing food and lodging. They would heal the sick and tell people that the kingdom of heaven had come near them. And hopefully, someone would invite them into their home and promote peace by showing the community that the disciples were accepted there.

This man of peace didn't necessarily have to receive their message; he simply needed to receive them. And the disciples were to remain in that person's home for as long as they were in that village. It was a brilliant strategy. They built relationship with the person and came to know their household and community through them. This granted them far more opportunities to minister to others than if they had remained strangers.

Once you and your ministry partner have prayerfully identified a target area and started ministering, watch carefully for someone who seems like a person who peacefully welcomes you. Perhaps they hang around you a lot. Perhaps they ask a lot of questions. Or perhaps they invite you to share a meal. No matter how they communicate their interest, seize the opportunity. Spend time with that person and ask them to introduce you to friends, family, and neighbors who need spiritual help.

If you're struggling to find such a person, don't be too quick to move on. Unlike Jesus's disciples, you have the luxury of not needing a place to stay for the night or food to eat, so you can take a few days searching. In verse 4, Jesus told them not to greet anyone on the road. This wasn't because Jesus didn't care about the people on the road, nor was it because they couldn't have meaningful evangelistic encounters there. Jesus simply wanted them to have the maximum opportunity to search for a person of peace in the city. Since your goal is to start an ongoing local ministry in this place, don't distract yourself with trying to make new disciples somewhere else. It's not bad to share the gospel with people you might meet elsewhere, but that's not your objective and won't lead to a church in your target area. Minister purposefully in the place where you sense the Lord has sent you.

People will either receive the message or not. (See Luke 10:10–11.) If they receive it, begin meeting with them regularly. If not, either keep looking for a person of peace in that area or else ask the Lord where he'd like you and your friend to minister next.

Perhaps your first convert will be the person of peace, or perhaps it will be one of their connections. Regardless, once you lead someone to Jesus, it's time to shift gears yet again.

Fourth Gear: Start Meeting Regularly

All you need is one disciple. If you and your ministry partner baptize this person and meet regularly with him or her, then you've planted the seed of a church.

Continue ministering healing and serving the community, but now bring the new disciple along with you and your ministry partner. Teach them to do what you do. Talk about hearing God's voice, healing ministry, and the Holy Spirit. Discuss matters of character like the struggle to maintain humility when you see results or the opposite struggle to avoid despair or condemnation when you don't. Model forgiveness, confession, love, and the nature of Jesus. Pray for them to receive the baptism in the Holy Spirit. Challenge them to share their testimony, pray for people, and minister like you do.

Introduce them to the Bible and teach them how to identify chapters and verses. Show them the Old and New Testaments, and teach them the difference between the two. Give them a reading assignment (I like the Gospel of Mark, followed by Acts, but follow the Holy Spirit). Whenever you gather, ask them what they're getting out of the reading. Take time to listen. Celebrate their insights and observations. Don't try to one-up them with more impressive revelation. Give them their moment. Encourage them and ask meaningful questions that help them think deeper about what they're reading and the conclusions they're drawing.

Fifth Gear: Grow!

You may find that it isn't long before your new friend starts inviting others. Or perhaps your evangelistic work will connect new people. Repeat the previous steps with this new person.

New disciples often have a lot of zeal that helps promote fast growth. This is exactly the sort of momentum you're looking for. Encourage your first new disciple to mentor their friends the same way you have been mentoring them. Help them out with wise counsel and biblical advice.

At your meetings, aim to include all the elements of a house-church meeting. Ask everyone what God is speaking to them that week. Study the Bible. Take communion together. Baptize new believers. Pray for each other. Continue to preach the gospel, serve people, and heal the sick in that community.

Once the group reaches around ten people, ask the Lord if someone present should be mentored or raised up as an elder in the group. We'll talk later about the dynamics of shepherding people, and perhaps this book will be helpful to you in training this person to pastor like Jesus. Don't be hasty in this selection. (See 1 Timothy 5:22.) In Acts 14:23, Paul and Barnabas appointed elders in each house church with prayer and fasting. They didn't take the task lightly.

Once a house church reaches around twenty people, the introverts start to shut down, and the conversations suffer. House churches larger than twenty people lose their intimacy and start to look more like traditional churches where only a few people actually do any ministry while the rest remain spectators. If you reach about twenty people, it's time to send some out to start a new church.

Sixth Gear: Multiplication

In chapter 18, we'll discuss various means of multiplying house churches. What matters now is the fact that you're ready to do so. If you wait too long to do it, my experience tells me that your meetings will stagnate. Your attendance will peak, and people will settle into a routine of maintaining what they have rather than continuing in the mission. All the momentum will be lost, and you'll see fewer new disciples.

But if you multiply, then the growth continues. It's emotionally hard to either leave a house church or see others leave, but it's necessary for the sake of the mission.

This, of course, is why forming a network is so valuable. You'll continue to see those people, making the transition much easier.

Another benefit is that you now have something you never had before: You have a church comprised of disciples who understand the mission and culture of house-church ministry. At this point, you can get out of the tractor and into the Tesla Roadster. You can start a house church with automatic disciples who can immediately implement everything you've taught them so far. You can glide right through the first five gears without ever needing to push the clutch. The second house church will grow faster than the first. Sending a team to launch the new church will also shrink the first house church so that they have room again to continue reaching and welcoming new believers.

All Vehicles Need Fuel

To some this sounds far too easy, and to others it sounds terribly intimidating. Both groups, however, need the Holy Spirit so they can minister effectively in the power and love of Jesus.

Tractors run on gasoline, and Tesla Roadsters run on electricity; neither vehicle can go anywhere on its own. Both need fuel, whether petroleum-based or electric. The gifts and graces you'll need from the Holy Spirit to start your first house church will be different from those needed to multiply and lead a network. But the same Holy Spirit provides both.

Even though Jesus had breathed on his disciples right after his resurrection and given them the Holy Spirit to live within them (John 20:22), he still told them to wait in Jerusalem until they had been clothed with heavenly power (Luke 24:49). Jesus commanded his disciples to go into all the world and make disciples, but then he told them not to go anywhere or do anything until they received power.

Jesus wants the world to be saved, so much so that he surrendered to crucifixion for their salvation. Then why would he put the Great Commission on hold when his disciples already had three years of firsthand experience following him in ministry? Why would he delay sending trained ministers into the most important mission?

The answer is simple: If the disciples had started multiplying before they received power, they would have multiplied disciples just like them—working in their own strength and striving to obey with their own abilities. But empowered disciples reproduce empowered disciples.

You can follow every step I listed above without being empowered by the Holy Spirit. You can shift through the gears and start multiplying. But it will be a monument to your own strength and ability rather than the Lord's, and the chances are high that you'll eventually burn out. Your tractor needs fuel. Your Tesla needs a charge. You need power for the mission.

I make no apologies for passionately preaching about the baptism in the Holy Spirit. I tell people not to bother engaging in disciple making until they know they've received this baptism. Some have expressed distaste toward that advice, but I'm only telling them what Jesus said. And didn't Jesus tell his followers to teach new disciples everything he had commanded them? (See

Matthew 28:20.) One of those commands was to wait for power. (See Luke 24:49 and Acts 1:4–5.)

If we jump immediately into ministry without power, then we will always have work with which to busy ourselves. But Jesus, in his love for us, has given us the liberty to be singularly focused on seeking his power before we are ever expected to go anywhere or do anything. It's the mercy of God that commands you to wait until you have spiritual power before trying to minister.

If it were difficult to receive the baptism in the Holy Spirit, then this might be an unfair command. But since he is freely available to all, you can receive his power right now.

If you're a Christian (and I'm sure you are if you've read to this point in the book), then you already have the Holy Spirit living within you. (See Romans 8:9 and 2 Corinthians 1:22.) He is there to save you, make you a new creation, and bring you into fellowship with God. But he also wants to overflow from within you and rest upon you to empower you for reaching others. He dwells within you for your benefit, but he comes upon you for the world's benefit.

In other words, you don't need to ask the Holy Spirit to come from some faraway place. He lives inside you. In reference to the Holy Spirit, Jesus said that "rivers of living water" will flow *from within* you (John 7:38–39). Simply ask Jesus to baptize you in the Holy Spirit so that you can have power to make disciples. The Spirit of God will overflow from your life like a river, and Jesus will immerse you in his presence and power.

The experience is a little different for everyone. When the Spirit came upon Jesus, he came like a dove. When he came upon the disciples, he came like fire. Some describe feeling electricity. Others, overwhelming peace. It doesn't really matter what it feels like. What matters is that it's him. And if you ask the Lord for the Holy Spirit, he will give you the Holy Spirit. (See Luke 11:13.)

As soon as you recognize that the Lord has answered your prayer and given you power, simply open your mouth, vocalize, and begin speaking whatever words and sounds the Holy Spirit gives you. You'll quickly discover the unspeakable joy of partnering with him, yielding to his influence, and letting him work through you.

In Jesus's name, be filled with the Holy Spirit.[36]

---

[36] For a more complete teaching about the baptism in the Holy Spirit, see chapter 5: "Real Power" in my book, *Rooted: Thriving in Your New Life*, which is available as a free PDF at https://www.RootsAG.org/how-to-follow-jesus.

CHAPTER 11:

LIKE IT OR NOT, YOU'RE A LEADER

We can't wait until every believer feels mature enough to minister because no one will mature unless they minister. This is one of those chicken and egg conundrums. Which comes first—ministry or maturity? According to the Bible, ministry comes first.

—Steve Murrell

"Who is leading this thing?"

My friend Tony's question bothered me. I thought I had been clear when we started our little house church that there were no leaders except Jesus himself. So I answered him boldly: "Jesus."

"That's all well and good," Tony replied, "but who is taking responsibility for the spiritual lives of the people and casting vision? It seems like it's you, but you keep dodging responsibility. Leaders are in the Bible. People need earthly leaders. If you won't obey Jesus by leading our group, I will."

My friend's ultimatum challenged me to rethink my convictions about leadership. Until that moment, I had avoided responsibility—probably because church leaders in my past had hurt me. Some hurt me because they were bad leaders, and some hurt me because their good leadership pressed on emotional wounds in my life. My bitterness and pride led me to reject the notion of church leadership altogether. So when I formed my first house church, I was deliberate about not leading—even telling people time and again that I wasn't their leader.

And yet, I was leading.

Leadership has less to do with what we say (though that's part of it) and more to do with the direction we're headed. If we're going in a direction that others like, they'll follow us. No matter how much we might say we're not leading, we are.

And that was precisely my problem. I was leading, but I was shirking responsibility. I wanted to head in my own direction and see how many would join me, but I didn't want to take responsibility for others or, frankly, care for them. A great deal of healing needed to take place in my heart.

Jesus is the Head of the church, but he told Peter, "Feed my sheep" (John 21:17). Jesus gave some people to the church to be shepherds (Ephesians 4:11). Jesus isn't bothered by earthly leaders in his church; in fact, he appoints them. My failure wasn't that I refused to lead. I was leading whether I liked it or not. My failure was that I refused to take responsibility for the people following my lead or serve them for their benefit.

I led with independence and woundedness, and that house church often attracted wounded people with an independent streak. I also led with bold faith and a passion for seeing salvations and miracles, so we attracted that crowd as well. Furthermore, I was passionate about letting God transform my heart so I could become more like Jesus. Accordingly, the culture of our group was that it became a safe place for wounded people to gather in God's presence, step out in spiritual gifts, and heal from their past hurts. That much was great. But it also became a safe place for people to complain about other churches and bad experiences they'd had in the past. I didn't realize I was leading anyone, but I was, and I wasn't leading in the best direction.

Leading on the Frontlines

In 2 Samuel 11:1, we read, "In the spring, at the time when kings go off to war, David sent Joab out with the king's men and the whole Israelite army. They destroyed the Ammonites and besieged Rabbah. But David remained in Jerusalem."

While other kings were fighting alongside their armies, David sent his armies out and relaxed in his palace. In the following verses, we read about the woman he saw bathing on her roof, his abuse of both her as a person and his own authority when taking her by force, and his subsequent murder of the woman's husband when she was later found to be pregnant.

When a lot of people think about what it means to lead others, they think about delegating tasks. Certainly, a fair amount of delegating must be done to accomplish big goals. But when delegation takes us out of the frontline fray, it's unhealthy. David should have been on the battlefront with his men, leading the charge. Rather than walking in his identity as a champion warrior, he took on the false persona of an adulterer and murderer.

Biblical headship or leadership is less like a king sitting in a palace, telling others what to do, and more like a king on the frontlines of battle, making the first kills. It's less like a ruler commissioning an expedition and more like a pioneer blazing trails that make it easier for others to follow. Healthy leaders do the difficult work that helps others succeed more easily.

Some think the people you lead will always be limited by your own lifestyle. I've heard it said that "leaders are lids," but I disagree. Those you lead can go beyond you if you lead them well. The best leaders show people what it looks like to be everything Jesus has created them to be, and that means partnering with the Lord to love people extravagantly. If we live wholly devoted to him, those who follow us will find it easier to be wholly devoted to him. Sure, they could do that without us, but we can make it easier for them. And it will be far better in the end for us to live rightly and make it easier for others to live rightly than if we live in sin and thereby make it easier for others to live in sin.

Real love seeks the success of those around us. A leader's personal success is found only in raising up and sending out others to fulfill God's plans for their lives.

How, then, do we ever fulfill our own missions and do everything God has called us to do if we are spending so much time, energy, and talent on helping others succeed? Easy. If we are leading people well, they'll follow our example of loving and serving others. As they're transformed by Jesus, they'll love us back and help us succeed.

Leadership is setting an example. If we live selfishly, others around us will see our selfishness and believe it's the source of our success. They will become selfish in order to share our success. If we live with emotional insecurity, lashing out at others and holding them back, the people we lead will learn that the way to gain influence is to use people and keep our emotional walls up. We don't merely lead people into tasks. We lead them into lifestyles.

Jesus modeled a lifestyle of frontlines evangelism, taking the brunt of persecution and rejection for his team, trusting the Father for extreme intervention, protecting the victims of legalism and false beliefs, living humbly, and refusing opportunities to exalt himself. He showed the disciples how to live and then trusted them to do the same in his name. (See Matthew 10 and Luke 9–10.) And Jesus did it so well that he told them their works would exceed even his own. (See John 14:12.)

In Luke 9:23, Jesus told his followers, "Whoever wants to be my disciple must deny themselves and take up their cross daily and follow me." In other words, Jesus would deny himself first. He would take up his own cross first. And the disciples would be those who joined him in that lifestyle. Jesus blazed a trail of self-denial, and his disciples eventually thrived along that path.

As leaders, we can make success easier or more difficult for the people in our care. We can blaze trails for them, or we can leave new territory uncharted. In a sense, we can make it as though the people following us are swimming upstream or downstream to accomplish God's purposes for their lives. We may not be their "lid," but we can certainly be pacesetters, for better or worse.

When geese fly in a V formation, the goose at the front tip takes the brunt of the wind resistance while the next geese in line flow along with a measure of ease in the pockets of updrafts spinning off his wings.[37] In a pack of wolves, the leading alpha wolf initiates hunts rather than waiting for others to bring him food.[38] A dominant male mountain gorilla will fend off a threat to his troop, allowing the weaker animals to retreat while he beats the ground and roars at the enemy.[39] God's design for leadership works hard and takes risks so others can succeed and thrive. As Jesus said about himself, "The good shepherd lays down his life for the sheep" (John 10:11).

Dead Shepherds

A quality shepherd doesn't spend his time daydreaming about a better life. Rather, he puts all his attention on the sheep and their surrounding environment, caring for their needs and watching

---

[37] Helen Thompson, "Scientists Solve Mystery of Birds' Flying V," *Smithsonian Magazine*, January 15, 2014, https://www.smithsonianmag.com/articles/scientists-solve-mystery-birds-flying-v-180949352/.

[38] Roger DeSilvestro, "President's Day: How Animals Lead," NWF, January 5, 2016, https://blog.nwf.org/2011/02/presidents-day-how-animals-lead/.

[39] Ibid.

vigilantly for predators and thieves. He doesn't lead the flock to comfortable neighborhoods where he can relax indoors. He leads them to green pastures and still waters where they can thrive. The shepherd lives, but he lives as a man dead to the world and wholly devoted to the flock in his care. "The good shepherd lays down his life for the sheep."

The word "pastor" only shows up one time in a typical English Bible, and that without definition. (See Ephesians 4:11.) But the Greek word from which it is translated shows up multiple times. The literal rendering is "shepherd." It's the same word used for the shepherds who witnessed Jesus's birth. And the verb form of the word (literally "to shepherd") is directly tied to the concept of elders in the church. In context, these elders are basically house-church leaders.

> To the elders among you, I appeal as a fellow elder and a witness of Christ's sufferings who also will share in the glory to be revealed: Be shepherds of God's flock that is under your care, watching over them—not because you must, but because you are willing, as God wants you to be; not pursuing dishonest gain, but eager to serve; not lording it over those entrusted to you, but being examples to the flock. And when the Chief Shepherd appears, you will receive the crown of glory that will never fade away. (1 Peter 5:1–4)

If you are leading a house church, you are a pastor, and you will one day give an account to the Chief Shepherd, Jesus. While this should put a certain measure of the fear of the Lord in us, it ought not to scare us to the point of inaction. It also ought not to drive us into slavery to a ministry role. Peter was clear that pastors are free from obligation or compulsion. He admonished us to shepherd God's flock "not because you must, but because you are willing" (1 Peter 5:2). Healthy pastoring is somehow both hard work and effortless when we trust the Holy Spirit to empower us. In Colossians 1:29, Paul wrote, "To this end I strenuously contend with all the energy Christ so powerfully works in me." This is how pastors are invited to work. We strenuously contend, free from obligation and empowered by the Holy Spirit.

Romans 12:8 tells us that the Holy Spirit can empower us with a gift of leadership. The beautiful thing about spiritual gifts is that they're straight from the Holy Spirit. That means they're not based on our own personal skills, intelligence, or personality. And since we are commanded to "eagerly desire spiritual gifts" (1 Corinthians 14:1), even those who have no innate leadership abilities can call on the Lord for a special dose of his supernatural grace to empower them to lead.

Accordingly, the commands in 1 Peter 5 are not rules you must follow in your own strength. Jesus said, "Apart from Me, you can do nothing" (John 15:5). We lay down our lives so that Jesus can become our lives. (See Galatians 2:20 and Colossians 3:4.) He alone is the Good Shepherd.

> "I am the good shepherd. The good shepherd lays down his life for the sheep. The hired hand is not the shepherd and does not own the sheep. So when he sees the wolf coming, he abandons the sheep and runs away. Then the wolf attacks the flock and scatters it. The man runs away because he is a hired hand and cares nothing for the sheep.
>
> "I am the good shepherd; I know my sheep and my sheep know me—just as the Father knows me and I know the Father—and I lay down my life for the sheep . . . . The reason my Father loves me is that I lay down my life—only to take it up again. No one takes it from me, but I lay it down of my own accord. I have authority to lay it down and authority to take it up again. This command I received from my Father." (John 10:11–18)

The death Jesus spoke of was followed by resurrection, all for the sake of the sheep. Likewise, when we die to the world, forfeiting our own lives, the Holy Spirit raises us into new life with Christ. This is the gospel message—complete surrender to the King of Kings so that his will can be carried out in the earth through us.

As pastors, we must die to the false identity of being merely hired hands so that we can be raised to new life as earthly expressions of the Good Shepherd. As Paul wrote in Galatians 2:20, "I have been crucified with Christ and I no longer live, but

Christ lives in me. The life I now live in the body, I live by faith in the Son of God, who loved me and gave himself for me."

You cannot be a good pastor in your own strength. The only Good Pastor is Jesus, and he will shepherd his flock through you if you will lay down your life for the sake of his sheep.

God Speaks Most Clearly in Bodily Form

When God wanted to shepherd his people in the Old Testament, he spoke through the Law and gave messages through prophets; yet the people remained largely unmoved and unchanged. Even miracles, signs, and wonders were insufficient to change them.

But when the time had fully come, he spoke his clearest message ever by putting his voice in human form. In John 1:14, we read, "The Word became flesh and made his dwelling among us. We have seen his glory, the glory of the one and only Son, who came from the Father, full of grace and truth."

Jesus perfectly reveals the Father to mankind. (See John 5:19; 14:8–11; and Hebrews 1:1–3.) He is the clearest revelation of God's heart and voice.

Someone once said that "a thousand words leave not the same deep impression as does a single deed."[40] Or perhaps you've heard the more recent and popular adage, "A picture is worth a

---

[40] Source unknown. Various internet sources attribute this quote to the nineteenth-century Norwegian playwright Henrik Ibsen. However, this has never been confirmed, and the quote is not found in any published work.

thousand words."[41] What God spoke through the Word-made-flesh was more than the sermons that came out of our Savior's mouth. The Father spoke through the Son's entire life. Everything Jesus said and did was a message from God. Jesus made the Father's voice both visible and tangible.

Today, Jesus has ascended into heaven and physically sits at the right hand of the Father. But his body has not entirely left this earth. We are the body of Christ. (See 1 Corinthians 12:27.) And that's not merely a beautiful metaphor. In 1 Corinthians 6:15, Paul wrote, "Do you not know that your bodies are members of Christ himself?" In other words, as a physical temple of the Holy Spirit, we have together become physical extensions of Jesus in the earth. That means we—the body of Christ—are a continuation of "the Word made flesh."

The same way God once spoke perfectly through his Son to lead his people, he continues to speak through his Son to lead his people—only now, he does it through those who have laid down their own lives so Jesus can live through them.

This is true of every Christian, not merely pastors. But if pastors are uniquely here to express the shepherding part of who Jesus is, then we shepherds need to die to ourselves and let the Good Shepherd flow through us. Jesus is a far better leader than any of us will ever be in our own strength.

---

[41] "A Picture Is Worth Ten Thousand Words," Quote Investigator, accessed March 24, 2023, https://quoteinvestigator.com/2022/07/22/picture-words/.

Whose voice speaks through your body? Is it the voice of your own selfish ambitions? If so, then no matter how perfect your verbal teaching, it will be drowned out by the louder and clearer message of your lifestyle. But if Jesus lives in you and you deny yourself so he can shine, then the message of the Lord will be seen, felt, and heard by those around you. Your life leads.

My friend Tony's question was an important one. I needed correction from the Lord. I needed to see that I had merely been a hired hand who didn't care for the Master's sheep. I needed to die to my independence and selfish ambition, and I needed the Good Shepherd to reveal himself through me.

I spent the next decade learning how to do that.

CHAPTER 12:

THE PRACTICAL SIDE OF SHEPHERDING

Pastor is not a title; it is a job description. It describes the gift that focuses on caring for the sheep, feeding them, tending them, and dealing with threats that seek to destroy.

—Steve Wilson

Bursts of wind whipped through the starlit canyon. The sporadic bleating of sheep echoed off rock faces on either side. The shepherd scanned the length of the gorge in either direction, keeping his back to the fire that warmed him so it didn't impair his vision.

A shadow moved in the distant darkness. The shepherd's heart began to race as he squinted to identify who or what might be approaching. *Is it a wolf?* he thought. *A thief?*

With one eye on the faint shadow, the shepherd carefully stepped backward around the fire, shielding his eyes from the flames. He stretched his arm behind him, and his hand met the wood of the sheep pen's gate. Noting with a quick jostle that it was secure, the shepherd stepped forward again and picked up his staff from beside the fire, his eyes still fixed on the darkness.

The shadow stopped moving. Two glints of light hovered low to the ground, dancing in harmony with the flames behind the shepherd.

Then, without warning, the beast raced for the flock, staying close to the cliff opposite the shepherd. The shepherd gripped his staff with both hands and circled along the side of the pen, glancing momentarily at the rest of the dark valley to ensure no other predators were on the hunt as well.

Soon pointed ears, hackled fur, and a bushy tail became clear. The shepherd shouted to scare off the wolf, but the creature's mind was fixed. The sheep burst into commotion.

Crack! The wolf yelped as the shepherd's staff met its head. The animal stumbled while the shepherd slowed down and regained his own balance.

The sheep instinctively huddled at the opposite side of the pen, raising their voices together in a drone of agitation.

The wolf turned his gaze to the shepherd and bore his teeth. A low growl rattled the shepherd's nerves. His hands tightened on his staff, and he planted his feet for a fight.

Fierce Guards of the Flock

Sometimes I hear people talk about pastors as though they're little more than softhearted, gushy counselors who just want everyone to get along and feel comfortable. But a real shepherd also has a fierce side.

When someone in my church is struggling in their marriage, I take responsibility to fight for their marriage before anyone else, sometimes even before the couple themselves. I pray for them with fiery intensity. I keep my eyes open for weapons—whether scriptural insights, educational resources like videos or books, or practical helps—that will help us fight off the spiritual attack. I remind them that "our struggle is not against flesh and blood, but against the rulers, against the authorities, against the powers of this dark world and against the spiritual forces of evil in the heavenly realms" (Ephesians 6:12). I tell them, "Your struggle is not with each other but with a common spiritual enemy. Instead of fighting against each other, fight together against the enemy." We then try to carefully identify the point of attack. Often the surface problem is not the root issue, and forgiveness is needed in other areas to eliminate the devil's foothold. (See Ephesians 4:26–27.)

Many times, I've sacrificed hours of my life to fight for someone else's marriage or family. Naturally, this requires me to fight even harder to keep my own marriage and family healthy and thriving. As Paul wrote to Timothy, "If anyone does not know how to manage his own family, how can he take care of God's church?" (1 Timothy 3:5). Real shepherds are mature believers who know how to live "by grace through faith," allowing Jesus to permeate every aspect of their home life. They shepherd their own earthly families first, and the stability and victory overflows to their extended, spiritual family.

Wolves come in many forms. While Jesus used the wolf metaphor for false prophets (Matthew 7:15), these are not the only dangers against which we must guard the flock in our care. Attacks come from all angles. It doesn't matter what metaphor you use for all the things that threaten believers—wolves, lions, bears, snakes, thieves, storms—the threat is just as real.

Our first line of defense is vigilance. Like the shepherd's campfire, prayer wards off most threats and exposes the rest. Pray regularly for the people in your church. Seek the Lord for words of knowledge, words of wisdom, and prophetic encouragement for them. In Luke 22:31–32, Jesus spoke a grave warning to strengthen Simon Peter before an attack, "Simon, Simon, Satan has asked to sift all of you as wheat. But I have prayed for you, Simon, that your faith may not fail. And when you have turned back, strengthen your brothers." Pray for the people God has entrusted to you. He will give you wisdom and insight in how to lead them.

Second, we must remember that the Good Shepherd who lives in us also lives in the sheep themselves. Trust the Lord to serve his people through other believers as well. Even though Jesus might have given you special revelation into his shepherding heart, if you train and equip the church to love each other well, they'll make your job easier. Sheep make all manner of noise when a threat approaches the flock. They warn each other. You are not the only member of Christ's body, and you don't need to be the solution to everyone's problems. You simply need to do what Jesus is leading you to do. He will do the rest through others. (See 1 Corinthians 3:5–9.)

During house-church meetings themselves, certain threats may appear from time to time. For example, keep the conversation away from trivial matters and fruitless arguments. (See 2 Timothy 2:23–26.) Instead, make sure everything is established on Scripture as our final authority. If you don't know what the Bible says on a matter (and even if you do), ask the group. If no one knows, model how to research an answer—even if it's just a web search on someone's smartphone. Sort it out together. As Proverbs 18:2 observes, "Fools find no pleasure in understanding but delight in airing their own opinions."

Opinions are great to discuss, but they're not the purpose of the house-church meeting. The real purpose is to encounter Jesus through each other. Anything that distracts from him is either something for Jesus to address through people in the meeting (thus revealing himself through the correction) or else is a threat to the group (because Jesus is not being expressed in a way that addresses the matter). As pastors, our role in the meeting includes discerning when to let a conversation happen and when to redirect it.

Also, from time to time, you may encounter what is popularly called "a wolf in sheep's clothing." Jesus said, "Watch out for false prophets. They come to you in sheep's clothing, but inwardly they are ferocious wolves" (Matthew 7:15).

> But there were also false prophets among the people, just as there will be false teachers among you. They will secretly introduce destructive heresies, even denying the sovereign Lord who bought them—bringing swift destruction on themselves. Many will follow their depraved conduct and will bring the way of truth into disrepute. In their greed these teachers will exploit you with fabricated stories. Their condemnation has long been hanging over them, and their destruction has not been sleeping. (2 Peter 2:1–3)

Some false prophets and false teachers are fully aware of their actions, fabricating stories and exploiting the flock. They come to gain influence over others and peddle their snake-oil (powerless) doctrines among unsuspecting victims.

Other false prophets and false teachers are ignorant of their harm. Some are merely teaching what they've been taught by well-meaning people who were taught by other well-meaning people.

Still others have formed errant conclusions from their own study of Scripture. But they come without interest in what God is speaking through others and proudly seek attention and followers for themselves.

A young minister came to one of our house churches years ago. He praised our emphasis on the moving of the Spirit and was rather excited about the interactivity in the group. He shared his YouTube channel with some of the people and started coming regularly. But his own teaching was legalistic, and he became more interested in convincing people to follow Old Testament rules in their own strength rather than being free in the power of the Holy Spirit.

Thankfully, the minister's false teachings were ignored—not because he was unlikable or distrusted by the people in the house church but because the house church's pastor had faithfully taught the true gospel for so long that the people in his church easily recognized the counterfeit. As Benjamin Franklin famously stated, "An ounce of prevention is worth a pound of cure."[42] Immunizing is generally better than doctoring.

Quality Veterinarians

Godly pastors care less about growing the numbers of the flock (although still important) and more about maintaining and improving the health of the flock. As with the false teacher just mentioned, sometimes you will need to make a choice between adding to the size of your house church and removing someone who is detrimental to the ongoing health of the flock. The pastor of that house church allowed the other teacher to attend for a time, hoping the man would catch on to truth and learn enough to repent. But when it became clear that he was more interested in arguing his points and peddling his own doctrines than

---

42 "Ounce of prevention, pound of cure," University of Cambridge, accessed April 19, 2023, https://www.cam.ac.uk/research/news/ounce-of-prevention-pound-of-cure#.

participating in an interactive community where his own views could be challenged and changed, the pastor asked him to leave.

Quality pastors watch for spiritual infections and illnesses in the sheep under their care. Some infections could be as insidious and obvious as bitterness or discord among the people. Others could be as subtle as a misunderstanding of God that only becomes apparent during conversation.

This is one of the primary reasons I prefer house-church meetings over traditional pulpit-to-pew ministry. In all church settings—whether house churches or more traditional models—people hold all manner of errant views about the gospel, God, and themselves. In the typical American church model, these views are rarely ever made known to the pastor because communication only moves in one direction. The congregation generally remains silent.

Many pastors mistakenly assume that the members of their congregations understand and believe what they teach each week. In reality, those who disagree rarely change their minds because of a sermon, and those who misunderstand the sermon may end up believing a warped version of what was taught. Furthermore, some people only attend once every few weeks, which means they don't receive a full teaching on anything shared in a series of sermons.

Any ignorance or errors are not exposed until one of these people is placed in a teaching or leadership role. And even then, they often remain unaddressed until someone with enough understanding of truth is bold enough to question what is being taught. By then, the damage has been done.

Shepherds do not merely throw food at sheep and expect the sheep to thrive. Shepherds interact with the sheep and gently inspect them, carefully doctoring any issues before they become serious. They quarantine and medicate infectious diseases before they spread. They wash and bandage wounds before they fester. They watch for signs of poor health and identify solutions.

Likewise, house-church pastors need not be high-quality public speakers. They simply need to be attentive veterinarians—caring for the sheep and doing what they can to maintain and even improve the overall health of the flock. This means spending quality time with people and listening carefully during conversations. It means gently correcting misconceptions with Scripture and feeding people truth. It means mediating disputes and discord, bringing reconciliation and helping people learn to love each other.

As an elder in a house church, your responsibility is to guard, feed, doctor, and serve the small portion of Jesus's flock that has been entrusted to your care.

Shepherds Don't Rule, They Serve

Peter encouraged pastors to be "eager to serve; not lording it over those entrusted to you" (1 Peter 5:2–3). Much of American church structure is borrowed from the hierarchy of corporate America. Senior pastors are often the CEOs of their nonprofit corporations, and they are therefore often expected to manage a thriving business.[43] There's nothing innately wrong with this, as long as it's helping the body of Christ make more disciples. But sometimes a blurring of the lines between the organization and the organism can lend itself to pastors operating outside their callings or skillsets—treating the flock more like a CEO treats troublesome employees than a shepherd treats his sheep.

I've been blessed to minister in hundreds of churches across twenty countries so far, and I've seen a wide array of leadership styles among pastors. I'm pleased to say that in most situations, I've encountered wonderfully healthy and loving ministers who truly care for the people entrusted to them. But I've also watched an African pastor announce to his congregation, "Clap for me. Give me the honor I deserve." I've seen Indian pastors who live in extravagant mansions while their congregations are mostly impoverished. I've been in lavish offices that look more like royal palaces than a pastor's study. And in these situations, which are rare experiences for me, I generally also see these pastors inappropriately exert authority, lording over the flock.

This pastor-at-the-top model would be foreign to the first-century church. Jesus taught them a different form of leadership—one of humbly raising up others while seeking no honor for oneself.

---

43 I offer this critique as a senior pastor and the CEO of two nonprofits—Roots Church and Wildfire Ministries International. I'm not speaking against organizational structure as much as I'm addressing the abnormal, extrabiblical responsibilities we expect from many pastors.

> Then Jesus said to the crowds and to his disciples: "The teachers of the law and the Pharisees sit in Moses' seat. So you must be careful to do everything they tell you. But do not do what they do, for they do not practice what they preach. They tie up heavy, cumbersome loads and put them on other people's shoulders, but they themselves are not willing to lift a finger to move them.
>
> "Everything they do is done for people to see: They make their phylacteries wide and the tassels on their garments long; they love the place of honor at banquets and the most important seats in the synagogues; they love to be greeted with respect in the marketplaces and to be called 'Rabbi' by others.
>
> "But you are not to be called 'Rabbi,' for you have one Teacher, and you are all brothers. And do not call anyone on earth 'father,' for you have one Father, and he is in heaven. Nor are you to be called instructors, for you have one Instructor, the Messiah. The greatest among you will be your servant. For those who exalt themselves will be humbled, and those who humble themselves will be exalted." (Matthew 23:1–12)

Toxic ministry culture comes in many forms. One extreme is the pastor who sits on a literal throne of honor (yes, this exists in many churches around the world), the people hanging on his every word and never allowed to question anything the pastor says. Someone—usually called an "armor bearer"—carries the man of God's Bible. When the church has food, he eats the first and best. And may God have mercy on whomever might challenge or question his authority!

But toxic ministry culture can also be as subtle as a structure that forces a shepherd into a role Jesus never intended. It's not wrong to lead a nonprofit corporation, so long as we realize this is not in itself pastoring. Shepherds are in the business of sheep, not barn-building. And while there are some wildly gifted pastors who do fantastic work shepherding large congregations (usually with help from other staff or pastoral people in the church), Jesus spent most of his own time and attention pouring into only a small group of leaders. The typical American church structure places expectations on pastors that are foreign to the expectations in the Bible.

In my network of house churches, all pastoral ministry happens at the house-church level. We do have an overarching nonprofit organization, which allows us to have a corporate identity, insurance, a bank account, a large missions budget, an official face in the community, and other valuable benefits. But our senior staff doesn't carry a title of pastor. Our senior leadership team is comprised of various directors who focus their attention on logistical areas that help the house churches in our network thrive. At Roots Church, the word "pastor" is reserved for those elders (in Christian maturity, not necessarily physical age) who faithfully shepherd the small flocks that meet in homes. Our pastors need not focus on church budgets, productions, planning outreaches and events, staffing ministries, or the like. They can invest all their time and attention into the work of loving and serving the people Jesus has entrusted to them.

In this role, pastors are free to lift others up. They don't perform their duties for attention or honor. With Jesus's help, they lay down their lives for the success of others.

We don't lead like dictators, lording over people. We lead by example, aiming to be the pacesetters for lives of victory and self-sacrifice. That's what Jesus did. "Take up your cross and follow me" (Matthew 16:24).

A Stern Warning to Shepherds

Shepherds are not unique to the Christian church. They also existed in ancient Israel. Even in the Old Testament, God expected certain people to serve the overall population, not lording over them but helping the people thrive.

But the shepherds failed. So God spoke a rebuke to the shepherds of Israel that rings through the ages as a stern warning to those of us who would pastor today:

> The word of the Lord came to me: "Son of man, prophesy against the shepherds of Israel; prophesy and say to them: 'This is what the Sovereign Lord says: Woe to you shepherds of Israel who only take care of yourselves!

Should not shepherds take care of the flock? You eat the curds, clothe yourselves with the wool and slaughter the choice animals, but you do not take care of the flock. You have not strengthened the weak or healed the sick or bound up the injured. You have not brought back the strays or searched for the lost. You have ruled them harshly and brutally. So they were scattered because there was no shepherd, and when they were scattered they became food for all the wild animals. My sheep wandered over all the mountains and on every high hill. They were scattered over the whole earth, and no one searched or looked for them.

"Therefore, you shepherds, hear the word of the Lord: As surely as I live, declares the Sovereign Lord, because my flock lacks a shepherd and so has been plundered and has become food for all the wild animals, and because my shepherds did not search for my flock but cared for themselves rather than for my flock, therefore, you shepherds, hear the word of the Lord: This is what the Sovereign Lord says: I am against the shepherds and will hold them accountable for my flock. I will remove them from tending the flock so that the shepherds can no longer feed themselves. I will rescue my flock from their mouths, and it will no longer be food for them." (Ezekiel 34:1–10)

Little commentary is needed here, but I wish to emphasize the consequences of poor shepherding. First, the flock suffered. Second, one could say God suffered (it's his flock, after all). And finally, the shepherds suffered—not so much because of the natural consequences of their own actions but because God himself turned and fought against them.

> He said, "Surely they are my people,
>   children who will be true to me";
>   and so he became their Savior.
> In all their distress he too was distressed,
>   and the angel of his presence saved them.
> In his love and mercy he redeemed them;
>   he lifted them up and carried them
>   all the days of old.
> Yet they rebelled
>   and grieved his Holy Spirit.
> So he turned and became their enemy
>   and he himself fought against them.
>
> (Isaiah 63:8–10)

When God's people are distressed, God is distressed. And he actively fights against those who grieve the Holy Spirit—especially leaders. In speaking of the body of Christ—which is the church, of which we are all members—Paul tells us that "if one part suffers, every part suffers with it" (1 Corinthians 12:26). We often forget that this applies also to the most important part of the body—the

Head: Jesus. So when shepherds rule over the body of Christ, they wrongly and sinfully lord over Jesus. When pastors cause the body to suffer, Jesus suffers. When God's people are distressed, he is distressed.

Your role is not to rule over the flock any more than your role is to rule over Jesus. Your role is to serve the flock as you serve Jesus. They are his body. And you, too, are part of that body. Even as a shepherd, you are a sheep too.

You Are a Sheep Too

In 1 Peter 5:3, the apostle instructs pastors to be "examples to the flock." This is only possible because we, too, are sheep.

Every metaphor only goes so far. In the real world, a shepherd can't be an example to his flock. Sheep are entirely incapable of standing upright and doing any of the things a shepherd can do. Real-world sheep have no opposable thumbs.

But spiritual shepherds—pastors—can be examples to the flock because biblical pastors are sheep too. Whatever we can do with the Holy Spirit's help, other Christians can do with the Holy Spirit's help.

Knowing you're a sheep is important because it keeps you from creating an artificial divide between yourself and the people in your care. When you see something lacking in the lives of people in your house church, first ask if it is lacking in you. As Jesus taught, "First take the plank out of your own eye, and then you will see clearly to remove the speck from your brother's eye" (Matthew 7:5).

If the people in your house church are not reading their Bibles, set an example for the flock by first pouring more of your own time and attention into Bible reading. If the people in your house church seem bitter against other people or churches, first identify whether you have been bitter. If you want the people in your house church to share the gospel more frequently, begin by stepping out to minister to people in public yourself. Share testimonies. Talk about your own struggles and how the Holy Spirit helps you overcome your flesh. Confess sin and discuss solutions. Be authentic, and the flock will become more authentic.

Being a sheep means you also need to be fed. Be careful that ministry doesn't overtake your personal walk with Jesus. If you want the people in your house church to value what Jesus is doing through everyone in the meeting, you, too, need to value what Jesus is doing through everyone in the meeting. The flock will value what the shepherd values.

Be Vigilant

The wilderness is full of wolves, bears, snakes, diseases, thorns, and more. It's more than one person can adequately guard against. That is to say, one *earthly* person. Jesus sees it all.

As you live surrendered to Jesus, he will fight the wolves through you. He will doctor the sheep through you. He will pull the thorns and bandage the wounds through you. Keep your eyes fixed on him.

And since you're an example to the flock, the people in your care will look where you're looking. As you fix your eyes on Jesus, so will they. As you receive your direction from the Lord, so will they. And when everyone is being led by the Chief Shepherd, pastoring becomes easier. It's much easier to fight off wolves when the sheep rise up with staffs too.

CHAPTER 13:

CREATING AN ENVIRONMENT WHERE SHEEP THRIVE

If you're not in a small group, you're not in the New Testament church, because the New Testament church met in the homes. And if you're not being vulnerable and real with each other, never confessing your sins to each other, and still being private, then you're just playing games—church hasn't happened yet.

—John Loren Sandford

Why do people own sheep? Only someone truly eccentric would own sheep for the pure fun of it. Most expect to gain something.

My father-in-law, for example, owns a petting farm and has around twenty sheep. The sheep are part of the attraction, enabling visitors to interact with live farm animals. The sheep earn him money. Most people who own sheep do so for other productive reasons—perhaps collecting wool or, in some cultures, milk. Whatever the case, they're not pets; they're producers.[44]

If I owned sheep, I would hire a shepherd who would ensure my sheep were top producers—not driving them, as though wool could be produced faster if the sheep just tried harder, but caring for them in such a way that they are healthy and thriving. The healthier my sheep, the more productive they'll be. Their wool will be better quality. Their milk will be richer. And they'll multiply faster and produce stronger lambs than if they're malnourished. The shepherd's role is to care for my sheep in such a way that they naturally produce more than if left on their own.

Whatever it is that sheep produce, they do so without effort. In the same way, the fruit that we produce as Christians is effortless for us. It's the work of the Holy Spirit, expressing Jesus through us. "Remain in me, as I also remain in you. No branch can bear fruit by itself; it must remain in the vine. Neither can you bear fruit unless you remain in me. I am the vine; you are the branches. If you remain in me and I in you, you will bear much fruit; apart from me you can do nothing" (John 15:4–5).

A good shepherd doesn't drive the sheep, demanding that they try harder and produce more (as though they could). Instead, a good shepherd guards the sheep against thieves and predators,

---

44 Remember, every analogy breaks down at some point. A father loves his child long before that child can do anything productive. Here, we are focusing strictly on the sheep metaphor so that we can gain insight about our roles as shepherds of God's flock.

leads them to green pastures and still waters, and basically monitors their health and manages their environment so the flock can thrive.

In any church, large or small, the environment that needs monitoring and management is called culture. In a healthy culture, people will know the Lord and be free to produce his fruit in the Spirit's power.

The healthiest church environment—producing the best spiritual health and multiplication—is a culture established on the gospel. As I've made the gospel our central theme and message, Jesus has added people to our church. When you create an environment where sheep thrive, the Good Shepherd seems to like to entrust more of his flock there.

Culture Is Cultivated

The word "culture" is traceable back to the Latin word *colere*, which means to till, cultivate, and tend land. This agricultural word implies intentional action on the part of the people shaping the environment. In a social context, culture refers to the ways in which people live—our social norms, group activities, language, and so forth.[45]

All culture is cultivated. Even when we think a component of our culture emerged by accident, a hand was at work. If the

[45] JR Woodward, *Creating a Missional Culture: Equipping the Church for the Sake of the World.* (Downers Grove, Illinois: InterVarsity Press, 2012), Kindle Edition, 35.

kingdom of God is not intentionally shaping a culture, the kingdom of darkness is.

The world's culture didn't become what it is today by chance. It has been carefully shaped for millennia by spiritual "rulers . . . authorities . . . powers of this dark world and . . . spiritual forces of evil in the heavenly realms" (Ephesians 6:12). The kingdom of darkness has carefully crafted an environment with just the right balance of sin and structure so that most people can live in sin but be just comfortable enough not to want to escape it. It's a deliberate environment where the devil has "blinded the minds of unbelievers, so that they cannot see the light of the gospel that displays the glory of Christ, who is the image of God" (2 Corinthians 4:4).

If you're comfortable in the world's culture, then you're part of the world. This world is not our home. As people of faith, we are "foreigners and strangers on earth" (Hebrews 11:3). We've been called out of this world's culture and into a different realm.

Immersive Christianity

David and Paula Mansfield started their house church in 2018 after a mission trip to Guatemala changed their perspective on life. Their Nazarene church sent them out as local missionaries, and with some pointers and vision from Francis Chan's "We Are Church" movement, the Mansfields began discipling people in their home with a house church.

David was helping mentor men at the Detroit Life Challenge ministry.[46] He knew men were being helped by the program, but he cared deeply about their success after graduation. He and his house church began looking for houses in the neighborhood that they could perhaps buy together, giving these men a place to live near their church and Christian community.

Then came the pandemic in 2020, and housing prices skyrocketed. David had a wild idea. He asked his wife, "What if we moved into my parents' house next door for a few months and try letting guys in addiction recovery live in our home?"

David, Paula, their four kids, and David's parents all took a leap of faith. They moved into one house, and the Mansfields offered up their previous home to disciple men in recovery.

Their house church continued meeting in the same home three times a week. Meanwhile, David's brother owned a restaurant down the street and helped employ the men.

I met David about a year later, and his family and house church soon joined our network. We're all better because of it. David and Paula's example (along with that of his parents) has been a powerful picture of Jesus's self-sacrificial love.

They continued to host the men in their own home for almost three years until a new opportunity arose for them to provide housing where the men could participate in a missional

---

46 You may know this ministry better as Teen Challenge or Adult and Teen Challenge. This is "a non-profit, faith-based, residential recovery program for men and women who struggle with addiction." For more information, please visit https://lcministries.org.

community, reaching their neighborhood. Other believers live in the neighborhood too, offering local stability and friendship to the men. David and Paula's house church has now multiplied and will soon multiply again. Meanwhile, the men are benefitting from an immersive culture of love and gospel truth.

The Mansfields' story is inspiring. Lives are being transformed because they've welcomed people into their home and family. The Mansfields are spiritually healthy, mature, and resilient, setting a powerful example in an environment that can sometimes be volatile. Their house is a gospel house with a gospel culture, and it's impossible to spend time in that sort of environment without being transformed.

Maybe you'll offer up your own house or a room or an addition or an apartment or a nearby rental. Or maybe not. What matters is following the Holy Spirit as you shine Jesus in whatever lifestyle he directs. Gospel people generate gospel cultures.

You Are a Culture Influencer

Everyone influences culture. Some have more influence than others, but every human relationship generates language, behaviors, and shared activities that reverberate through friend groups, workplaces, and even the church.

If I can change the way you think and behave through the words I've written here, then I have successfully influenced your culture. Those new thoughts and behaviors will play out in your real-life relationships, and the ways you and others once related will change.

Words either strengthen culture or redirect it. Actions do too. Even inaction can affect culture. Everything you do (or don't do) in a human relationship either strengthens or changes the cultural environment in which you and those close to you live. You can go with the flow, leaving the lost people around you blissfully ignorant of their doom; or you can shine a light in their darkened eyes that just might wake them up. Your words, thoughts, and actions matter.

What words are you believing? Are your thoughts and actions more in line with the kingdom of darkness or the kingdom of God? Which realm do you love more? Do you like the culture in which you live? Or do you love heaven enough to pray that it would come to earth? (See Matthew 6:10.)

Each of us is most likely to influence culture toward the homeland we most love. "Do not love the world or anything in the world. If anyone loves the world, love for the Father is not in them. For everything in the world—the lust of the flesh, the lust of the eyes, and the pride of life—comes not from the Father but from the world. The world and its desires pass away, but whoever does the will of God lives forever" (1 John 2:15–17).

Many Christians are too concerned about fitting in. They want to influence their culture, but they want people to still see them as "normal."

But what is normal? Normal is room-temperature. Normal is the status quo. Normal doesn't change things; it conforms.

We don't have to try to figure out how to fit into the world's culture. Our allegiance is to a different kingdom. Yes, we need to know how to engage the world culture, but we don't need to be anything like them—in fact, we shouldn't be. "Therefore, I urge you, brothers and sisters, in view of God's mercy, to offer your bodies as a living sacrifice, holy and pleasing to God—this is your true and proper worship. Do not conform to the pattern of this world, but be transformed by the renewing of your mind. Then you will be able to test and approve what God's will is—his good, pleasing and perfect will" (Romans 12:1–2).

Revelation 12:11 tells us that believers will ultimately overcome the devil with the blood of the Lamb (which is what Jesus has done), the word of our testimony (which is what Jesus has done in us), and not loving our lives so much as to shrink from death. In other words, we don't love the way things are so much that we'd rather settle into the status quo than risk our lives or comforts to change it. Instead, we love Jesus and his kingdom enough to die—whether physically or simply spiritually. We have been crucified with Christ and no longer live (Galatians 2:20). It's hard to scare someone with death when they're already dead.

Culture Is Pressure

When you walk into a library where everyone is quiet, you naturally whisper if you need to speak. When you walk into a crowded stadium as the home team faces its chief rival, you naturally shout and cheer. All cultures invite conformity.

When a person from one culture enters another culture, they feel a certain social pressure. If the culture is appealing, the pressure will move the person to conform. If the culture is repulsive, the pressure will move the person to action—either leaving the culture or acting to change it.

Abolitionists found a culture of slavery repulsive and rose actively against it. Meanwhile, certain other people found that evil culture appealing and fought to maintain it. On this issue and others, the American Civil War was a true "culture war." And culture wars continue today all over the world as some try to move the boundaries of society deeper into spiritual darkness (where they're comfortable) while others try to move them further into the light.

Some Christians are too comfortable in worldly culture, but other Christians are too comfortable in "churchy" culture. Neither option is kingdom culture. Those who are too comfortable in worldly culture never feel enough pressure to bother changing anything around them. They live for their own comfort and regularly fail to benefit others. Those who are too comfortable in "churchy" culture avoid interacting with the world whenever possible, always enjoying Christian meetings but avoiding and even complaining about outsiders.

God invites us to the uncomfortable position of living with our hearts anchored in heaven and our bodies fully present in the earth. We long for an eternal utopia in his presence, and we spend time, energy, and resources in this world, inviting broken and lost people to join us there. This requires that we sometimes enter cultures that are foreign to us—not condoning the evils that might exist within their cultures but also not requiring people to conform to our preferences before we are willing to serve them.

If we want to create an environment where sheep thrive, then we shepherds need to be culture-makers who are so at home in heaven that the pressures of this world rouse us to action. We need to create a new "normal" for people.

A twelve-year-old young man told me that he has never felt the presence of God at any other church like he has felt at my house church. Everyone here knows that it's normal to hear from God and expect miracles in everyday life. And this young man has shocked his parents as he has stepped out in ministering prophetically to others—seeing visions and conveying powerful messages to people. And all this has developed in him over the last three months as I write. Obviously, God is doing a work in his heart, but it's an easy work because this young man is immersed in a culture where such activity is normal.

What is the culture of your home? Does it look like the kingdom? If not, spend time studying the kingdom of God and seeking the Lord on the matter. Turn off the television, social media, and other entertainment long enough to detox from the world culture. A gospel house is marked by a gospel culture.

When someone steps out of a hot tub and dips their toe in a swimming pool, it feels like ice. But the people immersed in the pool say, "Come on! It's great once you get in!" But maybe the cold water isn't great. Some of us need to get out of the cold water entirely and immerse ourselves in the fiery presence of God until we adjust to a new normal. Then we can return to the world and more strongly feel how repulsive the darkness is. Perhaps the startling iciness will finally be enough to rouse us to action.

Relationships Define Culture

Since culture is shared, it is directly connected to human relationships. The stronger the relationships, the stronger the culture they create.

Naturally, the strongest relationships tend to be familial. Whether people are literally related to each other by blood, bound by a marriage contract, or close enough to think of each other as family, such relationships are strong enough to create a culture that may even transcend the societal culture in which they live.

Jesus understood this. And whether for theological reasons, practical, or both, he made this perspective clear, defining his family as those who obeyed the same Father he did.

> Then Jesus entered a house, and again a crowd gathered, so that he and his disciples were not even able to eat. When his family heard about this, they went to take charge of him, for they said, "He is out of his mind."

> . . . A crowd was sitting around him, and they told him, "Your mother and brothers are outside looking for you."
>
> "Who are my mother and my brothers?" he asked. Then he looked at those seated in a circle around him and said, "Here are my mother and my brothers! Whoever does God's will is my brother and sister and mother." (Mark 3:20–21, 32–35)

Jesus welcomes you into his family. Through believing in him, you are given the right to become a child of God. (See John 1:12.) The gospel tells us that we don't need to strive to be accepted into this new family. Instead, we have been born of God and are already full participants. Our Father loves us, not because we have performed well enough but simply because we belong to him.

The more you can see yourself as part of his family, the easier it will be to live according to his family's culture—a culture where the Spirit of God dwells in you and expresses the love and nature of Jesus through you. Kingdom culture and gospel culture are synonymous.

The gospel is therefore the ultimate culture-setter because, through the gospel, we enter God's family and receive his Spirit. If you want a healthy kingdom culture in your house church, then the gospel needs to permeate everything you say and do.

The Ultimate Culture Setter

In chapter 3, I stated that the gospel is the DNA of the body of Christ, and I shared a summary of our union with Jesus in his death, resurrection, and ascension to authority at the right hand of the Father. But this is only the core of the gospel. The full picture is much bigger.

Before Jesus died and rose again—meaning before those components were part of the story—he said, "And this gospel of the kingdom will be preached in the whole world as a testimony to all nations, and then the end will come" (Matthew 24:14). The good news we carry is about God's kingdom (his rulership and authority)—a true story that begins in eternity past with "the Lamb who was slain from the creation of the world" (Revelation 13:8). That story reaches its climax in the death, resurrection, and ascension of Jesus Christ and continues right up to today as Jesus's work continues to bring God's rulership and authority into hearts and minds all over the world.

There's only one way to enter this kingdom: death and rebirth. That's of course a metaphor, but it's also somehow true in a spiritual sense. Second Corinthians 5:14 tells us that "one died for all, and therefore all died." The author of this verse, the apostle Paul, spoke of himself as dying with Christ and commanded believers to consider ourselves "dead to sin but alive to God in Christ Jesus" (Romans 6:5–11). "I have been crucified with Christ and I no longer live, but Christ lives in me. The life I now live in the body, I live by faith in the Son of God, who loved me and gave himself for me. . . . May I never boast except in the cross of our Lord Jesus Christ, through which the world has been crucified to me, and I to the world" (Galatians 2:20; 6:14).

We who have placed our faith in Jesus have died to the world, and the world is dead to us. We are now part of a new world—a heavenly world. We have been born again and are now seated with Christ in the heavenly realms. (See Ephesians 2:6.)

This message of death and rebirth is the central theme of the entire gospel. Surrender to the King of this new kingdom looks like considering your old life dead and giving full allegiance to his rulership and authority. Yes, that means serving his will and working for him but not as mere servants. Rather, we work *with* him as dearly loved sons and daughters.

Those who have been born again have become new creations. God's Spirit lives in us, and we are being transformed daily to look more and more like Jesus. (See 2 Corinthians 3:18.)

The gospel transforms culture by transforming people. It's not just a method; it's resurrection power and life. In the gospel, Jesus is revealed through those who put their faith in him. We show his nature—his love, his mercy, his miracles, his authority, his humility, his holiness, and more—through the power of the Holy Spirit. The mature Christian life looks like Jesus.

The Gospel Is the Answer to Everything

When this message permeates every aspect of a house-church meeting, people become healthy. And this message is simple too:

Death to self and life in Christ. This becomes the application every single time we gather.

There's a lie in this world's culture that "God helps those who help themselves." The truth is that God empowers those who desire to obey him and admit their desperate need for him.

Do you want to have a healthy marriage? You can find plenty of great advice out there about love languages, intimacy, and conflict resolution. But if we never arrive at dying to ourselves and letting the Holy Spirit live through us to serve and bless our spouse, then all that great teaching is nothing more than empty philosophy. (See Colossians 2:8.) Only the gospel truly changes the heart.

Likewise, there's plenty of great advice about parenting, and we parents need it. But more than we need another method to try, we need transformation that makes us more like Jesus, enabling Jesus to parent our children through us as the Holy Spirit enables us. I don't need to worry about whether I'll be a good dad because I'm dead and the One who perfectly reveals the only perfect Father lives in me. I trust him to express righteous fatherhood through me. No more worry—only trust, rest, and obedience.

Do you want to be better at evangelism? Die to self and let God's Spirit live through you. Do you want to be a better coworker? Die to self and let God's Spirit live through you. Do you want to be a better neighbor? A better student? A better citizen? The answer is always the same. Die to self and let God's Spirit live through you.

Every healthy Christian knows that the way we come to Jesus is by grace through faith. It's not by works, so no one can boast. (See Ephesians 2:8–9.) But as grateful as we are to be saved by grace through faith, we sometimes forget to *continue* the same way. Colossians 2:6–7 tells us that the way we came to Jesus (by grace through faith) is also how we are to continue in him—"strengthened in the faith as you were taught."

People often ask me about my devotional life, but I rarely tell them. What most people really want to know is, "How can I do what you do so I can become who you are?" But that's not how it works. I do what I do, not to become anything but simply because I already am that person. My actions flow out of my identity; they don't produce it.

An environment where sheep thrive is an environment where sheep die. It's an environment where the life-giving power of the Holy Spirit gives them the grace to live in the image of Jesus. Sheep don't have to work hard to produce wool for their owner.

House church is not a magical methodology that automatically spits out mature Christians. If small-group gatherings were the answer on their own, then game nights and parties would be enough to transform us. The model we use (whether house church, traditional church, or whatever) is far less important than the message.

If your house-church meeting ends with assignments for people to complete in their own strength, then the gospel is not at work, the culture is worldly, and the sheep will not thrive. But if those assignments are given with the understanding that we can only do them by grace through faith and if we lead people again to a deeper death with Jesus and a fuller expression of the Spirit's resurrection life, then we will have success.

> I would like to learn just one thing from you: Did you receive the Spirit by the works of the law, or by believing what you heard? Are you so foolish? After beginning by means of the Spirit, are you now trying to finish by means of the flesh? Have you experienced so much in vain—if it really was in vain? So again I ask, does God give you his Spirit and work miracles among you by the works of the law, or by your believing what you heard? (Galatians 3:2–5)

Sheep Thrive in a Gospel-Centered Family

When this message permeates our meetings and when we see ourselves as parts of a real family who share the same Father, Christians thrive. We begin to honor each other above ourselves. (See Romans 12:10.) We treat older believers with respect as we would parents and younger believers with dignity as beloved siblings. (See 1 Timothy 5:1–2.)

In a healthy family, people experience appropriate affection—hugs of greeting, handshakes, pats on the back, and so on. Such appropriate physical touch has a powerful effect on human development and psychology, and it is one of the ways God brings holistic transformation to people.

As a family, we rejoice with those who rejoice and mourn with those who mourn (Romans 12:15). We have enough access to each other's lives that we know what they're going through. We support each other in difficult times—taking meals when people are sick, buying each other groceries when money is tight, and even paying bills or helping people in emergency situations that are beyond their ability to solve alone. This is what families do. Yes, we have a responsibility as Christians to be kind and merciful toward all people, but the biblical priority is first to the family of believers. (See Galatians 6:10.)

This is the environment where sheep thrive. If you want Jesus—the Chief Shepherd—to entrust his sheep to your care, then learn to articulate the gospel message in response to every situation. Be a gospel-centered person. Help people to die to their own abilities and receive the new lives that operate entirely by grace through faith. And help them see themselves as vital members of this new family.

As a shepherd yourself, apply this message so deeply and meaningfully to your own life that you become a living, breathing example of it for others. If you do, the natural result will be an overflow of God's unconditional love in your life. This is exactly the environment where Jesus wants his sheep.

CHAPTER 14: LOVE AND MESSES

God wants your ministry to flow from the realization that you are a beloved child of God. In that place, you don't worry too much about how people see you. You don't worry too much about whether they're nice or mean. You don't even worry about whether they love you or hate you. You don't worry because you're simply going to love them and love him. This comes from knowing who he is and what he thinks of you. This is what it means to grasp you are a child of God.

—Heidi Baker

I'm never coming to church again.

Robin read the text message. She knew this young woman was struggling through all manner of emotional turmoil. It wasn't that she was hurt by anyone at church. It's that she was in a dark place in her soul—spiraling in despair—and she was struggling with the love that was being shown to her so regularly.

Robin knew that she shouldn't reinforce the young woman's behavior, but she also knew her friend needed love. Partly in frustration and partly in wisdom, Robin simply replied, *I'll see you next week*.

It's hard not to paint our house-church network as some sort of utopia. The culture we have been experiencing is nothing short of a move of God. At times, I want to pinch myself to check if I'm dreaming. Lives are being transformed rapidly, and a real spirit of love and unity exists among us.

But scattered throughout this overwhelming beauty are plenty of messy situations. We've had people with mental illness lash out in slander and accusations. We've had people with immense physical needs leave because the house church couldn't help them to the magnitude they wanted. We've had people experience offenses and distance themselves, not wanting to confront the people who hurt them. And on rare occasions, we've also had to ask people to leave for the sake of protecting others. People we love have suffered divorce, drug overdoses, and tremendous loss.

Yet the magnificence of what God is doing among us remains. We're learning to love better and better all the time. And with the increase of love has come an increase of messes. Perhaps God trusts us more as our capacity for love grows. Perhaps we're seeing psychological reactions to our love—people self-sabotaging to see if this love is real. Perhaps there are other reasons. All I know is that no matter what, we are to keep growing in love.

House-church meetings can be messy. And networks of house churches are messier still. Love is always the appropriate response to messes. But sometimes, love is also the reason for the messes.

Love Invites Messes

I was in the last row of a twelve-passenger van. Beside me sat a fourteen-year-old young man whom I had just met. His mother signed him up for this youth retreat with a church I previously attended, but he didn't really want to be there.

As the van bounced down the highway, I asked him about his life. I listened. I showed genuine interest, probing with more and more questions, laughing at his jokes and encouraging him about the good qualities I saw in him.

About two hours into our three-hour drive, he stared out the window for a minute or two. I knew he was processing his thoughts and gave him some space. He spun his head back toward me and broke the silence. "I'm not a good person."

I raised my eyebrows with interest, inviting him to expound.

Over the next five minutes, I listened as he melted down in front of me. He confessed addictions, impure thoughts, shameful activities, and more. It was as though he were the prosecuting attorney in his own trial. He knew he had done wrong. But he wasn't confessing in repentance. Quite the opposite. He was trying to communicate to me just how terrible he was and how much he liked living this way.

The Lord dropped wisdom into my heart. It was as though I could hear his spirit crying out louder than his physical voice. I looked into his eyes and replied, "I know what you're doing. For the last two hours, you've experienced real love from me, and you don't feel like you deserve it. You believe that if I knew who you really are, I wouldn't love you the same way. But guess what? Nothing has changed for me. I don't take back anything I've said. I still care about you. I don't really care what you've done. I care about you as a person."

Tears welled in his eyes, and he turned back to look out the window. After a little more time, we continued our conversation. A couple of days later, I was with that young man as he surrendered his life to Jesus.

Sometimes when people experience a love that feels too good to be true, they self-sabotage as a way of testing that love, wanting to prove to themselves that it couldn't possibly be real. Why? Because if such a love is real, then their mental framework of lies will come crashing down. They can no longer believe that no one loves them. They can no longer believe that they are unlovable. And they're confronted with the reality that their life really does have value.

In our house-church network, we see such self-sabotage from time to time. I've witnessed public meltdowns, angry outbursts, and plenty of empty threats. And every time these actions are met with love, I've also witnessed powerful repentance.

Sometimes these issues are public because people feel safe to struggle openly. A culture of love is an environment with room to fail. Other times, these messes are public because people feel an inner need to reinforce the lie that they'll be rejected.

Love invites messes because it invites discovery. The house my children grew up in had spaghetti sauce on the curtains, paint on the carpet, and sometimes a pile of unwound toilet paper on the bathroom floor. Likewise, my house church has people learning to minister in spiritual gifts, developing an understanding of the Bible and theology, and discovering relational skills they never needed before. The result is the occasional mess as people make mistakes, but love invites those messes.

Basic Trust

Early childhood researcher and psychologist Erik Erikson famously observed that the first eighteen months of human development involves learning what he calls basic trust vs. mistrust.[47] As parents meet their child's needs, babies learn self-worth and develop a general outlook on life of trusting others and anticipating love. But if parents lack consistency in meeting those needs, their babies may grow up thinking the whole world is against them and they need to fend for themselves.

As we minister to people who have challenging histories, we frequently encounter those who never learned basic trust. They struggle to open up to others, ask for help, or even believe that

---

47 "Basic Trust Versus Mistrust," APA Dictionary of Psychology, American Psychological Association, accessed April 20, 2023, https://dictionary.apa.org/basic-trust-versus-mistrust.

they are loved and valued. Many don't even think they have any value. In many such cases, inconsistencies in the first eighteen months of life convinced them that they can't trust others to care for them.

Basic trust is learned through consistency. As we consistently demonstrate love and keep proclaiming the gospel message, the person's walls may eventually come down.

The ways we treat one another can penetrate emotional walls to the most broken parts of the soul and bring transformation. But the carnal mind puts up a fight. A person may intellectually agree with the gospel while still operating on an internal framework built of lies from past hurts. Such perspectives can be prayerfully loved out of us in a healthy, consistent, Spirit-filled, gospel-centered community.

Love Creates Messes

Sometimes love chooses a mess for the sake of health. Sin needs to be confronted as the Holy Spirit leads. In the best and healthiest scenarios, sin is addressed privately, just between you and the other person. (See Matthew 18:15.) But sometimes sin requires a public correction. (See Matthew 18:17 and 1 Timothy 5:20.) Neither is easy.

Confrontation is almost always uncomfortable for everyone present. It can be emotional and messy. When private sins escalate so that they are made public, sometimes observers don't know how to react. Sometimes people experience grief and other emotions—

especially when an elder believer falls. Real love dives headlong into the mess rather than trying to avoid it.

Adam and Jenny were dating when they joined our house church, and soon they were engaged. At some point, I learned they were secretly living together. They obviously knew they were in a sinful situation because they were hiding it, and my loving confrontation only confirmed it. I asked why they were so willing to compromise, and they told me about a challenging financial situation in which neither could afford to live alone.

I hurt inside for them. I knew they felt trapped. But I could also see that they were trusting their bank accounts more than the Lord, and I told them as much. They agreed that they needed to make some changes.

A couple of weeks later, another man in the house church came to me and asked if I was aware that the two were living together. He had confronted Adam as well, and he was coming to me to carry out the next step of Matthew 18—take two or three others with you to address the sin. The two of us and another mutual friend from the house church went to meet with Adam.

With love and gentleness, we asked him why he had not made any changes. Again, he cited his financial responsibilities in helping Jenny. He was struggling with wanting to do two right things—live righteously before the Lord and protect his fiancée from homelessness. He felt he could believe for himself but didn't feel right risking her well-being with his actions.

The three of us had discussed the matter ahead of time. I said to Adam, "Here's our offer: If you're on board, we will help you move this weekend, and we will pool our money to pay your rent so that you can keep sending help to Jenny. We care more about your holiness than our bank accounts."

That weekend, we helped Adam move back into his mother's house. As it turned out, he didn't need to live with his fiancée in the first place, and we never had to pay any rent for him.

Within months, the couple cancelled their engagement, and I believe rightfully so. They were not healthy for each other, and both married other people later. Jenny, especially, was better off in the long run and was spared a great deal of grief. The entire process was awkward and painful yet gloriously redemptive. Love knows that any mess it creates will be beautiful in the long run.

Love produces another sort of mess. In an interactive house church meeting, theological differences will emerge among the people. Sometimes it's no big deal, and the pastor's role is to help everyone celebrate unity in our diversity. Other times, one or more perspectives are clearly unbiblical. But you cannot pretend that such differences are compatible. False doctrine needs to be struck down with gentleness and careful handling of the Scriptures. Such direct challenges are uncomfortable and awkward, but love for the flock demands that we not dodge the issues. Such disputes are well worth the time and attention. Often people learn more from listening to these open, emotion-laden debates than from formal teaching.

Love Endures Messes

Jesus's love compelled him to spend so much time with tax collectors, drunkards, prostitutes, and sinners that religious people thought he was one of them. But Jesus never compromised. The sinners he visited knew exactly where he stood. Jesus wasn't afraid to enter their mess.

I've sat in a courtroom to offer emotional support to a congregant who had spent time in jail for assault. He knew I didn't condone his behavior, but he also knew I loved him. As it turned out, my presence helped demonstrate to the judge that he had a support system, and his charges were dropped.

We have people in our house-church network who struggle with addiction. We have people who are still battling sinful attitudes—confessing their sin but not yet experiencing the full freedom that is available in Christ. We have people in our network who are quirky or socially awkward. Some struggle with various forms of mental illness. Some have joked that my house church is like The Island of Misfit Toys.[48]

One minister at another church once commented to me, "Someone pointed out that you tend to attract a lot of difficult people and social outcasts—not that that's a bad thing. But it makes them question your ministry." I smiled, knowing I must be doing something right.

---

[48] A reference to a fictional land in the classic animated Christmas movie, *Rudolph the Red-Nosed Reindeer* (1964), in which weird, poorly designed, unwanted toys enjoy community together.

Love spends time with messy people. Love enters a messy world and doesn't change its mind. Love always perseveres (1 Corinthians 13:7).

Love Cleans Up Messes

A woman came to our house church with a variety of physical conditions. She was deeply hurt by Christians in past churches who blamed her for the fact that she wasn't yet healed. She was worn out from one person after the next telling her, "If you want to be healed, you need to do this . . . " She was tired of jumping through hoops and seeing no results. I knew these things from conversation with her, but most others were unaware.

As our house-church meeting neared its end, I asked for people to share prayer needs. Naturally, this woman asked us to minister healing.

Another woman in our group has grown tremendously in her faith by quoting Scriptures and claiming promises. With a genuine desire to see her friend set free, she said, "I really believe you need to start speaking the Word over your life and standing on the promises God has made."

As you may have guessed, the woman snapped back like a cornered animal. The wounds of her past had been aggravated, and she wasn't about to let one more person place a burden on her shoulders. Her response was angry and harsh.

The one who offered the advice had her own hurts to process and was deeply bothered by the way the other woman responded. She stood up and stormed out of the house.

Everyone else looked at me, wondering what I was going to do. I was wondering too.

Sometimes, like God, you leave the proverbial ninety-nine while you go after the one. (See Matthew 18:12.) I certainly could have asked someone else in the meeting to finish for me while I chased the woman down. But in this case, I felt it was more important to remain with the most vulnerable person and not demonstrate to my church that running is a way to capture attention. We need to be Spirit-led not crisis-led.

I explained my actions to everyone, we prayed for each other, and we finished the meeting.

Later that night, I called the woman who left and invited her over for dinner with my family the next day. And before I could call the other woman, she called me to say that she regretted the way she snapped at her sister and wanted to know how to clear up the issue.

Dinner the next day was great. The woman went home, called the other, and the two reconciled and came to understand each other better. And the following week, they sat next to each other in the house-church meeting, genuinely getting along.

In a typical large church, such messes still happen, but they are much easier to ignore. Pastors of large congregations are often spread too thin to deal with every little issue between congregants.

But in a house church, the group is small enough that a pastor not only knows what happened but can also give personal attention to resolving the matter. Love doesn't ignore a mess; it cleans up.

Meeting Needs

A couple in our house-church network was in financial trouble. The husband had lost his job. They had just enough money in the bank to pay their rent, but they didn't have enough extra for the ninety-five-cent electronic processing fee. Their payment was rejected, and their bank issued a steep overdraft fee. Now they faced an eviction notice and a court date. They didn't know what to do.

Their house church could have pooled their money and paid their rent. But the couple had been in a similar situation before. The house church decided they needed to help the couple in a different way. First, they assured the couple that they had a safety net. If the eviction went through, everyone had agreed on a calendar by which this couple could live with various families for a couple of weeks at a time, moving from house to house until they found a new apartment. Meanwhile, the church family would pay for a storage unit for all their belongings.

Additionally, one of the men offered to meet with the couple to go over their finances and figure out a strategy to help them thrive in the future.

The judge overturned the eviction, so the couple could stay in their apartment. The house church helped them cover the overdraft fee and replenish their bank account. The budget conversation led to the husband finding a job. The wife then received a significant increase in pay. Everything turned around for this couple because their church family was willing to do the hard work of entering their mess and genuinely helping—not merely looking for the fastest, easiest way out.

Love Embraces Messy People

Jesus welcomed many messy people into his circle. Peter was quite impulsive, often saying the wrong thing at the wrong time. Jesus called James and John "sons of thunder," which may have been a reference to their personalities (Mark 3:17). In response to a village that rejected their message, the brothers offered to call down fire from heaven and destroy them all! But Peter, James, and John were Jesus's closest disciples.

At the Last Supper—the Passover meal before Jesus went to the cross—Jesus showed his love to his disciples by wrapping a towel around his waist and washing their feet. This task was reserved for the lowest of slaves, but Jesus chose it.

Jesus didn't only wash the feet of Peter, James, and John. He also washed Judas's feet. Jesus knew all his disciples would abandon him in his darkest hour, but he also knew Judas would outright betray him.

Love embraces messy people.

As you make disciples, your house church may accumulate betrayers and hot heads. Furthermore, a loving, Spirit-filled environment will sometimes attract problematic people who hold strong, divisive opinions about certain fringe subjects. You'll bring in new believers with complicated issues and broken families. If you do your job right, you'll welcome the poor, sick, and struggling into your home. You may find yourself branded in the eyes of others as someone who is a friend of sinners and social outcasts.

A friend of mine once said that morgues are sterile while birthing rooms are messy. I would rather have a mess with life than keep everything tidy but dead. Disciple making is messy, and a gospel house welcomes that mess with love.

CHAPTER 15:

SHEPHERDING NEW CREATIONS

Before Peter could be trained, Jesus had to change his mental evaluation of himself and create in him an expectation of success.

—Rick Zachary

When I was a kid, I was part of a Christian scouting group known as Royal Rangers. Many times while camping with the group, we sat around the campfire to watch some variation of a scripted production that often included a skit called "pulling a rope."

At various times throughout the night, a skit or monologue was interrupted by a recurring character entering the scene, walking in front of the performers. In his hand was a rope that stretched out behind him and dragged along the ground. And all the while, he would mutter to himself, "Pulling a rope . . . pulling a rope . . . pulling a rope . . . "

This repeated four or five times at random moments throughout the night until, finally, the master of ceremonies stopped the man and asked in exasperation, "Bill! What are you doing?"

To which Bill would matter-of-factly reply, "I'm pulling a rope."

"Yes, I can see that! But *why* are you pulling a rope?"

Bill would stare blankly for a moment, stunned at his questioner's ignorance, and reply, "Well, have you ever tried *pushing* one?"

Far too many pastors have tried in vain to push their sheep. They know where the sheep need to be and what they need to be doing, so they use rhetorical force—perhaps shaming them for inaction or guilting them into action. They believe the sheep will never do the things they're supposed to do or leave the lifestyles they're supposed to be leaving unless someone exerts pressure on them.

Perhaps in reaction to these abusive ministry methods, other pastors decide it's better to pull the sheep along. They lead by example, preach the truth about righteous living, and invite the sheep to attend classes and sermons to learn how to better relate to their spouses, excel in business, parent more effectively, share their faith, understand the Bible, and so on.

Both of these groups of pastors, however, are dealing with the same problem:

The sheep are dead.

The Trouble with Dead Sheep

When sheep are alive, they'll run alongside you to the places you're leading them. But when sheep are dead, you'll spend all your ministry time either pushing or dragging their lifeless bodies, flopping them down in green pastures, and wondering why they aren't eating unless you shove the grass in their mouths and move their jaws for them.

"Knowledge puffs up while love builds up" (1 Corinthians 8:1). As we fill these lifeless sheep with Bible knowledge and psychological methods for improving their relationships and reaching their goals, rigor mortis sets in. They bloat. You might actually find them easier to move at this point. Bloated sheep can be rolled to the next pasture. Educated, dead Christians are easier to manage than ignorant, dead Christians. But from time to time, one of these bloated carcasses explodes and makes a mess of all the sheep around them—a mess that you'll likely need to clean up.

Dead sheep don't multiply. A flock of dead sheep only grows through either the snowball effect or through neglect. Either the flock happens across another dead sheep that gets swept into the lifeless flock as the shepherd shoves them from one place to the next, or worse yet, they find a living sheep that ends up dying because the shepherd only knows how to treat it like all the others—doing everything for it and pushing or dragging it from one pasture to the next.

Believe it or not, the main problem here isn't technically the shepherd. These shepherds generally have a strong sense of responsibility and truly care for the sheep. They know what the sheep ought to be doing and try their hardest to make it happen. Such shepherds wouldn't go to all the work described above if they weren't trying to honor God and fulfill his call on their lives.

The main problem isn't the shepherds.

The main problem is dead sheep.

Resurrecting Sheep

A shepherd's primary responsibility is not to feed the sheep or make them healthy. A shepherd's primary responsibility is to make sure the sheep are alive. Yes, this involves feeding them, caring for them, and monitoring their health; but these are all activities we do with living sheep. Otherwise, we find ourselves rolling carcasses from one pasture to the next, force-feeding and grooming them in hopes that something will change for the better.

The gospel is God's power for salvation. It's the mechanism that makes dead things live. And it's the one meal that provides eternal life to the sheep.

A moment ago, I said that the main problem isn't the shepherd. But this doesn't completely absolve shepherds of all responsibility. Yes, the main problem is dead sheep, but shepherds have been entrusted with a life-giving message that must be lived, proclaimed, and applied so that the sheep can live and thrive. When shepherds focus first on feeding and not on resurrecting, the work is hard, and messes ensue. Shepherds must make the gospel the priority in ministry to the sheep. As mentioned in chapter 13, it's the solution to every problem. All other teaching or advice must build on a gospel foundation so the Holy Spirit can express Jesus's life through each person.

Far too many pastors are tempted to shepherd the old man. They give advice that even a person dead in their sin could follow. They try to manage people's behavior. And when that behavior can't be managed, they find ways to cater to unsanctified personalities.

Living sheep are harder to control but far easier to lead and serve. And that's great because our mission was never to control the sheep anyway. Healthy, living, thriving sheep often take care of themselves. They eat on their own. They multiply without the shepherd forcing the issue. And they raise up the young with natural instincts and minimal help from the shepherd.

Jesus doesn't expect you to shovel dead sheep from one pasture to the next. That's not Christian leadership. He expects you to shepherd living sheep—people who have been made alive by the Spirit through the power found in the gospel of Jesus Christ.

Accountability

What does this look like in practical terms? It looks like trusting the Holy Spirit more than you trust yourself. And it looks like teaching the sheep to trust him more than they trust you.

Many times, someone has asked me to be their accountability partner. What they generally mean is that they have a besetting sin issue, and they want daily phone calls from me as a deterrent. They believe that if someone would hold them accountable, they would stop sinning.

But this is a faith problem. This person trusts me more than they trust the Holy Spirit, and I tell them as much. If that weren't true, then why do they expect a daily phone call from me to be more effective than the Holy Spirit who is always present with them and watching them sin? They're living by sight, not by faith.

So when people ask me to be their accountability partner, I tell them no. Instead, I explain the gospel to them. I ask if they're ready to consider their old way of living dead and trust the Holy Spirit to express Jesus's victorious life through them. If so, then I tell them I'm not going to call them because I don't expect them to mess up. Nevertheless, I assure them that if they do mess up, they can call me to confess, and I'll convey Jesus's forgiveness to them, pray for them, and give them a pep talk, reminding them of the gospel they received.

My mindset is simple: I believe *you're* dead to sin because I believe *I'm* dead to sin. I believe *you're* alive in Christ because I believe *I'm* alive in Christ. I trust the power of the gospel because I've seen it work in my own life. If I'm having a hard time believing someone who surrendered to Jesus is a new creation, it may be because I don't yet understand the gospel for myself.

Another bit of advice I often give is that the fruit of the Holy Spirit in your life includes self-control. (See Galatians 5:22–23.) And according to 2 Peter 1:3, you already have everything you need for a godly life because you know Jesus. In other words, you already have all the self-control you will ever need. Logically, then, it follows that if you choose to sin as a believer, then you chose it with your own self-control. Sin is no longer your master. (See Romans 6:14.) You're free.

The key here is giving people personal responsibility for their actions and helping them connect with the internal motivators for their freedom. Then we teach them to have faith in the Holy Spirit to express the life of Jesus through them. As one of their shepherds, I aim to have more faith in their transformed new-creation identities than they have. I model what it looks like to trust God's work, which assures them that they can trust his work too.

This form of accountability has borne far more fruit than anything else I've ever tried. I've seen people quickly set free from long-term addictions and habitual sins. And when people mess up, they're not met with shame or condemnation. They're met with mercy, a declaration of Jesus's forgiveness, and encouragement, assuring them that I still believe they are new creations. In time, they start to believe it and live it themselves.

Confession

Many traditional pastors teach new ministers to maintain a certain wall of separation between themselves and the people in their congregations. They warn new pastors against transparency or vulnerability, specifically with regard to their own sin issues. They seem to worry that this will give people a license to sin. But my experience tells me that this couldn't be further from the truth.

I openly confess sin to my house church. I model what it looks like to believe that the solution to sin is found in actively rendering it dead on the cross. When Jesus hung on the cross, his body was naked and exposed for everyone to see. If my sin is going to be up there with him, then it, too, ought to be naked and exposed for everyone to see. That doesn't mean I have to necessarily post my confession on social media or shout it from the rooftops. It simply means I'm not actively trying to hide it from anyone.

We learn in 1 John 1:9 that "if we confess our sins, he is faithful and just and will forgive us our sins and purify us from all unrighteousness." So not only are your sins forgiven but even the stain of unrighteousness is removed from you. Confession is the birth of a testimony—it's the first time we tell the story of God setting us free from any given issue.

"Without the shedding of blood there is no forgiveness" (Hebrews 9:22). If people choose to cover their sin with anything besides the blood of Jesus, that false covering prevents his blood from touching the sin. Healing from sin will not happen until we remove our false coverings and false comforts. "But if we walk in the light, as he is in the light, we have fellowship with one another, and the blood of Jesus, his Son, purifies us from all sin" (1 John 1:7). We must be transparent with others.

By modeling confession, people learn that they, too, are safe to confess sin in the house-church meeting—and they will. In fact, confession is often better at bringing repentance to others than merely preaching against sin. When we confess our wrong attitudes, we communicate that such attitudes are illogical for the born-again Christian. People who regularly practice the same attitudes will not only see that their actions are wrong but they'll see the solution to their attitude on full display. One person's confession of sin will commonly be followed by a string of other people confessing sin.

How you manage one person's sin will directly impact the culture of transformation in your church. So when someone shares their struggle—especially the very first time—don't flinch. Take it seriously, but don't let your expression convey repulsion or anger—only compassion.

Make sure you verbalize forgiveness to the person in Jesus's name. It's one of the roles Jesus gave us as his followers, filled with his Spirit. (See John 20:23.) Simply reply with something like this: "Scripture says that when you confess sin, God forgives you and cleanses you from all unrighteousness. So in the name of Jesus, I tell you, you are forgiven and cleansed."

Addressing Sin

In most situations, the above is sufficient. But suppose someone openly confesses something more serious than an attitude or addiction.

How we respond to sin depends on where that person is in their walk with the Lord, the type of sin committed, the person's relationship with you and the church, and how the sin was made known.

Where is the person in their walk with the Lord? If they're new believers, then we expect a certain amount of struggle. "Love covers over a multitude of sins" (1 Peter 4:8). Loving the person through the struggle will transform them. Gentleness and patience will go a long way. But suppose the person is a leader in the church. Paul told a fellow church leader, "But those elders who are sinning you are to reprove before everyone, so that the others may take warning" (1 Timothy 5:20).

What type of sin was committed? Suppose someone confesses that they beat their spouse. What do you do? Whatever your response looks like, it needs to include protecting the victim because love "always protects" (1 Corinthians 13:7). In most cases, what people confess—anger issues, poor financial management, unforgiveness, verbal insults against others, lies, lust, and so on—does not put others in danger. But when others are affected, restitution is usually needed. Have the person ask the Holy Spirit what they need to do to make things right with the person they wronged. Wait for them to reply with whatever comes to mind. And if the sin poses serious danger to someone else, ask the Lord what you need to do to help protect the innocent.

What is the person's relationship with you and the church? There's a difference between how you respond when the person is a Christian versus when they do not know the Lord. We judge those inside the church, not outside. (See 1 Corinthians 5:12–

13.) If the person is dead in their sin, then the only solution to their sin is faith in Jesus for their salvation. Share the gospel and invite them to know the One who will deliver them from their sin. Only when the person is a Christian does confession lead to real transformation. Furthermore, what's your personal relationship with the person? If the person confesses in your house-church meeting, then you're free to address the matter. But you don't have to feel responsible to address sins committed by people you don't personally know. Keep your attention local.

How was the sin made known? Did the person confess or were they found out? The way we respond to confessed sin is different from the way we confront discovered sin. Confessed sin is met with mercy. Discovered, unrepentant sin is confronted as Jesus taught:

> If your brother or sister sins, go and point out their fault, just between the two of you. If they listen to you, you have won them over. But if they will not listen, take one or two others along, so that 'every matter may be established by the testimony of two or three witnesses.' If they still refuse to listen, tell it to the church; and if they refuse to listen even to the church, treat them as you would a pagan or a tax collector. (Matthew 18:15–17)

A lot of people read the above passage as though it is meant as a pathway to excommunication—removal from the church. But

I see this passage as Jesus teaching us to try everything reasonable to avoid excommunication. Social accountability is supposed to help the person come to their senses and repent.

There's a difference between how love responds to sin and how fear does. In the story of Adam and Eve, we see that when they sinned, they realized they were naked, covered themselves, and hid in the bushes. (See Genesis 3:7–8.) But when God came walking in the garden, he confronted the sin and created garments to clothe the man and woman. (See Genesis 3:9–21.) In other words, fear exposes sinners and hides sin, but love exposes sin and clothes sinners.

For this reason, the repentant must be protected and restored to the community and to trust. As long as they're not putting anyone in danger, we have a responsibility to restore them to fellowship as though no sin was committed.[49] Real forgiveness means we will never weaponize their sin against them. It won't be joked about or brought up in any context other than as a testimony to help someone else and only ever with the person's permission.

We expect this standard from everyone in the community. A breech in this practice is its own sin issue that needs to be

[49] Note my disclaimer about danger. When sin is on the magnitude of, say, child molestation or assault, we are under no obligation to restore such a person to fellowship. Actually, the opposite is true. Be sure to check your state laws about mandatory reporters. In much of the US, clergy (including anyone assumed to be clergy) is required to report certain crimes to the state or face legal consequences. House-church pastors are generally included within this definition.

addressed. Those communities that take this practice seriously are the ones that produce the healthiest disciples.

Holiness

Holiness is a word that has been misinterpreted over the years. Some groups have assumed that holiness looks like dressing a certain way, not wearing makeup, never watching movies or playing cards, and other such rules. But history has proven that these behaviors are not what make someone truly holy.

To be holy is to be completely different from anyone else. It is to be set apart for a purpose. My toothbrush is, in a sense, holy. It is not used for anything other than brushing my teeth. If my toothbrush were used to clean a toilet, I would consider it defiled and throw it away. Holiness really matters when it comes to my toothbrush!

And holiness really matters when it comes to us. "Without holiness no one will see the Lord" (Hebrews 12:14). We, too, are set apart for a purpose. We are created for relationship with God.

> What agreement is there between the temple of God and idols? For we are the temple of the living God. As God has said:
>
> "I will live with them
> and walk among them,
> and I will be their God,
> and they will be my people."

Therefore,

"Come out from them

and be separate,

says the Lord.

Touch no unclean thing,

and I will receive you."

(2 Corinthians 6:16–17)

With all that said, holiness is a process. Thankfully, the Lord prepared a way to make us perfect in Christ even before we have become fully holy in every way. As Hebrews 10:14 says, "For by one sacrifice he has made perfect forever those who are being made holy."

As we shepherd new creations, we deal with people who are perfect positionally in Christ while still needing to work out their salvation with fear and trembling. (See Philippians 2:12.) The more we can help people see and believe what God has already done in them, the more fully they will surrender to that truth, becoming holier day by day—more and more set apart from the world.

For this reason, treat people as though they're perfect already. Expect the best from them. Teach them, prophesy to them, and encourage them as though Jesus has already finished his work in them because, in a very real sense, he has. Expect them to live in victory. And if they mess up along the way, be the sort of person who will help them get back on track and keep moving forward.

Your job is not to push or pull the sheep. Your job is to keep them alive and lead them.

CHAPTER 16:
WELCOMING JESUS BY WELCOMING CHILDREN

One of the most grievous errors we believers have made is assuming children are not capable of understanding or acting on the deep things of God's Word. Consequently, they are never seriously educated or discipled in Christianity, but are merely pacified for twelve years with entertaining little Bible stories via the latest technology.

—Becky Fischer

My two sons regularly minister healing to each other. So do other kids in our church. Some of our young ones prophesy over people at the grocery store. Some see angels and describe them, not knowing that a few days earlier, a prophet in our church described the same angel in the same location during a prayer meeting. Kids in our house-church network pray and worship. Some lead their friends to Jesus, some speak in tongues, and some lead their newly saved friends into the baptism in the Holy Spirit. While all are growing and need discipline, they're generally respectful, loving, and honoring of their parents.

They're still kids, and they still have their moments. They're not totally perfect. But overall, the kids in our house-church network feel free to grow in their faith—not forced or coerced into behaving a certain way. Why? Because we treat our kids the same way we treat everyone else. All the principles you've read in this book also apply to the youngest among us. We share the gospel with our kids, and we trust the Holy Spirit in them to help them live as new creations.

In Mark 9:37, Jesus said, "Whoever welcomes one of these little children in my name welcomes me; and whoever welcomes me does not welcome me but the one who sent me." In other words, the way we treat children is the way we treat Jesus.

For this reason, a gospel house prioritizes kids.

There are multiple ways to minister to children. Some house churches have a separate meeting for the kids, led by someone who is trained and gifted in leading young ones in an age-appropriate biblical discussion. Other house churches let the kids squirm in their seats and wiggle around the room, even participating in the house-church conversation if they so desire. Still other house churches let the kids play during the meeting, then parents have a separate meeting for the kids at a different time—either together or as separate family units. You may even think of another way to accommodate the children.

We have a lot of options, but what matters most is that we welcome Jesus by welcoming the children.

Expecting the Best from Children

When children ran to Jesus, the disciples feared they would be a burden to him. But Jesus told his disciples to let them come, then he laid his hands on the kids and blessed them. (See Mark 10:13–16.) Jesus wants children to encounter him and experience his love and blessings. Kids are just as capable of interacting with the Lord as anyone else, and since Jesus so frequently held them up as an example to adults, they may even be better at it than the rest of us.

We don't worry about kids making messes of our meetings. Babies crawl around our feet, babble, cry, and flick the springy doorstop in our hallway so that it buzzes on the wall. But we just keep going. We're a family, and that's what families do.

Even at our large gatherings, when the whole network comes together twice a month, we have children in the room with us during the worship time. After that is a time when people share testimonies of evangelism and healing ministry that happened throughout the week. We want our kids to see and hear these stories, and we want them to participate. And they do. Once in a while, one of the kids even comes to the mic and shares a testimony. Sometimes, they take a long time to get to the point. But our priority is not efficiency or performance. Our priority is welcoming Jesus by welcoming the kids.

We bring kids with us on outreaches. They pray for people in public and give prophetic words. They explain the gospel to their friends and family members.

But here's my favorite part: No one is forcing the kids to do any of these things. They're simply immersed in a culture where these activities are taught, explained, celebrated, and modeled as normal. My own children were shocked when they found out that some Christians don't believe in healing ministry or that every Christian can hear God's voice. One of my boys asked incredulously, "Why would they even want to be Christians?"

We don't pressure our kids to perform, but we do expect the best from them. We proclaim their identity in Christ to them, reminding them of the truth we know about them. We pray out loud, thanking God for the qualities we see in our kids that remind us of him. We speak words of encouragement and affirmation to our kids—not pretending they're something they're not but genuinely speaking forth spiritual truth about who Jesus has made them to be.

Parents: The First Ministers

The most important ministers in a child's life are the adults in his or her home. We could have perfect church meetings, but if families aren't consistent in their own homes, then the kids will struggle with their faith.

One of the best ways to prioritize kids is to prioritize parents. If the parents are truly saved and living according to the gospel, then the home environment will change.

Many times, parents have come to me for advice about how to help their kids through a particular issue. Before I give them advice, I give them the gospel. I work with them to identify areas in their own life where they need to die to self and let the Holy Spirit express Jesus through them. And by the end of our conversation, the parents typically know intuitively what they must do next. The gospel produces a change in the way people think, and suddenly, they can see their own solutions. This is far more helpful than if I simply play the role of a parenting expert.

We do encourage and train parents, grandparents, stepparents, foster parents, and surrogate parents to be the best caregivers they can be, raising their children to know the God who loves them so deeply. This sometimes makes its way into our house church conversations. But the goal is to equip parents with principles and tools that they can apply themselves, not to simply tell them what to do.

Furthermore, we're there for each other. When one of the young mothers in our church had to go through chemotherapy, sometimes people helped clean her house. Sometimes people took her three kids for the day. When a single mom had to stay home with her kids because one was sick, people made meals and brought them to her house. And when she couldn't pay her rent, people in our church pitched in to help get her back on her feet.

In a gospel house, no parent is on their own. Kids don't come with a manual, but a gospel house comes with a family.

Training Children's Ministers

A lot of small churches are lax about children's ministry. House churches often suffer from the same problem. Since there's a need, they'll fill it with any willing person. And because the church is small, the pool of possible candidates can sometimes be the bottom of the barrel—even hiring a babysitter from outside.

It's a hassle to make sure children's ministers are trained, vetted, and background-checked, but such actions indicate how seriously we prioritize children in our church.

As a house-church network grows, new options open up. For example, my wife attends one house church and manages children's ministry for another. She's also the children's director for our network and handles all the training and background checks throughout.

But before we were a network, we were only one house church. During our meetings, the kids played in another room, around the corner from where we met, and my wife listened from the kitchen between the rooms with one eye on the kids. At that time, my wife had been background-checked for her work in childcare, but she was never truly alone with any kids anyhow.

Later, as we grew, our responsibility grew too. As new families came who didn't know my wife personally, it became even more important for her to show herself trustworthy. And as other house churches in our network started to need children's ministry, we needed to make sure the same level of care, ministry, and safety was available network wide.

Children's ministry is one of those rare areas that actually needs a certain amount of bureaucracy. We make no apologies for making sure all our kids ministers are trained, experienced, and background-checked. And the parents who come to our house churches are grateful.

Plenty of YouTube videos teach basic principles of kids' ministry. You can create your own playlist according to your needs. You may even find it helpful to have your children's ministers read this chapter as part of their training.

You can also engage a background-check service. The specifics and prices will vary from state to state. A decent one will charge about twenty-five to thirty dollars per person. Contact a few mid-sized churches in your state to find out what systems they use. You may even find that a few of them aren't doing the needed background checks. But don't use this as an excuse for your house group. When you prioritize children, you prioritize Jesus. When you welcome them, you welcome him. Love always protects (1 Corinthians 13:7). If you want God's Spirit to move powerfully in your house church, go out of your way to accommodate children.

The Children's Meeting

As I already mentioned, a house-church meeting can accommodate children in many ways. This is what we do at my house church, and you can feel free to modify this or be creative according to your needs.

First, our kids' meetings are for ages two to eleven. At twelve years old, we let kids choose between being with the adults the entire meeting or spending the first hour with the kids and the second hour with the adults. And at thirteen, we expect them to be with the adults the entire time. Sometimes younger kids want to stay with their parents, and that's fine too.

When the ages of kids in the meeting are varied, we mainly teach to the primary age in the room while also making sure the youngest remain interested and engaged. Older children serve as helpers in a room of younger kids and may even be invited into the ministry process by reading to the kids or facilitating a part of the meeting they can handle.

Second, there's a children's minister and an assistant. This ensures no one is left alone with the kids, which is a safeguard that not only protects kids but also protects our children's ministers from false accusations.

The first hour of the meeting is play time. This offers flexibility if some families arrive late so that their kids can still participate in the lesson.

At the top of the hour, the kids gather for their own age-appropriate house-church meeting. They start with what we call a One Thing Moment where each child is invited to tell everyone one thing that they know about God, learned in the Bible, or have been thinking about him that week. Some little ones say the same thing every week, and some older ones might recount a whole

Bible story. The kids listen to each other, and the children's minister helps guide the conversation in a healthy way.

Next, we are in the process of developing our own curriculum for our network, but you may find another that works.[50] What matters most is that we want our kids to learn the gospel (how to die to self and let Jesus live through them), not moralism (how to be a good person). More on this in a moment.

Our kids practice a memory verse. They might sing a song or two together, then they play for whatever time remains of the adult meeting (which usually runs about two hours total).

What Are We Teaching Our Kids?

A lot of children's ministry is superficial and teaches a compromised pseudo-gospel of Moralistic Therapeutic Deism (MTD). The term "MTD" was first introduced in the 2005 book *Soul Searching: The Religious and Spiritual Lives of American Teenagers* by the sociologist Christian Smith and his co-author, Melinda Lundquist Denton. Smith's study interviewed more than three thousand teenagers and found that a remarkable number of young people believe in several moral statutes and spiritual ideas, some of which run contrary to real Christianity:

- A God exists who created and ordered the world and watches over human life on earth.

---

[50] When this curriculum is finalized, we intend to release it at SupernaturalTruth.com.

- God wants people to be good, nice, and fair to each other as taught in the Bible and by most world religions.
- The central goal of life is to be happy and to feel good about oneself.
- God does not need to be particularly involved in one's life except when God is needed to resolve a problem.
- Good people go to heaven when they die.[51]

MTD is as much a product of Western culture as it is an unfortunate byproduct of a poor understanding of the gospel among many children's ministers. The poor understanding of the gospel is then taught and spread among younger generations who never learn what it is to die to self and be raised to new life in the power of the Holy Spirit—knowing God and partnering with him in his mission. MTD is based on self-effort and pays little to no attention to the work of the Spirit in the life of the believer. Under such teaching, virtues like love, joy, peace, patience, and so forth are taught as ideal attitudes and behaviors that must be strived after in order to please God. These things are not presented as they ought to be: the natural outflow of the Spirit in a person's life.

---

[51] Christian Smith and Melinda Lundquist Denton, *Soul Searching: The Religious and Spiritual Lives of American Teenagers* (New York: Oxford University Press, 2005), 162–3.

The gospel is the central component of our house-church culture. It's the defining element of a gospel house. If you want to raise up children who know and love the Lord for a lifetime, saturate them with gospel truth through teaching, modeling, and encouragement.

Discipline

There's only a one-letter difference between "discipline" and "discipling." The words are related. But there's a major difference between behavior management and transformation. Behavior management is a set of practical tools that affects the frequency, duration, intensity, or practice of specific behaviors. Transformation is a work of the Spirit by grace through faith by which the life of Christ is internalized and works its way out through a person's behavior.

The gospel is not a behavior-management plan; it's a transformation plan. Jesus didn't come to manage our behaviors. He came to crucify our sin and give us a new life empowered by the Holy Spirit.

Behavior management makes us well-adjusted members of society. Transformation makes us more like Jesus. Behavior management can change actions and words, but it cannot change the heart. Behavior management can be applied by an external agent (parents, teachers, ministers, etc.). Transformation can only be applied by the indwelling Holy Spirit as a person willingly surrenders to Jesus.

While you can shape a person's behaviors apart from their will to change, the only way to change a person's heart is to pray, love, and share the gospel. Parents and children's ministers ought to learn and apply healthy behavior-management techniques to teach etiquette, ethics, and social skills. But at the end of the day, the gospel must be our priority.

It's important to know that discipline is not the same as punishment. Encouraging a child to make his bed is discipline. Trusting a pre-teen to do her own laundry is discipline. Teaching a late teen to drive responsibly is discipline. Bringing a child to church every week is discipline.

Proper discipline comes from a place of knowing your own identity in Christ. Many parents discipline their children out of fear. Fear-based discipline leads to unhealthy standards, unreasonable restrictions, and kids who look for loopholes to feel a sense of control. But proper discipline calls forth a child's identity. Proper discipline is encouraging. Proper discipline capitalizes on natural consequences. Proper discipline communicates age-appropriate responsibility.

Search online for such behavior-management tools as modeling, redirection, positive reinforcement, negative reinforcement, satiation, saturation, and extinction. All these tools in your toolbelt will give you a lot of options so that you feel a sense of clarity and healthy control of the group when you meet.

Ministering to People with Special Needs

People with special needs can follow Jesus. Physical and cognitive impairments are not spiritual impairments. This requires us to recognize that intellectual advancement in biblical matters does not equal spiritual growth. We need a definition of spiritual growth that does not rely on the accumulation of knowledge.

Over the years, my house church has included people on the autism spectrum, people with various learning disabilities, people with physical impairments, and more.

Years ago, my house church seemed to consist primarily of special needs. I had a man with high-functioning autism, another who struggled with schizophrenia, another who had been addicted to cocaine (and who still struggled off and on), plus a small handful of people who had various cognitive and social impairments. Only a minority were what one might consider neurotypical. But everyone exercised incredible patience and honored others above themselves.

My college degree is in early childhood development and education, and I also studied adult special needs, so I had some education and work experience in the field. For the most part, I enjoyed our unique gathering.

But after several months of pastoring this group, we experienced a particularly difficult meeting. I complained to the Lord in prayer later that night. "Why do you keep sending me such complicated people?"

His answer stunned me: "Because I trust you with them."

My whole perspective changed. In an instant, I went from feeling burned out to having an overflow of love and compassion. I didn't need any of my friends to change. They weren't projects; they were brothers and sisters.

We never stopped believing in or pursuing physical healing. It's possible to believe in miracles without making people feel like projects or treating them as though they need to be fixed. Love, compassion, prayer, and healthy interaction can go a long way in helping such people encounter the healing power of Jesus.[52]

I recommend that, in general, we treat people with special needs as we would treat anyone else. Be personable toward them. Greet them by name and with a smile. Introduce them to others in the church, just as you would introduce anyone else. If they're verbal, ask them questions about things they like. Speak like an adult—not in baby talk. Simplify your vocabulary if necessary. Model for your house church how to treat the person with dignity.

Be consistent. Routine and structure bring peace of mind, both to people with special needs and to their parents. Some people with special needs have significant difficulties with deviations from expected routines. Try to keep on a similar schedule each week.

---

[52] Do not attempt to minister deliverance when no demon is presently manifesting. Sometimes the problem is purely physical, but the suggestion of possible demons can send some people (or their parents) spiraling with unwarranted fears and anxieties. If no demon is obviously manifesting, there's no need to even suggest the possibility. Simply love the person and trust God's healing power to be sufficient.

For severe special needs, you may want to print out a schedule of what to expect (with or without timestamps, according to the needs). You may want to include pictures. Make sure everyone else present understands the value of the schedule in loving the person who needs it. Anyone who complains that such a schedule is not Spirit-led may need understanding. No one should prioritize a personal preference for spontaneity over the biblical command to love and honor others above oneself.

If possible, minimize environmental distractions. Some people are overwhelmed by too much sensory information. Flashing or flickering lightbulbs, lighting that is too bright or too dim, strong odors or perfumes, sudden loud noises, excessive clutter, noisy appliances, and so on can all be significant distractions or behavioral triggers for certain people.

Don't be afraid to offer some social coaching, even to adults with special needs. Some people need to be told what sort of behavior or speech (and how much of it) is acceptable in a meeting. Share with them in a loving, honoring way. Refuse to publicly shame the person.

You may also need to coach other Christians about how to interact with the person. Many Christians, who might come off as rude or standoffish, are simply unaware of how to interact with a person who has special needs. Filling them in on the person's needs and giving them a few pointers about how to talk to them (especially before they meet for the first time) can make all the difference.

Think of your house church meeting like a healthy family get-together. What would be expected of the person with special needs when a family comes together at someone's home? Is it acceptable for them to wander off into other parts of the house? Or are they expected to remain supervised? Does their parent or caregiver need to coach them through the social dynamics? Are other children and adults safe around them? If not, can you establish safeguards? Or do we need to find a better solution for helping them connect with God?

Be clear and literal, especially when it comes to people on the autism spectrum. Some people struggle with thinking abstractly or in metaphors. If you share a parable, be sure to explain it clearly. Avoid slang and colloquial phrases that do not have clear meaning.

Finally, value the person as a meaningful part of the Christian family. Ask them to pray for you. If they want to say something, let them share. You may have to offer some social coaching to help them *stop* sharing, but give them a little time to figure it out themselves.

If someone in your house church is having a hard time loving the person with special needs, address the issue with the person just like you would address anyone who is being unloving toward someone in your house church. Do not shrug off offenses simply because the person with special needs may not have understood the other person's words or actions.

In the case of adults with special needs, visit the person just as you would visit anyone else. Make time to communicate with him or her outside of scheduled meeting times.

Remember that Jesus said, "Whatever you did for one of the least of these brothers and sisters of mine, you did for me" (Matthew 25:40). The ways we treat kids and people with special needs are directly related to whether Jesus feels welcome in our meetings. If you want your house to be a gospel house, it's vital that Jesus wants to be there.

CHAPTER 17:

FOLLOWING THE HOLY SPIRIT

If we function according to our ability alone, we get the glory; if we function according to the power of the Spirit within us, God gets the glory. He wants to reveal himself to a watching world.

—Henry T. Blackaby

It's impossible to plan for a meeting where anyone can say or do anything, but it's entirely possible to prepare. We may not be able to map out the conversation ahead of time, but we can pray, study the Scriptures, and have our own hearts right before the Lord.

Many weeks, the Lord tells me before the meeting what he wants to do. Then, during the meeting, when someone inevitably brings up a subject that connects to what I already know God wants to do, I can keep the conversation focused on that subject and move toward application.

I have a shirt that depicts the day of Pentecost—a crowd of people with flames over their heads (Acts 2:1–4). One night, before the house-church meeting, the Holy Spirit told me to wear that shirt, and that night people would be baptized in the Holy Spirit.

I know there was no power in my shirt, but I also know there is power in obedience. So I changed my shirt before people arrived.

When the meeting started, one of the women asked, "I have to know. Why did you wear that shirt today?" I gave my answer, and she added, "I've never seen that shirt before, but last night, I had a dream where I saw that shirt, and God said he wanted to baptize people in the Holy Spirit."

It was the perfect setup. Because I knew what was coming, I already had a list of Scriptures in mind. I taught everyone on the subject for about fifteen minutes, let several people share their testimonies, then asked if anyone wanted us to pray for them to be baptized in the Holy Spirit.

God fulfilled his word.

I couldn't have planned for that meeting, but I was able to prepare.

Most weeks, I don't have such clear advance knowledge. Most weeks, I come to the meeting with nothing more than my own thoughts about what God has spoken to me in my own devotional time. But as the meeting progresses, I see where it fits in. I watch the common theme emerge. And because I have prepared myself in prayer, I'm able to recognize what God is doing as he's doing it.

Being Spirit-Led

A lot of Christians want to know how to be led by the Holy Spirit. It's quite simple. We've been led by a spirit our entire lives. "As for you, you were dead in your transgressions and sins, in which you used to live *when you followed the ways of this world and of the ruler of the kingdom of the air, the spirit who is now at work in those who are disobedient.* All of us also lived among them at one time, gratifying the cravings of our flesh and following its desires and thoughts. Like the rest, we were by nature deserving of wrath" (Ephesians 2:1–3, emphasis added).

Before we were saved, we were led by the ways of this world and the ruler of the kingdom of the air. That spirit was at work in us. How were we led by that spirit? We submitted to the culture he inspired. We agreed with the thoughts he inspired. We acted on our own desires for self-gratification.

In short, you had a thought that was inspired by that spirit, and you said, "Yes. Let's do that." Then you did it.

Now that we're saved, we are led by God's Holy Spirit. "But the fruit of the Spirit is love, joy, peace, forbearance, kindness, goodness, faithfulness, gentleness and self-control. Against such things there is no law. Those who belong to Christ Jesus have crucified the flesh with its passions and desires. Since we live by the Spirit, let us keep in step with the Spirit (Galatians 5:22–25).

How are we led by the Holy Spirit? It's essentially the same as when we were led by the spirit of the world. We submit to the culture the Holy Spirit inspires. We agree to the thoughts he inspires. We crucify the flesh and live according to the selfless desires of our new, alive, human spirits, which are in union with God.

In short, when you have a thought that is inspired by that Spirit, you say, "Yes. Let's do that." Then you do it.

The determining factor between whether we're being led by the Holy Spirit or "the spirit that is at work in those who are disobedient" is our mindset. We either have our minds set on what the Holy Spirit desires, or we have our minds set on what our own flesh desires.

> Those who live according to the flesh have their minds set on what the flesh desires; but those who live in accordance with the Spirit have their minds set on what the Spirit desires. The mind governed by the flesh is death, but the mind governed by the Spirit is life and peace. The mind governed by the flesh is hostile to God; it does not submit to God's law, nor can it do so. Those who are in the realm of the flesh cannot please God.
>
> You, however, are not in the realm of the flesh but are in the realm of the Spirit, if indeed the Spirit of God lives in you. And if anyone does not have the Spirit of Christ, they do not belong to Christ. But if Christ is in you, then even though your body is subject to death because of sin, the Spirit gives life because of righteousness. (Romans 8:5–10)

Children of God

In John 8:31–47, Jesus had a fascinating exchange with some Jewish people who had believed his message. But rather than celebrating their belief, Jesus clarified that they weren't truly free until after they put his teaching into practice (vv. 31–32).

This infuriated the listeners. They protested, "We are Abraham's descendants and have never been slaves of anyone. How can you say that we shall be set free?" (v. 33).

Jesus distinguished between slaves and sons and then said something that angered them further:

> "I am telling you what I have seen in the Father's presence, and you are doing what you have heard from your father."
>
> "Abraham is our father," they answered.
>
> "If you were Abraham's children," said Jesus, "then you would do what Abraham did. As it is, you are looking for a way to kill me, a man who has told you the truth that I heard from God. Abraham did not do such things. You are doing the works of your own father."
>
> "We are not illegitimate children," they protested. "The only Father we have is God himself."
>
> Jesus said to them, "If God were your Father, you would love me, for I have come here from God. I have not come

> on my own; God sent me. . . . You belong to your father, the devil, and you want to carry out your father's desires. He was a murderer from the beginning, not holding to the truth, for there is no truth in him. When he lies, he speaks his native language, for he is a liar and the father of lies." (John 8:38–44)

Did you catch that? "If you were Abraham's children, then you would do what Abraham did." The implication is that we are children of the one we look like. We prove who our father is by our actions. Those who lied and tried to kill Jesus were children of the devil, who lies and kills. Naturally, this is all contrasted with Jesus, who only did what he saw his Father doing. (See John 5:19, 21.) Sons keep their eyes on their Father and learn from him. Sons pattern their lives after their Father.

Those who are led by the Holy Spirit do and say what God is doing and saying. Romans 8:14 says, "For those who are led by the Spirit of God are the children of God." To be children of God means we do what our Father does.

But there's a catch. What God leads us to do is impossible to do on our own. Jesus said, "I am the vine; you are the branches. If you remain in me and I in you, you will bear much fruit; apart from me you can do nothing" (John 15:5).

Everything Jesus ever commanded is impossible to do apart from him. We cannot love our enemies apart from him. We cannot make disciples apart from him. We cannot "heal the sick, raise the dead, cleanse the leper, and cast out demons" apart from him (Matthew 10:8). And that means every command Jesus ever gave us is an invitation into union with him.

To be led by the Spirit is to be invited into the impossible. It is to find oneself nudged in the direction of doing things that don't make sense and then seeing miraculous results. Those who are led by the Spirit are children of God, doing what their Father does in partnership with Christ. If you *never* feel led to attempt the impossible, you are not being led by the Holy Spirit.

When we do our part in union with Jesus, he does his part in union with us. In Mark 16:20, we read, "Then the disciples went out and preached everywhere, and the Lord worked with them and confirmed his word by the signs that accompanied it." The disciples did their part in union with Jesus, then he did his part in union with them. This is what it looks like to be a child of God.

Gospel houses belong to children of God. And those children of God help others be children of God who do what their Father does. Only in that environment is God free to do what he wants to do through his people.

Let the Spirit Guide the Conversation

In a gold mine, a prospector chips away at worthless rock until they strike a vein of gold. Then they simply follow that vein until it runs out. Sometimes, the first part of a house-church meeting feels like chipping away at ordinary rocks. Three or four people might share nice words or stories, but their contributions don't feel like they're quite what the Lord wants to do that day. Sometimes up to an hour goes by, chipping away at the rock—having a nice conversation but still not landing on anything that has grace on it.

And then you strike gold. Something someone says feels right in your spirit. Other people connect with it as well. Now, pay close attention to what the Holy Spirit is doing in the room. If a subject doesn't seem resolved (with a practical takeaway), keep bringing the discussion back to that subject. If needed, let people know that you feel God's finger on this subject, and ask them to focus on it until it feels right to move on.

As you facilitate discussion, don't merely follow what seems interesting. Follow what stirs your spirit. The Holy Spirit often communicates with us through the realm of thought. As you prayerfully listen to what everyone is sharing, take note of the thoughts and impressions that suggest themselves to you in the moment. Listen carefully to what is being shared. Don't allow anyone to change the subject before you feel the present issue is resolved.

Always bring the conversation back to the gospel. Remember that the gospel is the solution to every problem. Discipleship is the process of applying the gospel to every part of your life—your emotions, physical health, finances, relationships, spirituality—everything. Our job as disciple makers is to help people apply the truth of the gospel to every problem and help them renew their minds to think gospel first.

The new creation is always the application. Do whatever you can to help people understand their identity in Christ. For this reason, many of our house churches take communion every week, using it as the application time. It forces everyone to think about the subject of conversation within the context of Jesus's sacrifice. The application is never *try harder*. It's always *be made new*.

Paul addresses this in the following passage: "That, however, is not the way of life you learned when you heard about Christ and were taught in him in accordance with the truth that is in Jesus. You were taught, with regard to your former way of life, to put off your old self, which is being corrupted by its deceitful desires; to be made new in the attitude of your minds; and to put on the new self, created to be like God in true righteousness and holiness" (Ephesians 4:20–24).

In all our discussions, we are listening for how we can put off the old self and put on the new. We do this by first being made new in the attitude of our minds by beholding Christ.

Sometimes, it is best to start house church with worship because that helps us keep Christ in view whenever we begin discussion. If someone brings up a problem, begin asking questions that reveal the character of Christ. Sometimes, simply seeing Jesus more clearly is rebuke enough for the wayward heart.

The Holy Spirit wants to exalt Jesus. If a thought comes to you that helps direct the conversation toward Jesus and the gospel of his kingdom, you can trust that it's probably him. Follow the veins of gold. You'll soon find Jesus is discipling everyone in the meeting, including you.

Make Frequent Room for Spiritual Gifts

Awkward silence is often a necessary precursor to prophetic utterance. As the leader, don't succumb to the pressure to fill that void.

Occasionally create a dedicated time for encouraging and prophesying over one another in a large group (not only in breakout prayer times). Sometimes ask if anyone has a word of knowledge or prophetic word that would be best offered in the group setting. When someone needs healing, coach others through ministering. You're pastoring the group, but you're not there to do everything for them. You're there to equip them.

If a message in tongues is given, let others interpret before you try. Don't bail everyone out of the awkward silence if no one else is interpreting. Sometimes people are working through an internal battle of wondering whether they really received the interpretation. Give them time to realize they did. Ask the group what they sensed, felt, saw, heard, or understood while the person was speaking in tongues. If you received any impressions, add your own thoughts after others have shared. It's usually helpful to provide a summary of the various interpretations if a synthesis is unclear. Have everyone exercise discernment with the various interpretations, and see what sticks.

Listen for the Holy Spirit to guide you as you guide others. Sometimes he'll tell you that he wants to speak, but he won't tell you what he wants to say. Let everyone know what you're sensing, and invite people to listen for a prophetic word.

Above all, help people prioritize love for one another. This isn't a talent show. We don't have interactive meetings so the super gifted can outshine the rest; we have interactive meetings so people can tangibly encounter Jesus's love in a variety of ways.

Exercise Discernment

Discernment is always necessary, even when everything looks healthy. In other words, even if you know a prophetic word someone gave is solid, remind everyone that we test prophecies. Ask them what they felt about the word. When we take the time to judge even healthy words, people learn not to feel insulted when we take time to judge what they say. "Do not quench the Spirit. Do not treat prophecies with contempt but test them all [not some]; hold on to what is good, reject every kind of evil" (1 Thessalonians 5:19–22).

Some healthy messages are true but are not for the moment. Sometimes we need to discern not correctness but relevance—not accuracy but the will of the Lord.

Discernment and discussion also help us hone our delivery of spiritual gifts. Sometimes what a person says is true, but the way they delivered it was confusing or convoluted. Asking the group to discern will likely lead to someone saying, "I've got to be honest.

I'm not sure I understood what that meant." This gives the person the opportunity to clarify. In time, they'll become better communicators of revelation.

Scripture is always the definitive measuring rod for all revelation. Paul taught Timothy that "all Scripture is God-breathed and is useful for teaching, rebuking, correcting and training in righteousness, so that the servant of God may be thoroughly equipped for every good work" (2 Timothy 3:16–17).

Because the Holy Spirit inspired the Scriptures, being Scripture-led is part of being Spirit-led. Naturally, Scripture doesn't speak to every matter of life. Although it does define what needs to happen in our meetings, it doesn't prescribe a specific order. In these scriptural gray areas, we need to practice sensitivity to the Lord, not only Bible knowledge.

The words of mature Christians who know the Scriptures and the Lord will carry more weight, but this doesn't automatically mean they're right. Test everything. Sometimes the mature need the most scrutiny.

In Hans Christian Andersen's classic fable "The Emperor's New Clothes," swindlers claimed they could weave a cloth that has "a wonderful way of becoming invisible to anyone who was unfit for his office, or who was unusually stupid."

The emperor sent his old minister to the weavers and asked him to report back. Naturally, he couldn't see anything at all, but he dared not admit it. He reported back to the king about the magnificence of the fabric.

This pattern repeated with others until the emperor himself went to see the fabric and, of course, saw nothing. But he certainly couldn't admit it! He didn't want to be exposed as "unfit" for the throne or "stupid."

The story culminates in the emperor parading naked through the town. All the townspeople marveled loudly at the "clothes," none wanting to admit that they might be the only person not seeing anything at all.

Finally, a little child announced that the king was naked, and little by little, the town came out of their delusion. But the emperor continued his march, refusing to end the parade out of sheer pride.

Sometimes a mature Christian or leader becomes so revered for their giftedness or influence that people are afraid to question anything they say. When this happens, the person will sometimes make statements that are nonsensical, unclear, or even wrong; and others will nod in agreement, not wanting to be seen as the only person who disagrees or doesn't understand. Others see this tacit agreement in the group and assume they must be the only ones not understanding. Thus no one says anything, even though everyone is thinking the same thing.

Sometimes it takes a new person, a child, a person with special needs, or someone especially bold to call into question what was said.

How we respond in these moments says a lot about our love, humility, and character. The right response is to listen intently, dialogue lovingly, and persuade gently until clarity is reached and the teaching or revelation can be appropriately discerned by the group.

If adequate conversation has taken place, Scripture has been consulted, and no one else in the group can vouch for what was said, it's right to reject it.

Don't be afraid to speak up when a word doesn't make sense to you or when it seems to contradict Scripture. Simply do so in love, giving the person a way to save face if possible.

As a leader, when you sense a word isn't right, ask the Holy Spirit what to do about it. If the warning signal in your heart seems intense, stop the meeting, explain what you're feeling, and ask everyone to pray along with you for discernment. Don't be afraid to linger in silence while people take time to discern together.

Respond to Jesus

Throughout the meeting, remember that Jesus is the most important person in the conversation. As the Lord speaks through people, take time to respond to him. Pause to worship or pray. If the Lord prompts the group to repent, take time immediately for the church to humble themselves before the Lord. Don't wait for the end of the meeting to direct your attention to Jesus. He's present throughout.

The end of the meeting is still important, though. People need a take-away from the conversation. Try to summarize what the Holy Spirit has been saying through everyone present.

If you can stay aware of Jesus throughout the meeting, you'll be Spirit-led. And as you model this awareness of Jesus, others will learn to be Spirit-led as well. Your entire meeting will be marked by children of God copying the example of their Father. You will have a house full of life-givers. (See John 5:21.) Anyone who joins such a meeting in your home will undoubtedly encounter God.

PART 3:
STEWARDING GROWTH

CHAPTER 18:

MULTIPLYING HOUSE CHURCHES

The highest demonstration of maturity for a local church is when it multiplies. Only something alive can reproduce, and it will do so only if it is healthy.

—Bob Roberts, Jr.

On New Year's Eve, 2019, we held house church at my home. I invited everyone to remain after our meeting for a party, followed by a time of prayer that would lead us into 2020.

Our house-church network had been officially incorporated since August. About fifty people were spread throughout three house churches that had slowly developed over the previous eight years.

As the calendar turned over to 2020, one of the ladies in our church, Patty Hartshorn, prophesied, "I believe the Lord is saying that this year, five new house churches will multiply out of this one house church."

That felt ambitious—especially knowing how slowly we had multiplied in the past. But it felt like an accurate word to me, and I figured I couldn't go wrong saying "amen" to something so in line with God's heart. I knew if it was going to happen, Jesus would have to do it. But that's how the church has always grown. Jesus is the one who builds his church. (See Matthew 16:18.)

Later that month, Patty started the first new church in her own home. Shortly after that, Greg and Theresa started a church.

One young couple, Justin and Kayla, had been radically impacted since joining our house church in the spring of 2018. When they first started coming, the two of them drank excessively and were pretty rough around the edges. Both had grown up in church, but they had certainly embraced a worldly form of believing in God while living for themselves.

But by December 2019, they were helping us lead worship at large gatherings, hosting our school of ministry in their apartment, and had come with me on a missionary trip to Uganda. They were new creations.

After Patty's prophetic word, Justin came to me and said, "I think we're supposed to start one of those house churches."

"Great!" I answered. "When?"

"I keep hearing April."

It doesn't take a student of world history to remember that April 2020 was a tumultuous time. Churches everywhere were shutting down as governments tried to curb the impact of a pandemic we truly didn't understand. In hindsight, we can easily cast judgment on those days, but as it played out in real time, no one quite knew what was happening.

Schools, stores, and businesses shut down the week before Justin and Kayla were supposed to start their house church. Justin asked me, "What should we do?"

"Well," I answered, "for the last few months, you've been telling me that God said to start in April. Do you think God didn't see this coming?"

So Justin and Kayla started our third house church that year as thousands of other churches were closing their doors.

Meanwhile, Judy had a friend named Emma who lived in Texas but wished she could be part of our network. Together, they started a house church that met exclusively on Zoom. That was our fourth house church.

Then in September, Joe and Emily left to start a fifth new house church.

Every time another house church started, we sent out a group of people from my own house church to help launch it. And every time a group left my house, the Lord filled their seats with new people.

The Lord fulfilled his prophetic word. Truly, Jesus builds his church.

Make Disciples to Make Churches

As discussed in chapter 5, the goal is not to plant churches. The goal is to make disciples. If you start a house church but never make any disciples, you're not yet doing what Jesus commissioned you to do. If you haven't started a house church but want to, maybe start by making a new disciple.

Over the course of perhaps one year, if your house church isn't growing, it's probably because you aren't making disciples. And if your house church isn't multiplying, it's probably because you haven't effectively trained others in your house church to make disciples. If that's the case, don't beat yourself up. Just make some course corrections.

One of the key factors in house churches that reproduce is planning to multiply. House churches that talk about the vision of multiplication are far more likely to multiply than those that don't. And this is especially true for house churches that set a date for their multiplication.

Yes, the Lord multiplied my house church network in 2020, but the vision God cast and the time constraint he offered in Patty's prophetic word also had a psychological impact on our church. People stepped up because they believed it was possible.

After leading a network for a few years, I have observed that it's fairly simple to start a house church. But the determining factor in whether that church remains is whether new disciples are made. House churches that simply gather those who have already been Christians for a long time eventually run their course and close. If you want your house church to thrive and last, make disciple making a priority.

Multiply or Die

While preparing a lesson about multiplication for our network's school of ministry, the Lord led me to a box of my old prayer journals. I felt led to a particular one, and the pages fell open to December 12, 2004. There, I wrote down the following dream:

> Last night, I had a dream in which I was pregnant with twins. I'm not sure what it means, but only God could come up with something so weird.
>
> Come to think of it, there were a few obvious details: First, I could feel them moving. Second, I knew it was time for them to be born. And third, I wouldn't let them come out because I was afraid of the pain that would be involved.
>
> One last detail—as depressing as it might be, both twins died before delivery. Then I woke up.

Healthy house churches grow, and as they grow, they eventually reach a size where it's time to divide into two new churches. It will be painful. But if you avoid acting when the time is right, both groups will die.

I've seen this to be true. In my experience, house churches that grow beyond a certain point and never multiply new groups will eventually collapse on themselves—either shutting down entirely or retracting in participation until only a fraction of the church remains.

What happens to all the other people who were once part of the church? Some go to other churches. Some stop attending church meetings altogether. It's far better to catch these people before they leave and offer them a third option: Help start a new house church.

They're leaving your house church anyway. It might as well be productive.

So what's the magic number when multiplication becomes necessary? There seem to be two factors. First is what church growth consultants call the 80 Percent Rule. This is a statistical anomaly where church attendance tends to eventually average out to approximately eighty percent of the seating capacity of the building.[53] I've observed this to be true in house-church settings as well. Your house may fill with people for a few months on end, but attendance will eventually drop to about 80 percent of your home's seating capacity.

One might think that the solution is to buy some folding chairs to expand the seating, but don't move too quickly. There's another factor. I have found that when a house church reaches

---

[53] As noted by the Duke Divinity School, no one knows the origin of the 80 percent rule. But countless church-growth consultants have anecdotally observed this and generally agree it is true. ("The 80 Percent Rule: Fact or Fiction," Duke University, August 11, 2006, https://alban.org/archive/the-80-percent-rule-fact-or-fiction/.)

about twenty people, the introverts in the church shut down and the interactive dynamic of the meeting suffers.

The sweet spot for multiplication appears to be when attendance is regularly exceeding 80 percent of seating capacity and ideally before attendance exceeds twenty people.

Yet one more factor exists. House-church experts like Rad Zdero and Joel Comiskey agree that a healthy house church should expect to multiply about every six-to-eighteen months.[54] This shouldn't be a mechanical constraint by which we force something to happen that isn't ready. We need to follow the Holy Spirit. But this common window for multiplication ought to at least inform our expectations. If two years pass without multiplication, we probably need to evaluate what we're doing and see if we need to make a course correction.

Life Stages of a House Church

Three People: Fellowship Begins—While two people can certainly fellowship with each other, only when a third person joins the conversation are people exposed to a new and important dynamic: Rather than wondering how to reply to the person talking, we're challenged to think, *What does the other person here have to say?* In this way, there is an opportunity to love in the presence of three people that does not exist with only two.

---

[54] Joel Comiskey, *Planting Churches that Reproduce: Starting a Network of Simple Churches* (Edmond, Oklahoma: CCS Publishing, 2009), 144; Rad Zdero, *The Global House Church Movement.* (Littleton, Colorado: William Carey Library, 2004), 113.

Five–Six People: Critical Mass—At this stage, the house church includes enough people that newcomers feel as if they're joining an established group, and the church becomes more sustainable. In our network, we try to start all our new house churches with this number of people by sending what we call a seed group—a small group of people who are already part of our house-church network and who will commit to at least six months of attending the new church to help launch it.

Seven–Fourteen People: Fellowship Thrives—This is the most enjoyable stage in a house church's development. New disciples are being made, people are open about their lives, hearts are being transformed, and the family of believers cares for each other.

Fifteen People: Fellowship Peaks—Once a house church crosses this threshold, many people tend to stop opening up about their lives. This needs to be remedied by prayer times when the larger group divides so that smaller clusters of people can be vulnerable with each other. When a house church reaches fifteen people, a house-church pastor should begin actively identifying future leadership (either to start a new house church or take over the present house church while the current leader plants elsewhere).

Twenty People: Fellowship Declines—When a house church reaches about twenty people, the introverts in the group tend to shut down, and only the minority of extroverts in the group tend to converse. If everyone present is an extrovert, not enough time exists for everyone to meaningfully share. When a house church reaches twenty people, the best course of action is to divide the group into two (or even three) new house churches.

Thirty People: Fellowship Dies—Whenever house churches grow to thirty or more people, participants are rarely vulnerable with the group. Even when groups divide for smaller prayer times, a person can gather with different people each week and may never open up there. If a house church reaches thirty people, multiply quickly before the culture becomes unhealthy.

I should note that the above applies to the number of people in the main meeting and does not include children who might be meeting in a separate room.

Multiplying Leaders

Part of making disciples is raising up and multiplying leaders. Jesus demonstrated that the largest impact is often made by investing in a small group of people. He spent most of his time with the twelve, and he spent even more purposeful time with Peter, James, and John.

I'm shocked at how unready the disciples were when Jesus finally handed over the church to them. He had much more that he wanted to say to them, but there was no way for them to bear it in such a short time. (See John 16:12.) Jesus trusted the Holy Spirit to empower his disciples and take them further in ministry than even he went. (See John 14:12 and 16:13.)

Jesus knew that the Holy Spirit could do more in a person from the inside than he could personally do in that person from the outside. He trusted the Holy Spirit to finish the work, then he entrusted the church to eleven men who barely made it through his crucifixion—some of whom still doubted him even after he raised from the dead. Even after washing his disciples' feet at the Last Supper, they were still arguing over who was the greatest. (See Luke 22:24.) But Jesus trusted the Holy Spirit to transform and teach these people.

We learn two things about leadership multiplication from this example. First, we will make the greatest impact with the smallest group of people. Don't get distracted trying to reach the biggest crowd. Put the most attention into pouring into a select few. And second, don't wait until those people are perfect before you send them. Simply prioritize their relationship with the Holy Spirit. If you can help them to know the Holy Spirit and learn from him, they will thrive in ministry, and he will teach them everything they still need to learn.

Model healthy leadership. Paul instructed Timothy to "set an example for the believers in speech, in conduct, in love, in faith and in purity" (1 Timothy 4:12). The example you set will always speak louder than the words you say.

Leading requires both *talking* and *doing*. When it comes to doing, leadership involves blazing trails. Leaders are breakthrough-makers, benefitting others with their own hard work on the others' behalf. And when it comes to *talking*, leadership also requires communication—explaining, encouraging, and equipping others so they can effectively do the same things. Explain how you minister, how you love, how you think, and how you live the way you do. Encourage others that they can do the same in the power of the Holy Spirit. And equip them with teaching, skill development, opportunities to practice, and meaningful feedback.

The best leadership is self-sacrificial (John 10:11), honoring of others (Romans 12:10), and expecting the next generation to run further and do more than the present leader (John 14:12).

In addition, we learn from Jesus's example that he didn't choose his successors on earth the way the world chooses. In Jesus's day, rabbis would choose the best students as their disciples. Those who were not chosen by the rabbis would go work a trade. The fact that Jesus chose tradesmen proves that he didn't choose the most educated or learned Israelites. Even after three years of walking with Jesus, the Jewish leaders still recognized that the disciples were unschooled and ordinary, but "they were astonished and they took note that these men had been with Jesus" (Acts 4:13).

How did Jesus choose these unique and ordinary men? Luke 6:12–13 says, "One of those days Jesus went out to a mountainside to pray, and spent the night praying to God. When morning came, he called his disciples to him and chose twelve of them."

In the same way, Paul and Barnabas were chosen and sent as the church worshipped and fasted. (See Acts 13:1–3.) And in the very next chapter, Paul and Barnabas established elders in the new churches while praying and fasting. (See Acts 14:23.)

The biblical pattern is to bring the question of leadership to God in prayer and fasting. Then, we select people based on his guidance—not natural qualifications or special skills. He may guide you to a particularly talented person, but don't let that person's talent be why you select them for leadership. We don't need skills nearly as much as we need the Holy Spirit.

In their book *Hero Maker: Five Essential Practices for Leaders to Multiply Leaders*, authors Dave Ferguson and Warren Bird recommend calling out qualities you see in people.[55] If you want to raise up disciple makers, then have personal conversations with individuals where you point-blank tell them, "Here's what I see in you that would make you an excellent disciple maker . . ."

Invite such people to serve as apprentices and learn from how you lead your house church. Share with them about what you believe God could do in their home through their leadership. You may even find it helpful to give them a copy of this book.

Then start a process of training with them. That process generally looks like:

- I do, you watch.
- I do, you help.
- You do, I help.
- You do, I watch.

---

[55] Dave Ferguson and Warren Bird. *Hero Maker: Five Essential Practices for Leaders to Multiply Leaders* (Grand Rapids: Zondervan, 2018), chapter 6.

Each step of the above process can take one to four weeks, depending on the person's confidence, ability, and growth. During these four steps, the leader and apprentice should debrief after every meeting. Discuss the mechanics of leading the meeting, challenges and opportunities that arose, whether situations were handled well, and how aspects of the meeting could have possibly been improved.

Remain humble. You're learning too. Don't be ashamed of admitting when you could have handled a situation better. You may even want to ask the person if they can identify what you could have done better. You might be surprised what you learn.

Before long, the other person will have confidence that they, too, can lead a meeting in their home. And the people in your house church will have seen that person in enough of a leadership capacity to know whether they want to go along with them to start a new church.

I must confess, I haven't walked out this specific process with every single person I've sent out from my house church. Sometimes the Lord accelerates the process according to his own agenda. Sometimes he wants to launch five or more new churches during a pandemic. But whenever I have followed these steps, the churches have thrived under the leadership of high-quality disciple makers.

Three Ways to Multiply a House Church

Once you have trained a leader, I recommend one of three options to multiply.

The most common way I have multiplied house churches (which is my personal favorite) is to ask people in your house church to pray about going with the new leader to start their house church. Ask them to commit to at least six months at the new house church to help establish it. Then have a special send-off meeting as you all pray for and prophesy over the new pastor (and perhaps over others as well).

Alternatively, if you haven't been hosting your house church in your own home, you might want to hand off the already established meeting to the new pastor and see who feels led to go with you to start a new church in a new location. In this case, the send-off meeting will be for you. I have seen this work well in certain situations.

And the third option, which is my least favorite but still needs to be mentioned, is to simply divide the church down the middle and send half of the people with the new pastor. The division could be based on geography, relationship, or any other factor. If you choose this option, make sure it is done with much prayer and open planning with the other pastor.

The Holy Spirit may lead you to multiply in other ways, but these three are the simplest I've found. Remember, you're multiplying not only churches but disciple makers. And if you do this well, you'll be amazed at how quickly a network forms.

CHAPTER 19:

JOINING GOD'S GLOBAL PLAN

If we want to be on mission with God we simply must *pause long enough to understand* how *God is on mission. Only then can we know with some degree of certainty that we are aligned as his instruments and not misaligned as his obstacles.*

—David Garrison

I boarded a small leaky wooden boat with eight people—mostly from my house church—and about ten Ugandan pastors and believers. We traveled about forty minutes on Lake Victoria in east Africa, eventually reaching Dagusi Island.

The churches I serve in Uganda wanted to plant a new branch church on the island, and they invited us to preach the gospel, heal the sick, and cast out demons.

The islanders largely practiced witchcraft and Islam. The pastors said there was no gospel influence on the island—only two Dutch so-called missionaries on the other side who were apparently only known for their drinking.

Our boat landed on the shore, and we entered the village. We wove between goats, chickens, fires for cooking, and mud huts with grass-thatched roofs until we reached a place where the Christians had erected some poles and worn-out tarps for the meeting. Then we sang, danced, and played drums until a group of villagers assembled around us.

The culture of our house church traveled with us and was powerfully expressed in this unique context. The Ugandans have a custom of introducing each person of honor at an event. So rather than simply preaching a sermon and inviting people to salvation, I took the time to introduce my team and let each one share.

As each person stood before the crowd to introduce themselves, they also spoke whatever the Holy Spirit placed on their hearts. Some shared testimonies. Some shared visions, dreams, and prophetic words they'd received. Some shared Scriptures. Some preached short sermons. And when everyone had shared, I came forward and tied up the loose ends. Finally, eight children and one man responded to the call for salvation.

We then asked who had a physical problem and wanted to be healed. No one responded, so I turned to our team and asked, "Is anyone receiving a word of knowledge?"

One by one, team members called out physical conditions, and one by one the people responded. The first healing to happen was when a little boy, who had just given his life to Jesus, laid hands on an old man who had back problems. The man was healed instantly. I then had our team minister to all the remaining people.

Twenty-seven people reported they were miraculously healed of various conditions, including snakebites, deafness, blurry vision, chest pains, and more. Even with our strict standards—pressing people to see if they were telling the truth and asking them to do something they couldn't do before—every single person without exception who responded for healing reported that they were healed. After experiencing and witnessing every person being healed, the village took notice. We planted a church on the island that remains to this day and has since multiplied.

Not everyone in my house church could go to Africa. The rest prayed for us, gave financially, encouraged us, and prophesied over us. And because of this, each of them was equally as responsible for the testimonies as those of us who traveled.

The Philippian church gave financially to support Paul's ministry. (See Acts 18:1–5[56] and Philippians 4:10–19.) Paul praised God for their partnership in the gospel (Philippians 1:3–5). He elsewhere said that they shared in his service to the Lord's people (2 Corinthians 8:4). Because of their teamwork in the mission, Paul said, "all of you share in God's grace with me" (Philippians 1:7). In other words, Paul's victories became their victories, and they even

---

[56] Philippi is in Macedonia, and this church is apparently the only one in the region that helped Paul financially. (See Philippians 4:15.) The Macedonians—specifically the Philippians—are known to have supported Paul on multiple occasions. Arguably, the reason Paul could stop making tents and devote his time to preaching after Silas and Timothy came from Macedonia is that they brought with them the finances mentioned in 2 Corinthians 8:1–7 and Philippians 4:10–19.

considered his troubles to be their troubles (Philippians 4:14). They were partners in prayer, finances, and the mission.

Gospel houses have a global impact. We support missionaries, and we even go ourselves as the Lord leads. Whether we're going or sending, whatever testimonies happen on the field are our testimonies. We are partners in the work. Thus we, the body of Christ, participate in Jesus's mission to spread the gospel to the ends of the earth (Acts 1:8).

Missio Dei

Sound missionary training includes discussion of *Missio Dei*, which is Latin for "the mission of God."[57] In short, the mission to make disciples of all nations and bring redemption to the entire world does not belong to the church—it belongs to God. We are not a church with a mission that God helps us fulfill. We are a church whose God has a mission that we help fulfill.

I've been serving a collection of rural churches in southeast Uganda for over a decade now. The church on Dagusi Island is one of them. Whenever I go, my first question is, "God, what are you already doing among the people here?" My second question is, "God, how can I join you in it?"

Most of the time, I simply ask the indigenous church leader I work with how I can most be a blessing to him and his ministry.

---

[57] The coining of this term is credited to German missiologist Karl Hartenstein in 1934, and it has been used in Bible colleges and missiological studies ever since. Karl Hartenstein, "Wozu nötigt die Finanzlage der Mission," *Evangelisches Missions-Magazin* 79 (1934): 217–29.

But I still need to pray so I know I'm serving the Lord's agenda and not wasting time with man's agenda.

The same is true of our local house-church network. The people in our network are not here to serve my vision. We are all here to serve God's vision. And we don't have a vision for how to reach Metro Detroit with the gospel; we have a vision for reaching the world. That's God's vision, and we're here to serve him.

If you want your house church to be truly gospel centered, then we must recognize that this gospel is for all nations, and we play a role in proclaiming it.

Revisiting the Great Commission

As noted in chapter 6, making disciples is a team sport. The commission was not given to individuals but to a people.

In Acts 1:8, what Jesus taught became an outline for the book of Acts and a practical example to us: "But you will receive power when the Holy Spirit comes on you; and you will be my witnesses in Jerusalem, and in all Judea and Samaria, and to the ends of the earth."

Just as the book of Acts follows the pattern of the gospel spreading first in Jerusalem and then to Judea and Samaria, finally launching out into the rest of the world, so we, too, begin locally, then reach our region, and so on. Jerusalem is our city. In my case, this is Metro Detroit, but it can be anywhere. Then Judea is the region that encompasses that city. My Judea might be understood as Wayne County or even the entire state of Michigan. Samaria, then, is the next region over, and it could even be seen as the people we don't necessarily want to go to (sorry, Ohio). And finally, we have the ends of the earth. A gospel house focuses on local ministry with an eye to the nations, partnering with God in his global work.

Evangelism looks different when we reject the idea that God partners with us in our mission and recognize that we are partnering with God in his mission. Only about six weeks prior to writing this, a man was on a business trip in Tennessee. While attending a conference for his work, a church gathered in the conference center on Sunday. This man attended, surrendered his life to Jesus, and returned home to Michigan.

A month ago, three ladies in our network—Sunni, Tammy, and Betti—stopped at a coffee shop on their way to a house-church meeting. They met this same man and engaged in some small talk. "I know this is strange," said one of the ladies, "but do you want to come to church with us in twenty minutes?" To their shock, the man joined them. It turned out he had been thinking about how he needed to find a church to attend, then the Lord sent these ladies. He attended the Saturday house church, then another Sunday morning house church, and then a large gathering for our network on Sunday night—three meetings in twenty-four hours. A few days ago, he was baptized at a Wednesday night house church.

We didn't lead this man to salvation. God did. We're only part of Jesus's body, but we are playing our role to love and equip this new disciple.

A few months ago, I sent my friend Greg, along with about ten other people, from my house church to start a new church in another town. About a month later, Greg was hungry for lunch and felt nudged by the Spirit toward a particular sandwich shop. There, he struck up a conversation with the young man behind the counter and offered to pray for him. The man was eager to share his struggles and asked, "Are you a pastor?"

Greg answered, "No, I'm just a Christian."

"Where do you go to church?"

"Well," Greg replied, "I'm part of a network of house churches. In fact, I lead one on Tuesday nights. Actually . . . wait . . . yeah, I guess I am a pastor!"

As it turns out, the young man had never been part of a church, but he had recently been watching YouTube videos of people like Todd White and wished to be part of something similar. This man is now part of Greg's house church and is growing in faith and spiritual gifts, receiving words of knowledge and praying for people on the streets.

Greg didn't have to do much. He simply showed kindness and offered to pray for a man. God was already working on this man, and Greg, following the Holy Spirit, found himself right in the middle of God's work.

> What, after all, is Apollos? And what is Paul? Only servants, through whom you came to believe—as the Lord has assigned to each his task. I planted the seed,

> Apollos watered it, but God has been making it grow. So neither the one who plants nor the one who waters is anything, but only God, who makes things grow. The one who plants and the one who waters have one purpose, and they will each be rewarded according to their own labor. For we are co-workers in God's service; you are God's field, God's building. (1 Corinthians 3:5–9)

When you see your house church as part of Jesus's global church, you become part of a much larger family of workers. Suddenly, everyone's ministry is *our* ministry.

To the Ends of the Earth

Jean-Philippe Gadbois, or as I know him, J.P., reached out to me in an email. He is a French Canadian who, at the time, had been a Christian for about six years. Through YouTube, he had been inspired by testimonies and videos of my work in Uganda and decided to try something similar in Rwanda. There, he partnered with local believers and ended up leading more than one hundred people to Jesus.

Seeing a clear need to disciple these precious people and seeing what God was doing through our house churches in Detroit, he reached out to me for advice. After a few emails and only a couple of hours of conversation on a video call, J.P. went to work organizing the churches.

A few months later, he crossed the border into Burundi to minister with a local evangelist there. The Lord blessed their work, and many people came to salvation.

Since this was happening during the height of the COVID-19 pandemic, Rwanda closed their borders, and J.P. was stuck in Burundi for about another month. During that time, the twelve churches in Rwanda became stronger, and the work in Burundi grew to more than forty house churches with hundreds of people involved.

What God has done in Rwanda and Burundi is nothing short of miraculous. My role in it was embarrassingly small—a few hours of conversations, a few emails back and forth, sharing some documentation from our network, and encouraging J.P. Nevertheless, I can't help but feel like we at Roots Church are family with these believers, even though I have only met a couple of their leaders.

Kingdom culture is meant to be exported. We need to recognize the difference, though, between kingdom culture and our own national, regional, family, or church culture. It's not that house churches are the only way to minister, but J.P. and the local church leaders felt this was the best means of establishing a resilient church during such tumultuous times. The ways of the world need to bow to the ways of our King, and we ought to be careful only to export the latter. We're gospel missionaries first, but house churches are a fantastic tool for making disciples.

The ways of God's kingdom transform the world. These ways are somehow both offensive and attractive to any culture. Our flesh bristles at the idea of dying to live, surrendering to win, giving to receive, and losing one's life to find it. Meanwhile, we can't help but be drawn to the love, humility, honor, faithfulness, authenticity, and power of real kingdom people. Persecution can't stop it, and challenging terrain won't slow us down. This message is for the uttermost parts of the earth.

Supporting Global Missionaries

Every house church officially connected to our network supports at least one missionary on a monthly basis. We prioritize missionaries who share our core values—especially those planting house churches. But we also support missionaries in more conventional contexts. We're one body with diverse ministries.

From time to time, we welcome itinerating missionaries to tour our house churches. When they come, we have a normal house-church meeting where the missionaries participate like anyone else. Then, we give them a window of maybe ten minutes to share about their work, leaving room in the schedule afterward if people have questions. We collect a cash offering for them and offer individuals the option of supporting them monthly. Finally, we pray together for them, and various people speak prophetically over them to encourage, strengthen, and comfort them in their ministries.

Many times, missionaries have raved about how blessed they were after a week of being loved, encouraged, supported, and prophesied over in multiple house churches.

Sending Global Missionaries

As a house church matures, so do the people who comprise it. And as Christians mature in an environment where God's mission is a priority, some will be called to work in other lands.

At the time of this writing, we have sent three missionary families from among us, although all three felt called to global work before joining us. We expect more missionaries to arise from among us as the Lord continues his work, and it's already happening

When those who attend conventional churches feel called to the mission field, they often establish conventional churches in new contexts around the world. We praise God for this! In our network, however, we have some Christians for whom house church is the only form of church they've ever belonged to. What will it look like when some of them are inevitably sent into world missions? I believe we will see tremendous fruitfulness.

In one sense, every person in your house church is a missionary. We're all called to spread the kingdom in the world, whether locally or abroad. Additionally, every person in your house church is invited to participate in God's global mission by sending and supporting those who are called to preach and plant churches in other nations.

A house church that doesn't participate in the global body of Christ is misaligned with God's mission. Whether we go or send will vary according to our unique callings and abilities. The Holy Spirit must lead us. Perhaps you will take teams to the heart of Africa like I do, or perhaps you'll send others. What matters is that you join God in his mission, both locally and abroad. You'll soon find yourself surrounded by a multiplying kingdom, sharing in testimonies and victories all over the world.

CHAPTER 20:

CLOSING A HOUSE CHURCH

Thriving churches have the Great Commission as the centerpiece of their vision, while dying churches have forgotten the clear command of Christ.

—Thom S. Rainer

Gospel houses never really go away. As long as you're still a gospel-centered person, your home will always be a place for people to encounter the Lord.

House-church meetings, on the other hand, may happen for seasons. Some house churches last for a year or two. Others last indefinitely. And sometimes the same meeting happens at the same time for years, but a complete turnover of people takes place, making it essentially a different church—and this turnover may happen two, three, or four times in a decade.

Whatever the case, it's helpful to know that starting a house church is not necessarily a lifelong commitment. Following Jesus is. And that means you'll always be a disciple maker as long as you walk this earth. But you're not under any obligation to host a regular house-church meeting. Some things are only for a season, and you can make disciples with others apart from a church meeting in your home.

A gospel house is a lifestyle; a house church is an organized meeting. Organized meetings may come and go, but your lifestyle of obeying Jesus and making disciples is inescapable for children of God. Follow the Holy Spirit.

Reasons to Close a House-Church Meeting

There are several valid reasons to close a house church meeting. Here are a few.

Moving: If you're physically relocating, no one else in the house church wants to host, and if no qualified leader is available to take your place, it makes sense to close a house-church meeting. But if at all possible, try to raise up a new leader and hand over the ministry to them (likely in a new location) before you move away.

Change in work schedule: Occasionally, circumstances beyond your control require you to move your house-church meeting to a different time, but this may conflict with everyone else's schedules. In these cases, the best course of action is to raise up a new leader and host for the current meeting, hand it off, and start from scratch with a new meeting at a different time.

Mission-drift: When people forget their mission to make disciples, they passively enjoy community and only ever invite Christian friends who might be in the market for a new church.

Church shoppers sometimes come with a consumeristic mindset: "What's in this for me?" Thus, the culture of self-focus continues. When people forget their vision is to multiply disciples, their natural tendency will be to default into what they know about church from popular culture: Keep inviting more and more people to make the biggest crowd possible. When new disciples haven't been made in so long that the culture has stagnated into an inwardly focused group, it may be preferable to stop meeting altogether for a few months and then restart only after there is a new disciple or two.

When God Closes a House Church

When God's Spirit is moving with power, lives are transformed, and people naturally want all their friends and family to experience this. But when spirituality becomes stagnant, people forget their mission and begin focusing on all the negatives—offenses, frustrations, selfish feelings and desires, etc.

As Larry Kreider points out, the closer we look at our faces in the mirror, the more imperfections we will see.[58] The more inwardly focused a church becomes, the more we see problems and the less we behold Jesus and hear his commands.

When John wrote the book of Revelation, he addressed what was essentially a collection of house churches throughout Asia Minor. When John wrote to the angel of the church in Ephesus,

---

[58] Larry Kreider, *Micro Church Networks: A Church for a New Generation* (Lititz, Pennsylvania: House to House Publications, 2020), 122.

Jesus had a stern warning: "Yet I hold this against you: You have forsaken the love you had at first. Consider how far you have fallen! Repent and do the things you did at first. If you do not repent, I will come to you and remove your lampstand from its place" (Revelation 2:4–5).

What's all this about a lampstand? It comes from the first chapter of Revelation, when John saw Jesus, shining in all his glory, standing among lampstands that represented the seven churches. (See Revelation 1:9–20.)

As my friend JonMark Baker points out, a church is only a church when it has representation in heaven. Names, websites, incorporations, buildings, and crowds are irrelevant. If there's no lampstand in heaven—and if the church doesn't have an angel assigned to it—then it's not a church.

According to Jesus, the church in Ephesus wasn't so far gone that it couldn't turn around. But the warning was dire. If the situation didn't change soon on earth, then it would change soon in heaven. It's not that God would remove his Spirit; it's that the church had already lost sight of God's Spirit. He would therefore remove their place in heaven. Without spiritual vibrancy expressed in love for Jesus, the church simply cannot continue being a church.

Spiritually dying churches either need revival or death. To maintain the status quo is to lock people into a lifeless, aimless disobedience club.

Low Attendance Is *Not* a Reason to Close a Church

Alex and Gracie Perry are members of our senior leadership team in our network. Alex started his house church when he was only twenty years old and Gracie was eighteen. They averaged a group of about six-to-eight friends who primarily met in their youth group as teenagers. Attendance has risen and fallen a number of times over the last five years since his church began. But the Perrys have remained faithful.

Early on, Alex and Gracie were praying about their house church, and Gracie felt led to text their friend Roman and invite him. For close to a year, Roman was the only person to attend most weeks. Alex and Gracie didn't consider the meeting a dud just because only one person came. Instead, they utilized the time to pour into Roman—reading the Scriptures, discussing, and praying together.

In time, the house church started to gain more traction. And as one might expect, Roman was eventually sent out from that house church to launch a thriving house church of his own. At the time of this writing, Roman's house church is actually bigger than Alex and Gracie's. But size is not our metric for success. Roman's thriving house church is the direct fruit of the Perrys' faithfulness to obey the Lord, even when attendance was low.

A Church that Loves Jesus

If a house church has drifted so far from its love for Jesus that it can't find its way back, God will shut down that church. He might not shutter the doors of their meeting space, but he will remove their representation in heaven. A cut-off branch will wither with time.

Love for Jesus is paramount. How, then, do we know if we love Jesus? "Jesus replied, "Anyone who loves me will obey my teaching. My Father will love them, and we will come to them and make our home with them. Anyone who does not love me will not obey my teaching. These words you hear are not my own; they belong to the Father who sent me" (John 14:23–24).

John, who witnessed and recorded these words from Jesus, later wrote: "We know that we have come to know him if we keep his commands. Whoever says, 'I know him,' but does not do what he commands is a liar, and the truth is not in that person. But if anyone obeys his word, love for God is truly made complete in them. This is how we know we are in him: Whoever claims to live in him must live as Jesus did" (1 John 2:3–6).

You can know if your house church is in love with Jesus by noting whether you and the rest of the people are obeying him. Obedience is Jesus's love language. And we successfully obey by living as Jesus did.

How did Jesus live? "Very truly I tell you, the Son can do nothing by himself; he can do only what he sees his Father doing, because whatever the Father does the Son also does" (John 5:19). Jesus lived completely dependent upon the Father. And that's how he taught us to live when he said, "I am the vine; you are the branches. If you remain in me and I in you, you will bear much fruit; apart from me you can do nothing" (John 15:5).

As discussed in chapter 5, the twelve were commissioned to make disciples for Jesus and then teach them to obey everything he ever commanded them. (See Matthew 28:19–20.) This is what making disciples looks like. It's an ongoing lifestyle of obedience to Jesus, no matter the cost—an obedience that is only possible through union with him, born out of love.

All our love for God comes from the overflow of his love for us. "We love because he first loved us" (1 John 4:19). So if you recognize a need to love God more, then the first thing to do is spend time with Father God, allowing yourself to recognize and receive his love for you. The same is true for your church.

Receiving love from God produces love for Jesus. And love for Jesus looks like obedience, which is only possible through union with him. In short, it's the gospel in action. Remember, the gospel is the answer to every problem.

If you feel like your church has drifted from obedience, don't start by demanding obedience from the people. Start by returning to your first love. Start by discussing God's love, practicing spiritual gifts like prophecy, and spending time in prayer together, simply receiving from God. You'll know when you've rightly connected to him when the natural outcome is obedience to Jesus, empowered by the Holy Spirit. And this is how you'll know that your church is still a church.

CHAPTER 21: ESTABLISHING A NETWORK

Isolated house churches tend not to be healthy and do not survive for too long. Vibrant house churches, however, unite together into networks for mutual encouragement, accountability, resourcing, and training.

—Rad Zdero

Some were weeping. Some were laughing. Some were praising God in English while others were speaking or singing in tongues. Some stood with arms raised while others knelt with their faces to the ground. Some collapsed into a couch or chair under the weight of God's glory while others trembled in his presence. There was no music, no stage lights, no hype or fanfare—just a small group of house-church pastors and people considering becoming house-church pastors.

Every second Sunday of the month, all our house-church pastors gather for what I believe is the most important meeting in our network. Each pastor has an opportunity to share wins and challenges from the last month, and others are there to cheer them on and help troubleshoot and pray as needed. Sometimes one of our network leaders will bring a teaching, and sometimes the entire meeting is a conversation. Then we finish with prayer, which has been known to last as long as four or five hours when the Holy Spirit is moving like I just described.

At one time, I was isolated—trying to shepherd a group of disciples on my own. Thankfully, I had two other friends in ministry—James Loruss and Jonathan Ammon—who thought out loud with me and helped me process challenging situations in our church. But that season of ministry was still challenging. I regularly had to navigate uncharted waters, agonizing over the best solutions to problems in my church and often trying several options before finding one that worked.

But pastoring my house church now is completely different as I gather monthly with these other leaders. We pastor our network together, valuing and honoring each other. We benefit from collective wisdom, camaraderie, and heartfelt love for each other. There's nothing like a healthy network.

Accelerated Growth

When I only had my lone house church, I gathered with the same group for almost four years before we finally multiplied the first time. Three years later, we multiplied again.

But when we officially organized as a network, our fruitfulness exploded. Three house churches and forty people combined to form Roots Church. While the Lord is certainly the one who added to our numbers, I can also say that something positive happened in the psychology of our people when we suddenly had a leadership team, name, website, and logo. It felt somehow more real for people, and they started seeing that they were part of something bigger than their one home group. In only one year, during the 2020 pandemic, the Lord grew our network to nine house churches and more than eighty people. Today, it continues to grow, with roughly three hundred people participating in fifteen house churches.

Our network has made us all healthier. Our slogan is "One mission. One family. Many homes." We truly have a unique sense of unity among us as we join Jesus in making disciples together.

The apostles among us push for multiplication and keep our eyes focused on Jesus and his mission. The prophets among us make sure we're sensitive to God's heart, calling us into worship and fellowship with him, and encouraging us to hear him for ourselves. The evangelists among us are pacesetters in street ministry, urging us all forward in our own proclamations of the gospel and populating our network with new disciples. The teachers among us contend for pure doctrine and help us remain faithful to God's Word and sound theology. And the pastors among us provide watch with care for the entire flock while especially focusing on those who gather weekly in their homes.

Meanwhile, all the people of God in our network love and serve one another. We pray for one another, encourage each other, prophesy over one another, and bear one another's burdens. We help each other through trials, celebrate each other's victories, and gather for informal times of prayer, worship, ministry, and fun. We're truly a family on mission together.

Benefits of Networking

I've experienced ministry in a single house church, a large, conventional church, and now a network of house churches. My single house church was a wonderful environment for discussing Scriptures, loving each other, growing in spiritual gifts, and being transformed in a close-knit family. My conventional church, however, had a face in the broader community, influence with city leaders, wonderful programs for families, fantastic events, corporate worship, great teaching, and a much stronger impact on world missions. When I was in one setting, I loved the positive aspects of ministry there but missed the benefits of the other.

Our network, however, unites the best of both worlds. All the benefits of a house church are accentuated by large, network-wide events, practical training from gifted equipping ministers, special meetings for kids and teens, large worship gatherings, tens of thousands of dollars going to world missions, and more.

There are many benefits to networking house churches:

Networks of house churches have more resources available. Material resources can be shared, enabling house churches in more impoverished neighborhoods to benefit from the generosity of those in more affluent areas. As Paul wrote: "Our desire is not that others might be relieved while you are hard pressed, but that there might be equality. At the present time your plenty will supply what they need, so that in turn their plenty will supply what you need. The goal is equality, as it is written: 'The one who gathered much did not have too much, and the one who gathered little did not have too little'" (2 Corinthians 8:13–15).

Additionally, human resources are drawn from a wider selection of people, enabling key ministries to emerge that benefit the larger network. Equipping ministries like apostles, prophets, evangelists, pastors, and teachers might not exist in a specific house church, but networks provide access to more people and more gifts.

Networks of house churches can make a greater impact on a region. One house church can reach a handful of people. Without multiplication, their impact will remain stagnantly limited to that one small area.

If a house church multiplies but never officially networks together with the new church(es) they planted, each group remains an entity unto itself, limited by its own resources and relationships. But a network can refer new people to churches that are the best fit for them—whether because of location or demographics. Families with children can attend a house church that has a children's meeting. Young people can connect with a house church that has some peers close to their age. Senior citizens or disabled people can be recommended to house churches that are more accessible (ramps, fewer stairs, etc.).

Furthermore, networked house churches can come together under one name to serve their community in a more public or official capacity, participating in or hosting large community events.

Networks of house churches have healthier leadership. As I noted at the beginning of this chapter, house-church pastors who are committed to a network gather at regular intervals to grow in their leadership skills, troubleshoot with each other, encourage one another, confess sin to each other, pray for one another, and so forth.

Additionally, if a house-church pastor becomes unstable or unhealthy, members of the house church can reach out to trusted and respected network leaders for accountability.

Networks of house churches have healthier participants. Participants in networked house churches have more teaching and training opportunities available to them. At Roots Church, we offer conferences, events, Encounter nights twice per month, and a school of ministry that helps ground people in sound theology, practical ministry, and a culture of Spirit-filled disciple making.

And of course, participants in networked house churches are led by healthier pastors who are regularly encouraged and resourced—never isolated.

Networks of house churches have psychological and social benefits. People generally want to feel part of something bigger than themselves. A large, growing network communicates that they're part of a healthy, thriving, bigger entity than their own little group.

As house churches multiply, an organized network enables key relationships to continue even when friends no longer attend the same house-church meeting. This makes multiplication socially easier and therefore more likely.

Networks of house churches grow faster than individual groups. Due in part to all of the above factors, organized networks of house churches tend to grow much faster than individual house churches.

How to Start a Network

If you're applying the principles of this book in the small-group ministry of a conventional church, then in some ways, your network already exists because of the umbrella organization. But even then, the groups are not truly networked unless the shepherds in those groups are meeting regularly and using training to help groups multiply.

If you're applying these principles outside the official oversight of a conventional church as I did, the road is a bit longer.

The first step is to multiply a house church. I recommend bringing the two churches together at least quarterly for a worship night or large meal or fun event. In this way, multiplication will be easier because those leaving house churches know they will still see the friends they're leaving or sending.

I also recommend not officially organizing until you have at least three stable, sustained churches. In my experience, a single house church that registers as a corporation rarely multiplies and sometimes doesn't organize in a way that even could multiply, but a network that forms a corporation already has multiplication in its DNA.

You should also consider the leadership issues of organizing too soon. A single house church that organizes can also be top-heavy, establishing the leadership needed for a large ministry while only a few people gather in a home. Not to mention, the pool of human resources in a single house church is much smaller than in a growing network. When I formed my senior leadership team for our network, I chose people from all three house churches in our network. All of them are top-notch leaders who are phenomenal at what they do.

Network Leadership

Those who oversee networks of small churches have a responsibility to identify and appoint qualified elders to oversee each small flock of Jesus's sheep. (*Elders* are also called "pastors," which is a word that literally means "shepherds." See 1 Peter 5:1–4.) In Titus 1:5, Paul wrote, "The reason I left you in Crete was that you might put in order what was left unfinished and appoint elders in every town, as I directed you."

At Roots Church, we have two forms of leadership: organizational and organic. Our *organizational* leadership includes our senior leadership team plus help from a board of five members from the congregation. And our *organic* leadership is comprised of all the house-church pastors throughout the network.

Organic leadership: As an organization, we do not desire to interfere with the multiplication of God's kingdom. All house-church pastors are authorized and encouraged to identify and raise up new leaders organically. Together, the community of house-church pastors in our network approves or removes other house-church pastors who might want to participate with us. Mutually, we all keep watch over the entire flock (including each other)—not only our own individual house churches.

Organizational leadership: This exists to strengthen and protect the integrity of the organization—approving those house churches that wish to be officially associated with the network, addressing matters of organizational membership, and credentialing pastors in our network.

Our leadership team is home-grown, comprised of people who have earned influence organically in our network. Organizational leadership is therefore also organic. It is not less than or greater than our organic leadership; rather, it comes alongside the pastors of our network to help them minister more effectively to their house churches and communities.

Follow the Holy Spirit in how you organize. We decided to have a senior leadership team that functions together as one unit rather than implementing a strong hierarchy. While as the leadership director, I am technically the senior pastor on paper and oversee the leadership team, I have told everyone on our team to dream, implement, and serve people as though they, too, are the senior pastor. My job is to ensure we're healthy, loving each other, and staying on track with our vision and purpose. But I have relinquished a great deal of control, knowing that it's the only way for an organization like this to thrive long after I'm gone.

In addition to my role, we have a spiritual life director who is essentially the pastor to the house-church pastors. This person organizes pastor gatherings each month and keeps their finger on the pulse of spiritual health throughout our network.

We also have an executive director who is responsible for keeping our network legally and financially sound. They interact with our bookkeeper, CPA, and board, sending out monthly stipends to our house-church pastors and maintaining records.

We also have an evangelism and discipleship director who oversees our program for new believers and ensures that people throughout our network are effectively making disciples who make disciples. Our community-outreach director oversees large-scale service projects throughout our network. And we also have a children's director and a youth director who organize meetings, events, and more for age-specific ministries that serve our entire network.

Your leadership may look different. We started with a team of five and only recently expanded to seven. We've also shuffled some roles and responsibilities as the organization has evolved and our leaders have matured. Perhaps we'll add more in the future. The goal is not to have structure for structure's sake but to create a structure that effectively serves the local context.

Multiplication happens best under decentralized leadership. While our organizational leadership is centralized, our organic leadership is not. We try to push autonomy to the fringes of the network, allowing the outermost edges of our family tree the liberty to make disciples and multiply without the need for special permission from a central office. Accordingly, people and their leaders are accountable to those with whom they have a personal relationship—not distant figureheads who rule from afar.

Money

Whether we like it or not, the topic of money must be discussed. There are many ways to handle money in a church, but the culture of a house-church network requires a certain amount of transparency.

Paul wrote to the Corinthians about giving an offering, saying, "We want to avoid any criticism of the way we administer this liberal gift. For we are taking pains to do what is right, not only in the eyes of the Lord but also in the eyes of man." (2 Corinthians 8:20–21). Integrity before the Lord is one thing, but we also need to do what is right in the eyes of man. This requires man's eyes to actually be able to see what's being done.

At the same time, we don't want the money stuck in a complicated web of committees, votes, or bureaucracy. In our network, individuals on our senior leadership team manage various accounts within the budget. We also have a savings account, which we call our vision account, that requires agreement among the leadership team.

In addition, a congregational board of five members from throughout the network provides accountability in how funds are allocated and received.

While we do have a network-wide fund for widows, orphans, foster families, and single moms, most benevolence happens at the house-church level as individuals give directly to each other. This money never touches our books and is simply seen as personal gifts from one person to another. House churches do, however, have locked collection boxes for giving tax-deductible donations to our network. These are brought to our large gatherings and emptied into the general offering. Most people, however, tend to give electronically on our website.

Leveraging Technology

One of the most beneficial expenses we've made was to create a smartphone app for our network (which can also be accessed online). Each house church has its own dedicated group, but there are also network-wide groups for prayer, announcements, general discussion, parents, and so on. People can join as many or as few groups as they like, and they can toggle specific groups to receive push notifications.

Our prayer group is one of the most active. People post prayer requests, and others reply within minutes that they're praying, sometimes even typing out their prayers in the comments. Sometimes people follow up with testimonies of answered prayer.

This has been tremendously unifying for our network. People who used to be part of the same house church but have since gone to start a new one can still interact regularly with people they would otherwise miss.

Additionally, we thought carefully about our website, tailoring the homepage for unsaved people who might interact with people in our church in an evangelistic context. We didn't see a need for targeting our homepage at Christians who already attend church.

At the same time, our website is robust in its articulation of who we are and what we do, helping other Christians understand our unique ministry model.

We also included an easily accessible curriculum for those who are introducing new disciples to the Christian life, plus we have free evangelism training.

Whatever technology you have or can afford is worth investigating to determine which is a waste of money and which is an investment in the kingdom.

If, like us, you're a true house-church network with no physical building, don't skimp on graphic design. Spend the time or money to make a truly professional brand for your logo, website, print materials, and so forth. Other organizations receive a certain amount of legitimacy in the public eye from their brick-and-mortar establishments, but you don't have that advantage. Instead, your real estate is your online presence. So make your materials something your church can be proud of. This will also be your face to the community, so make sure all your materials are attractive. Don't fall into the trap of trusting your own eye unless you're already a professional graphic designer.

Legal Considerations

When you're just starting out, you probably don't need to be bogged down with burdensome issues like insurance, accounting, policies, bylaws, and so on. But the sooner you begin thinking about such matters, the sooner your budding network will be poised to multiply healthfully.

Once you have three or four house churches, I recommend finding an insurance agency that specializes in church insurance and is willing to work with your unconventional model. The agency we use offers coverage for various liabilities, including defending pastors and kids ministers from false allegations (when accountability protocols have been practiced) and more. We have yet to need this insurance, but we can appropriately mitigate some risk for those who want to make disciples in their homes.

You're also eventually going to want to hire a certified public accountant who can help your organization remain compliant with tax reporting and so on. In our network, we have an executive director who oversees the finances, a bookkeeper who manages our accounting software and makes sure all funds are accounted for, and our CPA. All three work together to maintain accountability and financial health for our network.

I also recommend developing policies for how you will handle allegations of sexual misconduct and so forth. While no one expects poor or even illegal behavior, you don't want to find yourself blindsided by a situation that puts you in a difficult position, forcing you to make rushed decisions when you need to take the time to think about an effective course of action.[59] Think carefully about what policies and procedures need to be in place for the ongoing health and safety of all. You may want to consult a local nonprofit lawyer to help craft the language.

When the time comes to organize, develop your bylaws thoughtfully. House-church networks sometimes struggle to outlast their founders. Create an organization that depends more on a healthy team than on you personally. Design everything with longevity in mind.[60]

Large Gatherings

Before I started our network, I had a conversation with a friend of mine who had previously pastored a cell-based church. I asked him what he'd change if he could do it all again. I only remember one recommendation.

---

[59] If you'd like to see our policy, which was crafted with the help of a Michigan nonprofit lawyer, please visit https://rootsag.churchcenter.com/pages/sexual-harassment-policy.

[60] If you'd like to see a copy of our bylaws and customize them for your network, feel free to reach out to Roots Church at www.RootsAG.org.

He said, "I'd only have a big meeting once a month. I wanted people to see their cell as their church and the big gathering as a celebration. But no matter how hard I tried, as long as we had a Sunday morning meeting every week, everyone thought that was their church and the cells were optional."

In our network, we meet on the first and third Sunday night of each month. We don't own a building. Instead, we partnered with a small church in our area that doesn't have any Sunday night meetings. When we outgrow the building, we'll partner with a larger church. And if we can't find a larger building or when we outgrow one, perhaps we'll partner with two or three smaller churches and multiply our large gatherings as well. Time will tell.

Each gathering begins at 5:30 p.m. with prayer. At 6:00 p.m., we transition into worship. Around 6:40 p.m., we begin a time of testimonies—specifically pertaining to evangelism and healing ministry. After about fifteen–twenty minutes, we dismiss the kids to the nursery (ages one–four), children's ministry (ages five–eleven), and youth group (sixth–twelfth grades). We share a few announcements during the transition, and the teaching usually starts by about 7:00 p.m., lasting forty-five–sixty minutes. (Sometimes much of this is replaced by prayer or extended worship.) Next, we spend time seeking the Lord, usually ministering to one another. Many linger for hours in the presence of the Lord, eventually breaking into groups to chat and finally leaving around 11:00 p.m. or later.

We call these meetings Encounter Nights because we want to be clear about why we're gathering. This is not a typical church meeting. It's a time to encounter God together as a large network.

We also have a special prayer meeting every fourth Sunday that we call Hunger Night. These meetings don't have kids ministry or a worship team. We simply gather to seek the Lord. It's essentially an old-school, Pentecostal prayer meeting. People prophesy, pray, and seek the Lord for a fresh outpouring of his Spirit in our churches.

Second Sundays, as mentioned, are reserved for our house-church pastors and anyone considering becoming a house-church pastor. And we generally leave the occasional fifth Sunday open as a family night and encourage people to invite each other to dinner or something fun.

Training

None of the house churches in our network meet on Thursday nights, allowing everyone interested to participate in our school of ministry. This centralized training has been a tremendous catalyst for multiplication, raising up leaders who are spiritually vibrant, doctrinally sound, and practically trained and equipped to lead house churches.

We have a core curriculum that lasts thirty-five weeks along with ongoing teaching modules on various topics.

We don't require anyone to attend or graduate from any of these classes—even our house-church pastors (although we encourage it). Classes are entirely voluntary. Nevertheless, people come because the training is exceptional and has resulted in many people experiencing transformation and launching into ministry.

Reserve time in your network for training, even if you don't begin right away. Make the training fit your context and culture. Follow the Holy Spirit.

Don't be shy about going deep. Our thirty-five-week core curriculum covers the life of Christ in all four gospels (first forty-five minutes), plus thirty-five topical studies (sixty–ninety minutes each). With a short break, every class session is two–two-and-a-half hours long. We include Scripture reading and other assignments during the week. And our students eat it up.

Multiplying Networks

Eventually, if the Lord blesses the work, the house churches in your network will likely become so geographically diverse that gathering for large meetings will become less and less practical. At this time, it may be wise to consider sending four or five house churches to launch a new network with its own leadership, board, and gatherings. You might even consider dividing your current leadership team so that you have experienced people in both networks, filling in the empty seats with new ministers.

The multiplication of a network essentially happens in the same way as multiplying a house church, only on a larger scale. Leadership is raised up, trained, and equipped. And just like individuals deciding whether to move to a new house church, those house churches that want to join the new network are welcome to do so. Those who want to stay with the original network may remain if desired. Both networks are then free to grow and thrive in unity, following the Holy Spirit.

Dare to Dream

Perhaps you're reading this book before ever starting a single house church. Forming a network may feel years away. That may be. Or it may happen suddenly. Be prepared for the Lord to bring a miraculous awakening in your region.

Be creative. What worked for us at Roots Church may not be the right fit for you. Seek the Lord for your own context and develop ideas with others who share your passion.

Finally, refuse to see your region as hard ground. It doesn't matter if you're living under an oppressive government, a violent majority religion, or an atheistic culture. Lift up your eyes. The harvest is ready. There's no reason to delay. In John 4:35, Jesus said, "Don't you have a saying, 'It's still four months until harvest'? I tell you, open your eyes and look at the fields! They are ripe for harvest."

Remember, you're not here to build a network of house churches. You're here to make disciples. If you make disciples, you'll have a house church. And if you keep making disciples, you'll have to start another house church. And once you have a couple of house churches, you have the birth of a network.

When I started pastoring a group of young adults in my home in 2011, I had no idea it would become what it is today. I never dreamed I would see such a movement. I never set out to start an organization or a network. I simply said a small yes to Jesus. "Yes, I will meet weekly in my home with a group of young adults."

The Michigan AG superintendent, Aaron Hlavin, often says, "Greatness is goodness, compounded over time." You don't have to do big things. You have to be obedient to Jesus—faithful with the few things he has entrusted to you. And if you partner with him, always growing in faith and godly character, he will do great things in due time.

Lift up your eyes to the harvest fields. Make some disciples. You'll soon have a gospel house.

And then another.

CHAPTER 22:

PARTNERING WITH GOD IN REVIVAL

They didn't need the word "revival" in the Bible because they were living it. And here's the thing: Personally, as someone who mainly preaches at "revivals," I don't even care if you don't like the word. Here's revival: It's the present-day work of the Holy Spirit flowing in your life, which requires repentance, obedience, and partnership with Jesus. What's revival? It's New Testament Christianity.

—Jeremiah Johnson

What would you do if revival broke out in your home meetings, and God brought hundreds of new converts to your doorstep? Sure, you could direct them to other churches in your city (assuming there are healthy ones), but God didn't bring these people there. He brought them to you. What would you do?

In 1992, Abraham Sekhar pastored New Life Fellowship, a church that had four conventional congregations and about eight hundred members in Mumbai, India—a city of fourteen million. Abraham and his church prayed fervently for their city for several years, believing God to bring salvations. But Mumbai is the commercial capital of India. According to Abraham, multitudes were either entirely wrapped up in making money or else suffering in poverty, bound by alcoholism, drugs, and prostitution.

Abraham and his church leaders were doing all the work of the ministry while the people enjoyed their labor. Church attendance and membership had plateaued for nearly two decades. The leadership decided a focused door-to-door campaign was in order. They mobilized their eight hundred members alongside four hundred volunteers from other evangelistic organizations.

In four weeks, taking breaks only on Sundays, they distributed literature to more than five hundred thousand homes. More than ten thousand people responded to the campaign, agreeing to come to a follow-up meeting at a football field.

The day of the event came, but the only people in attendance were the church leaders and their eight hundred members. Despite their discouragement, they continued singing for a half hour, all the while feeling the sting of their failed efforts.

But as darkness spread over the land at sunset, thousands of people started pouring onto the field. An estimated crowd of eight thousand people stood to hear the gospel. Abraham told me,

> While worship continued and my elder later started to share the Word, my heart was pumping with excitement inside. At the same time, I was full of burdens and anxiety,

asking God for a strategy on how to bring the harvest into the fold and how to teach and disciple them.

The Lord spoke to me clearly and inspired to divide the harvest of eight thousand souls into groups of ten each and to appoint the eight hundred committed members to become house-group leaders overnight to take care of the ten allotted to each.

This was a risky move for the church leaders and a great challenge to the church members. About 30 percent of them were new converts themselves. But when God brings in a tremendous harvest, every worker is needed.

Within a week, and with inspiration and help from the Holy Spirit, Abraham and his wife wrote a seven-lesson book for new believers and had them printed. They gave a copy to each of the newly appointed house-church leaders to teach the new believers.

At the end of three months of weekly meetings, their church had grown by more than five thousand souls. More than sixty new worship centers sprang up. Fivefold ministry and operation of spiritual gifts became their lifestyle. Salvations, deliverances, and healings became normal.

As the Holy Spirit moved, the gospel spread to the family members and relatives in the cities and villages from where these five thousand had come to live in Mumbai. More than eight hundred additional village and town churches were established in thirteen states of India.

Today, three decades later, the movement has more than thirteen thousand house churches and village churches across almost every state of India. And it all began with prayer, obedience, and a Spirit-led willingness among the leadership to relinquish control, risking new converts to the care of ordinary Christians in house churches. The result is an ongoing movement where God is regularly pouring out his Spirit upon small gatherings of Christians throughout India.

You may think, *That's easy for a church of eight hundred in a city of fourteen million, but what does this have to do with my little home group?* There's good news for you too. Many revivals started with small groups.

In the 1700s, the Methodist movement was birthed out of small face-to-face, interactive house churches (called classes) that met weekly in the local neighborhoods of their participants. Unlike the revival I just described in India, where a large group divided the harvest into small groups, the Methodist movement worked the other way around. In the early days, people weren't even allowed to come to the large gatherings without first integrating into a home group.[61] Like Abraham Sekhar in India, John Wesley, leader of the

---

[61] Howard A. Snyder, *The Radical Wesley: The Patterns and Practices of a Movement Maker*, originally published as *The Radical Wesley and Patterns for Church Renewal* ((Wilmore, Kentucky: Seedbed Publishing, 1996, 2014), 64–65.

Methodists, put one of ten believers into significant ministry and leadership roles, and some estimate as many as one in five.[62]

If you will be faithful to make disciples in your home, there is no limit to what can happen as God pours out his Spirit.

Seeking Revival

Spirit-filled believers ought to long for outpourings of God's Spirit. Yes, he is omnipresent (meaning everywhere at once). (See Jeremiah 23:24 and Psalm 139:7–10.) Yes, he dwells within us. (See 1 Corinthians 3:16.) Yes, he will never leave us nor forsake us. (See Hebrews 13:5.) But there is a difference between God's generic omnipresence and the unique ways he manifested himself in the tabernacle and temple with such a thick cloud of glory that no one could enter. (See Exodus 40:34–35 and 2 Chronicles 7:1–3.) There's a difference between God's omnipresence and the glory that passed by Moses in the wilderness and nearly killed him. (See Exodus 33:15–23.) Scripture is filled with divine encounters that transcend mere omnipresence.

The Bible commands us to be continually filled with the Holy Spirit. (See Ephesians 5:18–20.) But history invites us to experience special moments of God's manifested presence. The Christian life is supposed to look like sustained spiritual vibrancy, marked with thrilling outpourings of God's Spirit.

---

62 Ibid., 75.

Those outpourings are generally unique. The same apostles who encountered God's Spirit in Acts 2:1–4 needed a fresh outpouring in Acts 4:23–31 as they faced imminent persecution, but these two events looked different. One was marked by the sound of wind, supernatural flames, and empowered languages. The other was characterized by an earthquake and bold preaching. Then, these same apostles spent time in the temple courts, preaching the gospel and healing every sick, diseased, and injured person who came to them. (See Acts 5:12–16.) The book of Acts contains one story after the next of both God and his people being discontented with mere quiet, routine omnipresence.

While spiritual maturity does look like obeying and rejoicing in the Lord no matter how spiritually dry we might feel, holy romance refuses to settle there. A healthy marriage will have dry spells, but those dry spells must turn into longing for one another lest the relationship grow cold.

God is longing for you. He has gone to extreme measures to rescue you from sin and reconcile you to himself. And if you will allow your heart to long for him as well, he promises, "You will seek me and find me when you seek me with all your heart" (Jeremiah 29:13).

Hosting Revival

You may think that revival is something that happens in a big church meeting or out in a field with a crowd, but in Acts, God often poured out his Spirit in homes. Pentecost happened in a house. (See Acts 2:1–2.) Ananias brought the gospel to Saul, healed his blindness, and laid hands on him to receive the Holy Spirit in a house. (See Acts 9:17–19.) Non-Jews first received the gospel and experienced a spiritual outpouring in the home of a Roman centurion named Cornelius. (See Acts 10.)

Sure, other outpourings happened in the streets and seized entire cities, like when the former sorcerers of Ephesus burned fifty thousand days' wages worth of witchcraft scrolls in a public display of repentance. (See Acts 19:17–20.) But these macro-outpourings began with micro-outpourings that often occurred in homes.

A gospel house is a revival hub. It's a place where tired, dry, dissatisfied believers can encounter refreshing and renewal from the Lord. It's a place where the Holy Spirit regularly pours out—working miracles, inspiring worship, delivering prophecy, performing signs and wonders, healing hearts, and more.

If we start a house church out of mere duty, thinking that will automatically bring an outpouring, we will be disappointed. God doesn't pour out his Spirit in response to performance—as though we have to earn his attention. But if we start a house church in faith—believing that our loving Father wants to pour out his Spirit even more than earthly fathers want to give good gifts to their kids (Luke 11:13)—then God will indeed respond to our actions. As Paul asked the Galatians, "Does God give you his Spirit and work miracles among you by the works of the law, or by your believing what you heard?" (Galatians 3:5). Simple faith attracts God's Spirit.

Preparing for Revival

Jesus came to start a movement that has swept the world. Even though he paid attention to the multitudes who flocked to him, he spent most of his time away from the crowds. He prayed long hours alone. He primarily trained twelve men while focusing most intently on three.

We and billions of Christians throughout the earth today trace our origin to the three years Jesus spent investing in a small group. He taught them to pray, explained God's kingdom, sent them to preach and minister healing and deliverance, reminded them to remain humble, and set an example of self-sacrifice and joy in suffering.

Then, after he rose from the dead, Jesus sent the promised Holy Spirit to empower them. The mighty wind and tongues of fire at Pentecost were only for a moment, but they inaugurated a movement. On the day of Pentecost, a church of only 120 people grew by 3,000. That's a sudden influx of 25 new converts for every established disciple.

But Jesus had prepared his church well. We don't know exactly how they facilitated the revival, but we do know that the people benefitted both from large meetings in the temple courts and small gatherings in homes where they prayed and broke bread together. (See Acts 2:42–47.) All the while, God continued to add new believers to their numbers.

Surely, Jesus knew this revival was coming. And the way he prepared for it was to be personally devoted to his Father and then model love to a small group. He didn't spend hours discussing strategies or planning marketing campaigns. And even though he was a builder by trade, he never constructed a cathedral. Jesus was intimate with the Father and invested in people, which was enough to incubate a movement that was soon born in a spiritual outpouring.

Recognizing Revival

As I write this chapter in February 2023, thousands of people are gathered at Asbury University in Wilmore, Kentucky. After a normal chapel service, a small group of students remained to pray and worship God. They prayed through the night as others joined in, moved by the Holy Spirit. This 24/7 prayer meeting continued for days and quickly snowballed until the main auditorium and overflow chapels filled with visitors while hundreds more remained worshipping, praying, and confessing sin outside in the cold.

Meanwhile, social media exploded with debate about whether to truly classify this event as a revival. Countless critics questioned every detail, and even Christians quibbled over the meaning of the word "revival." But none of this stopped the throngs of students and pilgrims at Asbury from having their hearts rekindled with holy passion in the presence of God and his people. If you're going to see revival in your house church, don't be surprised when the criticism intensifies alongside the glory.

One can read about revivals like Pentecost, the first and second Great Awakenings, Azusa Street, Brownsville, Toronto,

Asbury University, or what happened with Abraham Sekhar in India and assume that every true revival must look exactly like some or all of these special seasons in church history. But this can sometimes cause us to miss what God is presently doing right in front of us. I don't much care what word we use, as long as God is moving. A holy visitation is the wrong time to debate semantics.

Along these lines, we would do well to celebrate even the smallest breech in the dam—the slightest trickle of God's manifested presence. Don't allow cynicism to fool you into rejecting what God is doing just because it isn't at the magnitude of whatever full-blown revival you've studied or experienced in the past. Celebrate what God is doing, no matter how small.

Elijah prophesied rain and then prayed seven times, seemingly without results, seeking God to end a years-long famine. The seventh time he sent his servant to look for results, the servant finally reported a tiny cloud, only the size of a man's hand, rising in the sea. At that moment, Elijah knew the famine was over and a downpour was imminent. (See 1 Kings 18:41–45.)

Don't scoff at the tiny cloud and say, "That's not rain!" Faith looks at the tiny cloud and sees the end of famine. Celebrate the small things God is doing, and he will trust you with greater blessings.

If you have started a house church, what is God presently doing? Celebrate those breakthroughs as you hunger for more.

Embracing Revival

Every revival in history has been marked by refreshed zeal in God's people. This will inevitably lead to salvations, but revivals don't always start there. Generally speaking, revivals begin with believers.

That's the very nature of the word *revive*. Something must have once been alive before it can be revived. We love it when sinners come to repentance, but that's not revival—that's "vival" (there is no "re-"). Revival is first an atmosphere of life and regeneration among the people of God.

The primary preacher of the Second Great Awakening in the United States was Charles G. Finney. In 1835, Finney wrote, "Revival is the renewal of the first love of Christians, resulting in the awakening and conversion of sinners to God. A revival of true Christianity arouses, quickens, and reclaims the backslidden church and awakens all classes, insuring attention to the claims of God."[63] In other words, according to one of the most qualified authorities on the subject, revival starts with Christians before spilling over to the lost.

When God is refreshing his people, some may look at an absence of new converts and ask, "What's the point?" The point is people encountering God's love. What greater point could there

[63] Charles G. Finney, "What is Revival," in *Lectures on Revival: The Only Edition of This Masterful Classic Edited for Today's Reader* (Minneapolis: Bethany House Publishers, 1988), 15.

be? Give people time to soak in what God is doing. If we're patient, they will eventually take it to the world.

Revival is often messy and confusing. Sometimes the things God wants to do will offend our sensibilities. His Spirit shatters perceptions of normalcy. This makes revival difficult to embrace.

Don't be surprised if you see strange physical manifestations. They are biblical.

- All the people of Israel trembled when God came to Mt. Sinai (Exodus 19:16).
- Ezekiel fell face down in God's presence (Ezekiel 1:28).
- Daniel collapsed into a deep sleep (Daniel 8:17–18).
- In another encounter, Daniel lost all his strength, went pale, and became physically helpless. He was speechless until God opened his mouth, but even then, he was filled with anguish, physically weak, and could barely breathe (Daniel 10:8–9, 15–17).
- Peter, James, and John fell to the ground in terror (Matthew 17:5–6).
- Saul collapsed to the ground and heard Jesus's voice, becoming physically blind (Acts 9:3–4).
- John fell at Jesus's feet as though dead (Revelation 1:17).

In the 1600s, a group of Reformed French Protestants, known as the Huguenots, experienced a revival. Physical manifestations of various kinds occurred, including people of all ages falling under God's power, their bodies twisting, trembling, and flailing.[64]

Also in the 1600s, George Fox led the Society of Friends. Observers gave them the derisive nickname "Quakers," partly because the people regularly gathered for prayer and waited for a moving of the Holy Spirit that caused their bodies to physically tremble and quake.[65]

In the 1700s, the founder of the Methodist movement, and perhaps the best-known preacher of the First Great Awakening—a revival that struck America in the 1730s and 40s—was John Wesley. On January 1, 1739, Wesley wrote in his journal about a meeting in a home with about sixty people. He recorded, "About three in the morning, as we were continuing constant in prayer, the power of God came mightily upon us, in so much that many cried out for exceeding joy, and many fell to the ground."[66]

Meanwhile, a contemporary of Wesley, George Whitfield, began seeing wild manifestations in his meetings as people cried out, collapsed to the ground, and convulsed under God's power. Wesley journaled on July 7, 1739, that as Whitfield called sinners to

---

[64] Paominlen Kipgen, "History and Theology of Pentecostal Movement," accessed April 2, 2023, https://www.academia.edu/34842608/HISTORY_AND_THEOLOGY_OF_PENTECOSTAL_MOVEMENT, 8.

[65] *Encyclopedia Britannica Online*, s.v. "Quaker," accessed August 23, 2021, https://www.britannica.com/topic/Quaker.

[66] John Wesley, *The Complete Journal of John Wesley: Wesley Student's Edition Volume 1,* ed. Martin Mostert (n.p.: 2022), 236.

repentance, "four persons sunk down close to him, almost in the same moment. One of them lay without either sense or motion. A second trembled exceedingly. The third had strong convulsions all over his body, but made no noise, unless by groans. The fourth, equally convulsed, called upon God, with strong cries and tears."[67]

Around this same time, the famous revival preacher and theologian Jonathan Edwards preached in a private home meeting and reported:

> In the month of May, 1741, a sermon was preached to a company, at a private house. Near the conclusion of the discourse, one or two persons, that were professors, were so greatly affected with a sense of the greatness and glory of divine things, and the infinite importance of the things of eternity, that they were not able to conceal it—the affection of their minds overcoming their strength, and having a very visible effect upon their bodies. When the exercises were over, the young people that were present removed into the other room for religious conference; and particularly that they might have opportunity to inquire of those, that were thus affected, what apprehensions they had, and what things they were that thus deeply impressed their minds; and there soon appeared a very great effect of their conversation; the affection was quickly propagated throughout the room; many of the young

---

67 *Ibid.*, 253.

> people and children . . . appeared to be overcome with a sense of the greatness and glory of divine things, and with admiration, love, joy, and praise, and compassion to others, that looked upon themselves as in a state of nature; and many others at the same time were overcome with distress, about their sinful and miserable estate and condition; so that the whole room was full of nothing but outcries, faintings, and the like. Others soon heard of it in several parts of the town, and came to them; and what they saw and heard there, was greatly affecting to them, so that many of them were overpowered in like manner, and it continued thus for some hours; the time being spent in prayer, singing, counselling, and conferring.[68]

I could continue with report after report from revivals both ancient and recent. I've been present in such gatherings myself and have experienced God's overwhelming power on many occasions. It's holy. It's terrifying. It's awe-inspiring.

Can you imagine such an outpouring in your own home? What if prayer and worship in your house church rolled into the next day as people trembled, convulsed, and cried out under God's power? What if others from your neighborhood, town, or apartment building heard what was happening and flocked to your home? Would you welcome such holy chaos? What if you had to

[68] Jonathan Edwards, "Memoirs of Jonathan Edwards, A.M.," in *The Works of Jonathan Edwards, Volume I,* ed. Edward Hickman (Carlisle, Pennsylvania: Banner of Truth Trust, 2011) Kindle Edition, Loc. 3409.

work the next day? Would you let people linger unsupervised? What if there were no conversions taking place? Would you reject the occurrence as a mere distraction? Or would you still embrace what God is doing, knowing salvations will soon come?

We had all best think through such possibilities now before we find ourselves in the moment, struggling to process a move of God.

Enduring Revival

The laughing, crying, trembling, and other manifestations of revival look like foolishness to the world. The onlookers at Pentecost thought the believers in the house were drunk. (See Acts 2:13–21.) If an outpouring is to be sustained, then we who have been entrusted with leadership will need grace to persevere.

I guarantee the experience will be messy. As discussed in chapter 14, life produces messes. The avoidance of messes often requires the suppressing of life. Expect complications. Expect to be tired after late nights of prayer and worship. Expect people to sometimes act in their flesh, presuming to be in the Spirit. And as sinners are drawn to your meetings like moths to a flame, know that sin is inevitable too.

Nevertheless, none of these problems negate God's work. Rather, they are the reason for God's work. He comes to purify and set free. Your role is to facilitate the meeting in such a way that people can understand and be transformed by the outpouring of God's love among you.

Paul's rebuke of the Corinthian church was not to shut down all the spiritual phenomena taking place. He encouraged them to eagerly desire even more spiritual gifts. (See 1 Corinthians 14:1.) Yes, he noted that they were carnal, not spiritual. (See 1 Corinthians 3:1–3.) But at the same time, he celebrated, "You do not lack any spiritual gift" (1 Corinthians 1:7). Despite all the Corinthians' disorder, immorality, divisions, and other problems, Paul identified that the Holy Spirit was indeed working among them.

When Paul told the Corinthians that "God is not a God of disorder but of peace," he wasn't saying that the presence of disorder is the absence of God (1 Corinthians 14:33). That would negate his earlier recognition of the Spirit's work among them. Rather, Paul was inviting them into meetings where their regular experience of God's power would be met with a simultaneous experience of God's nature.

John Wesley famously prayed, "Oh, Lord, send us the old revival, without the defects; but if this cannot be, send it with all its defects. We must have revival!"[69] Revival comes with defects because it comes for broken people. We address the defects with love and the Spirit's wisdom rather than quashing them in a fleshly clamor for control. We don't ignore problems, but we also don't focus on them. We address them as the Spirit leads.

---

[69] Frank Bartleman, *Azusa Street* (New Kensington, Pennsylvania: Whitaker House, 1982), 43.

Sustaining Revival

A fire burns as long as new fuel is added. If God pours out in your house church but no one ever goes out to share the fire with others, the embers will eventually die out once again. In every revival, a time must come when those who are burning hot must share what they've received. More people need to come, so those who are present must go out. Revival in a house church will inevitably lead to bigger meetings or, better yet, Spirit-led division into more churches.

In his book *Keeping the Fire*, missionary Rolland Baker shares five principles that have helped maintain a worldwide revival for over two decades. Thousands of churches have been planted since the Holy Spirit first began to pour out on Rolland and his wife, Heidi, in the late 1990s. These five principles are:

1. Find God.
2. Depend on miracles.
3. Go to the least.
4. Suffer for him if necessary.
5. Rejoice in the Lord.[70]

Everything starts with encountering God personally and allowing that experience to overflow to those around us. From

[70] Rolland Baker, *Keeping the Fire: Sustaining Revival through Love: The Five Cove Values of Iris Global* (Weedon, Northampton, England: River Publishing & Media, Ltd., 2015).

there, we must anticipate the miraculous, regularly stepping into situations that will only work out if God intervenes. With this, we open our doors to the poor and visit the sick and the prisoner, knowing that Jesus is found among them. If we suffer, we endure with God's strength. And in all things, we choose to rejoice.

These principles don't belong to Rolland and Heidi Baker—they're simply the Christian life as shown in the Bible.[71] They are the lifestyle found in God's kingdom as it breaks into this fallen world.

In other words, if we'll live focused on Jesus and his love, there will always be fuel for the fire. Revival may begin with an event, but the flame can be kindled and maintained as we continue in the life God provides.

A Vision for the Future

A common refrain I have heard during the present revival at Asbury (which has now spread to many other universities) is that there are no big-name preachers or famous musicians. This isn't a necessary description of revival—John Wesley, George Whitfield, Jonathan Edwards, Charles Finney, and countless others prove otherwise. Nevertheless, God seems to be doing this right now. The current outpouring in which I write proves that you don't need a famous preacher to come to your house for God to pour out.

---

71 Rolland says as much in the introduction to his book.

What we're watching God do on university campuses is a glimpse of what he will soon do in homes. In my spirit, I see homes filled with people laid out on the floor, some laughing with heavenly joy, some weeping in repentance, some trembling under God's power. I see people peeling themselves off the floor and going out to the streets, healing the sick, raising the dead, casting out demons, and preaching the gospel with fiery boldness. I see new converts flooding home meetings faster than we can raise up new leaders, and I see God leading us to multiply in unique ways that may not even be covered in this book.

Like Abraham Sekar, we may need to start entrusting new house churches to relatively young believers. Those who are mature in Christ can mentor them along the way. It will probably be a glorious mess. But Jesus made it, so we might as well join him.

These sorts of meetings will spring up all over the world. Some will be small groups attached to larger church organizations, some will be unofficial gatherings of Christians, and others will be house churches. A specific person won't be leading the revival—only Jesus. That said, various new voices will arise, but only because of evident fruit in their ministries. Those voices will emerge, not through self-promotion but because they can't hide what God is doing. God will promote them—not for celebrity status but to be a blessing to the body of Christ.

I cannot help but wonder what a blessing it would have been if the eight hundred members of Abraham Sekhar's church could have read this book before launching their home meetings. I believe you are now more ready than ever to host an outpouring in your home and join believers around the world in multiplying God's kingdom.

Just before sending this book to my editor, I was at a prayer meeting for our network, and my friend JonMark Baker prophesied, "You have seen what you can do in your own strength. I will show you what I can do in my strength. The churches are going to be full. The net is already cast, but there aren't enough boats." I wrote this book so you can build a boat. A miraculous catch is coming, and it's more than our current churches can handle.

Jesus sees the multitudes, and he needs more shepherds: "When he saw the crowds, he had compassion on them, because they were harassed and helpless, like sheep without a shepherd. Then he said to his disciples, 'The harvest is plentiful but the workers are few. Ask the Lord of the harvest, therefore, to send out workers into his harvest field'" (Matthew 9:36–38).

I believe many will read this book after these prophetic words have been fulfilled. Perhaps you are one such reader, looking back on a movement of gospel houses that has swept the world. It's not too late to partner with God in this revival. If you will open your home, God will open the heavens.

No matter what, now that you've read this book, you're well equipped to plant, grow, and multiply a movement of Spirit-filled house churches. I pray God moves powerfully in your home and that many lives are transformed in your living room. You are ready. It's time for your house to be a gospel house.

CONCLUSION

Any Christian's home can be a gospel house. It doesn't matter if you attend a traditional church on Sunday or if your weekly home meeting is the only church you experience. What matters is that Jesus is present.

Jesus will be present when you welcome him by welcoming the least of these. And he loves a heart that loves his bride—free from bitterness against other churches and loving unity with the global body of Christ.

There is no competition in gospel houses. The goal is not to attract as many people as possible. The goal is not to make money. The goal is not to validate ourselves or prove something about our effectiveness or spirituality. The goal is to love God and love people, making disciples for Jesus along the way. One could even say that the goal is to help other people succeed in being disciple makers, setting them up for success and helping them start gospel houses that thrive even better than our own.

You are called to join God's mission by making disciples. I don't know how many sheep the Chief Shepherd will entrust to you. But I do know that the first step is entering a world of lost people and inviting them into the kingdom to which you belong. This will require opening your home to complete strangers—untrustworthy people who will eat your food, stink up your furniture, and use your bathroom (sometimes poorly). It's a risky endeavor, but the reward is eternal.

After living this way for the last eighteen years, I can say it's well worth the extra wear-and-tear on your carpet and furniture. It's well worth the late-night phone calls with people in crisis. It's well worth the extra food costs and extra scrubbing around the toilet. I wouldn't trade this lifestyle for anything.

I wrote this book because I believe in you. With the right teaching and encouragement, your house can be a gospel house. You can see the same sorts of wild testimonies I've witnessed and then some. One day, you and I will sit under a fruit tree beside a golden street, and you'll tell me story after story of the lives that were transformed because of your obedience to Jesus. I can't wait to hear it.

When my wife and I moved into our home, we prayed and dedicated that place to the Lord's work. We prayed that people's lives would be radically changed as they visited our home—not only in house-church meetings but also for social gatherings, parties, and play dates with our kids. Our home is a sacred space, set apart for the Lord's use. And this is enacted through our daily commitment to living for Jesus at all times.

The decision to make your house a gospel house is entirely yours. If you want this to be your lifestyle, start by walking through the rooms of your house, apartment, RV, or whatever the Lord has entrusted to you. Pray over each room and dedicate it to the Lord's service. Ask him to give you visions in your heart about what he wants to do in that home, and write those things down in a journal or a note on your phone. Agree with what he shows you and pray that you would see those promises come to pass.

Then start spending time with people who need to know Jesus. Live a gospel lifestyle, and soon your house will be a gospel house.

ABOUT THE AUTHOR

Art Thomas is the leadership director at Roots Church, Assembly of God—a Spirit-filled network of house churches in Metro-Detroit, Michigan.

Since 2011, Art has served as a missionary-evangelist who travels the world to train and equip Christians for Spirit-filled ministry. He is the president and CEO of *Wildfire Ministries International*—a global ministry that has spread the gospel to difficult and unreached regions, trained pastors, planted churches, and built a self-sustainable orphanage and primary school in rural Uganda.

Art is the producer and director of *Paid in Full*, a film that has trained tens of thousands to minister healing in Jesus's name, and *Voice of God*, a two-part film about hearing God's voice and prophetic ministry. He has authored several books, including *The Word of Knowledge in Action*, *Limitless Hope*, and *Empowered Creativity*.

Art and his wife, Robin, have two boys—Josiah and Jeremiah—and live in Romulus, Michigan.

For more information, please visit www.ArtThomas.org.

APPENDIX A:

QUALIFICATIONS OF A HOUSE CHURCH PASTOR

The following are biblical standards for church leadership, but they are also technically the expectations of any mature Christian. If you feel like this list doesn't describe you, ask Jesus how to apply the gospel to that area of your life. What needs to die so the Holy Spirit can live through you? Who do you need to forgive? What lies have you believed that need to be replaced with God's truth?

If you will faithfully and prayerfully address the areas that need transformation, the Holy Spirit will reveal Jesus through you.

- ❑ above reproach (1 Tim. 3:2)
- ❑ faithful to one's spouse (if married) and not in a sinful marital/extra-marital situation (1 Tim. 3:2; Titus 1:6)
- ❑ temperate (showing moderation or self-restraint) (1 Tim. 3:2)
- ❑ self-controlled (1 Tim. 3:2; Titus 1:8)
- ❑ respectable (1 Tim. 3:2)
- ❑ hospitable (1 Tim. 3:2; Titus 1:8)

- ❑ able to teach (1 Tim. 3:2)
- ❑ not given to drunkenness (1 Tim. 3:3; Titus 1:7)
- ❑ not violent but gentle (1 Tim. 3:3; Titus 1:7)
- ❑ not quarrelsome (1 Tim. 3:3)
- ❑ not a lover of money (1 Tim. 3:3)
- ❑ manage their families well (as applicable) and have obedient, believing children (under twelve years old), raising them in a way that is worthy of full respect (1 Tim. 3:4–5; Titus 1:6)
- ❑ shows signs of being a mature believer and has been a Christian for at least a year, preferably longer (1 Tim. 3:6)
- ❑ has a good reputation with outsiders (1 Tim. 3:7)
- ❑ blameless (Titus 1:6–7)
- ❑ not overbearing (not "unpleasantly or arrogantly domineering") (Titus 1:7; 1 Pet. 5:3)
- ❑ slow-tempered (Titus 1:7)
- ❑ not pursuing dishonest gain (Titus 1:7; 1 Pet. 5:2)
- ❑ loves what is good (Titus 1:8)
- ❑ upright (Titus 1:8)
- ❑ holy (Titus 1:8)
- ❑ disciplined (Titus 1:8)
- ❑ holds to the clear tenants of Christianity, defined in our church by our statement of faith (Titus 1:9)
- ❑ eager to serve (1 Pet. 5:2)
- ❑ exemplary in Christian conduct (1 Pet. 5:3)
- ❑ humble before others (1 Pet. 5:5)

Roots Church Network Additional Guidelines

If you're starting a network of house churches or if you're part of Roots Church, you may find this information helpful.

Before our senior leadership team will officially lay hands on a house-church leader and affirm him or her as an official pastor in Roots Church, he or she must meet the following criteria:

1. be or become a mission partner (official member) of Roots Church in good standing
2. either (1) serve in the capacity of house church leader or co-leader for six months, (2) serve in the capacity of house church leader or co-leader for three months and hold any level of active ministerial credentials with the General Council of the Assemblies of God, or (3) successfully graduate from the Roots School of Ministry (RSOM)
3. have three people from one's own house church fill out a confidential character-reference form that will be sent to the spiritual life director. (If married, one character reference shall be one's spouse, otherwise no character references shall be from one's own family.)
4. regularly attend Sunday encounter nights and second Sunday house-church pastor gatherings for at least three months

5. meet, along with one's spouse (if applicable), with at least two members of the senior leadership team for an interview and discussion about life, family, and ministry

APPENDIX B:

DISCIPLESHIP PATHWAY

What does intentional relationship look like? In what stage are your current relationships?

The following descriptions will help you assess your relationships with people you're trying to reach, then I'll offer advice for how to move them to the next step.

Contact

- You've met the person and had a conversation.
- You know each other's names.

Friend

- They know you're a Christian.
- You've prayed for them out loud, in-person.
- You have their phone number, and they have yours.
- You know something substantive about their life.

Pre-Convert

- You or someone in your house church has verbally shared the gospel with them.
- They understand both the cost and the reward of following Jesus.
- They know what they need to do to follow Jesus.
- They have visited your house church at least once.

Convert

- They believe the gospel.
- They want to be baptized.
- They are regularly attending and participating in your house church.

New Disciple

- They have been baptized in water.
- They are deliberately learning:
  - Bible reading
  - church participation
  - asking questions and seeking answers
- They have started an active prayer life.
- Their life shows signs of transformation and repentance.

Mature Disciple

- They have been baptized in the Holy Spirit.
- They are *still* deliberately learning.
  - Bible reading
  - church participation
  - asking questions and seeking answers
- They maintain an active prayer life.
- They hear God's voice and minister to others accordingly.
- Their life is actively being transformed into the image of Christ.
- They know how to share their faith, and they do.
- They actively engage in the mission of making disciples.

Note: Most Christians will remain at this stage, growing healthily in Christ. Some will show a gifting in the ministries of prophets, evangelists, and teachers.

Approximately one in ten disciples will stand out as chosen by the Lord to pioneer new works and shepherd some of his growing flock. The following two steps are for them.

Apprentice

- The house church (and especially the pastor) has identified consistent Christlike character traits that qualify this person for leadership.

- They have demonstrated a capacity to teach others effectively.
- They are being apprenticed by the house-church pastor to learn how to lead a house church-meeting.
- They begin searching for a person of peace in the field to which they feel called.

Leader (Missionary-type or Pastor-type)

- **Missionary-type**
  - They have found a person of peace and are actively reaching out to that person's sphere of influence with the gospel.
  - The house church has laid hands on them and commissioned them.
  - They have reached out to a handful of believers they know to join them as part of their seed group.
  - They are actively engaged in reaching people, making disciples, and establishing a new church.
- **Pastor-type**
  - If the current leader is a missionary-type:
    - The previous pastor has handed off shepherding responsibilities in the house church to the new leader.
    - The previous pastor goes out as a missionary to start a new house church elsewhere.
  - If the current leader is a pastor-type:

- The current pastor and the new pastor divide the group along a Spirit-led line—perhaps geographically or based on relationships—and divide the house church into two smaller groups with room to grow.

From Evangelism to House Church

Experience has shown that the number-one indicator of whether a person will commit to a house church is their level of relationship with the people within the church. Rarely—and perhaps statistically never—will a person show up because of a one-time conversation with a stranger. Intentional relationship-building is key.

One-on-one: Most evangelistic interactions begin with a personal encounter—perhaps praying for the person, ministering healing, or showing them an act of kindness. Whenever possible, this should include sharing your testimony and a brief presentation of the gospel.

But this one-off conversation is not enough to make a disciple. More rapport is needed, so you will need to follow up. This could include exchanging contact information or purposefully coming back to meet the person in the same place at a later date.

As soon as a person decides to follow Jesus, invite them to your house church—even if this happens during your first interaction. Some people will say they'll come but may still need more intentional follow-up.

Follow-up interaction: The second time you interact with the person, see how their life has progressed since your introduction. If you ministered healing at the first interaction, ask how they've been feeling since then. If you prayed for something specific, ask if the situation has yet changed.

This particular step can be combined with the next step, bringing another believer along for the follow-up.

Introduce a fellow believer: Prayerfully select someone from your house church to bring with you to meet the person you're reaching. This could be someone who you know with similar interests, or it could be a newer believer who you're mentoring in evangelism and disciple making.

Spend time getting to know the person and listening to their story. Look for ways to meet specific felt-needs that the person might have. Offer to pray once again, and remain sensitive to the Holy Spirit.

Invite the person to a social gathering with other believers: Do something fun as friends with people from your house church. Give the person an opportunity to meet and interact with believers who you know represent Jesus well. This may lead to prophetic words, testimonies, more prayer opportunities, etc. for the person you're reaching—especially if the friends understand that this is a missional opportunity.

If the person has not yet chosen to follow Jesus, this is the time to work on bringing the person to a place of decision.

In many cases, it's perfectly fine to skip this step before inviting the person to your house church, but sometimes it can make all the difference.

Even if the person has already attended your house church, it's still important to engage in social activities outside of the house church meeting. This helps strengthen the relationships.

Invite the person to your house church: If the person has not yet come to your house church, it's time to push the issue a little harder. If they're already hanging out with friends from your house church, it's clear they want to be around you and your church family. Explain to them all the reasons they ought to come.

At the house church, everyone should be intentional about meeting the person and showing an interest in their life. And if the person still has not given their life to Jesus, every effort should be made to help the person come to a place of decision. If they want to follow Jesus, baptize them as soon as possible.

APPENDIX C:

IDEAS FOR GROUP EVANGELISM

The following activities are ideas to help fuel creativity. Anything we can do to make disciples is a valuable use of time, effort, and resources. Use these ideas as they're presented, or let them stir your creativity. Follow the Holy Spirit, and he will bless it.

House-Church Party

A house church can plan a backyard BBQ, bonfire, block party, etc. and invite various people in the neighborhood. Hold the party at the host house for the house church. Those with gifts of administration would help organize the event while others make food and help create a fun and welcoming environment.

At the event, everyone in the house church intentionally includes and incorporates all the new people into everything they are doing—making conversation, building rapport, playing games, etc. House church participants are intentionally sensitive to the Holy Spirit, sharing words of knowledge and their testimonies, offering prayer, and even explaining the gospel.

Everyone who connects with a new friend invites them out for coffee or dinner with their family. In other words, follow-up is managed not by the house church pastor but by the people of the house church taking responsibility for the connections they each made. Every person who connects with a new friend intentionally continues to love, listen, pray, and look for ways to bring the kingdom of God into this person's life. (Follow "Appendix B: The Discipleship Pathway" explained earlier).

Neighborhood Service Project

One of the best ways to reach people is by meeting their felt needs. Raking yards, buying groceries for shut-ins, helping with spring cleaning, pulling weeds in sidewalks, giving out holiday cookies, and other acts of kindness can open doors for meaningful conversation about Jesus.

Generally speaking, such activities tend to be ineffective at making disciples on their own, but they do build rapport with neighbors and create opportunities for gospel ministry. For this reason, participants must be intentional about sharing Jesus with those they're blessing.

If you are using this activity to gain contacts and friends in the discipleship pathway, perhaps include a handwritten card with your contact information and an offer to pray for the person. You might also want to use such a service project as a means of blessing your neighbors before inviting them to a house church party as described above.

Modified Treasure-Hunt Evangelism

Typical treasure hunt evangelism involves purposeful trips into the community, following the Holy Spirit's guidance to specific people (usually through words of knowledge written down beforehand). As each person (the treasure) is found, prayer is offered, and occasionally, this leads to opportunities to share one's testimony and the gospel.

But typical treasure hunt evangelism rarely leads to long-term relationships and disciple making unless the ministers are intentional.

When treasure hunters aim at making disciples, conversations end up being longer and more in-depth, contact information becomes more important, and the geographical target area ends up being deliberately closer to the house church. The goal of the outing ends up being less about quantity (how many people get healed or prayed with) and more about quality (how many meaningful contacts and friends were made).

Houseless Church

A house church may choose to hold their normal meeting in a public place—perhaps a public park, a beach, the normal home's front lawn, etc. As the group meets, sometimes neighbors or passersby may stop to see what's going on.

In houseless-church meetings, the primary objective is outreach, so such people should be immediately engaged and welcomed. Food, drinks, and seating within the circle are important to have ready before people arrive. Welcome the person, introduce yourselves, talk about what you're doing (learning from Jesus together), and offer to pray for the person. Don't make it high pressure, and don't make that person the center of attention for too long. Simply make them feel welcome, invite them to stay, and continue with your normal meeting.

As always when a new person is present, make sure the conversation includes a gospel presentation. See "Appendix D: Tips for Hosting New Believers."

Deliberate, Ongoing Disciple-Making Mission

If your house church is near a homeless community, a low-income neighborhood, an immigrant population, or some other disenfranchised community, you may want to consider choosing a second time each week to try to establish a new church in that place. Your house church can work together, pooling resources and coordinating schedules, to purposely minister to that community.

Make contacts through compassion ministry (offering food, groceries, clothing, assistance with government forms or job applications, etc.). Before offering anything or doing any sort of outreach, two to four people can go on an exploratory trip to meet the gatekeepers in the community and ask what the needs are. See if they would welcome your church to help meet some of those needs.

Seek to learn from them as much as you intend to teach them. Ask them about their stories and take time to really listen.

Build rapport through learning their culture, eating whatever food they offer you, and if applicable, learning a few words in their language. Show gratitude for their time and anything they offer you. Pray for them and bless them.

In the process, follow the concepts outlined in Luke 10:1–12. Talk about the kingdom of God and heal the sick. As you talk to people about Jesus and his love for them, search for a person of peace (Luke 10:5–7)—someone who welcomes your house church and its message, shows hospitality, and helps you relationally gain access to others in the community. Suggest starting a church in their living space, whether that be a house or even outdoors. If they're not open to the idea, ask them if they know anyone in the community who might be.

Finally, if the Lord helps you start a church there, continue to meet with the people and make disciples. Prayerfully help raise up a leader from within the community to shepherd that church. Give that leader more and more responsibility for the church while you discuss multiplication. Encourage that church to do the same thing your church did and intentionally reach out to others with the goal of launching another church.

If the initial response is tremendous, you may need to launch two, three, or more churches, led by different qualified people from your house church. At any point, if you're part of a network, feel free to reach out to other pastors for assistance, resources, or additional ministers. If God is moving faster than your house church can keep up, the rest of us are here to partner with you to accomplish great things.

APPENDIX D:

TIPS FOR HOSTING NEW BELIEVERS

Healthy house-church meetings tend to include believers from varied stages of spiritual development. Each meeting presents new challenges as new disciples are being made, as established disciples are being matured, and as people invite pre-converts to experience church life.

For house-church meetings to be valuable to everyone in attendance, take care to help everyone connect with what Jesus is saying and doing among the people.

The following advice will help you create an environment where new people feel free and safe to share.

Establish a Low Bar for Encouragement

Especially when new people come, be sure to encourage people when they share: "That's really good," or "I like that." Such phrases communicate that people are on the right track.

If you only ever praise truly profound statements, (1) there won't be many, (2) people will start dismissing what's on their hearts for fear it's not profound enough, or (3) people will start trying to sound profound, minimizing any practical value.

Don't worry about encouraging too much. If the people in your house church hear you encouraging what sounds like bottom-shelf revelation—the stuff everybody knows, like that God loves us—they will be more likely to share and less likely to fear not being profound enough.

Will this inspire over-talkers? Possibly. For this reason, especially encourage when someone says something concisely.

This, of course, raises a question: How do we manage false teaching or unbiblical assertions? Do it with love and grace. Sometimes the best move is to ask the group what they think of what was said, or ask if anyone knows a Scripture that would support or contradict the concept. Many times, the group will correct itself. Other times, you might sense that turning the matter over to the group could become unhealthy or argumentative, in which case you may want to simply handle the reply. You might say, "I understand why you would hold that perspective, but there might be a different way to look at this. Let's see what the Bible says." In everything, bring the conversation back to Scripture and practical application.

Avoid Intellectual Showmanship

People should leave your house church feeling smarter, not stupider. When you dazzle them with a large vocabulary and theological jargon, they may be impressed with your intellect, but they won't know what you were talking about and may not feel qualified to speak in the future.

But this doesn't mean your meetings need to be devoid of intellectual topics. People come to your house church because they want to learn and grow. They know they don't know everything. The key is to introduce big words and concepts in a way that helps people feel included rather than excluded.

A great phrase is, "Here's a word they teach in Bible college . . . " Or for a larger concept, "Let me give you an overview of this subject to catch everyone up to speed and frame our conversation." Then explain it all with down-to-earth terms and analogies that are accessible to the least educated person and the newest believer in the room. If you don't feel like you know enough about the subject to do so, ask if anyone else does. Make sure everybody understands as you go. Keep the discussion rooted in the Bible. And whenever possible, ask questions that help people discover answers for themselves.

Make Sure Everyone Benefits

Sometimes a married person will talk about issues relevant to marriage, not realizing that half the people in the room are single. Sometimes a person will talk about a particular author or music artist in a way that assumes everyone knows who that is. Sometimes someone will make an off-the-cuff reference to an obscure Bible story—or even a *popular* Bible story—not realizing some people in the room have no idea what they're talking about.

People can talk past each other in a house-church meeting in many ways. House-church pastors should watch for these issues and try to figure out ways to connect everyone in the room with what is being said.

For example, a passing reference to a Bible story could be followed up with, "Let's quickly read that story." As you read, watch for fresh revelation. See if what the person said about that passage really applies.

Define words. You may want to explain who various authors are. Give an overview of a particular topic so people have enough of a foundation to engage in a meaningful discussion.

Manage Discussion with Everyone in Mind

When new believers attend, they will ask two types of elementary questions: relevant and irrelevant. If what they're asking is relevant to the conversation or if the answer would benefit others in the room, take time to discuss the matter. But if the question would distract from what Jesus appears to be doing in the meeting, say something like, "That's a fantastic question, but I think it might distract us from the issue at hand. Let's write it down and chat after the meeting."

On the other hand, a new believer can sometimes feel overwhelmed when it comes to conversations about topics such as spiritual warfare, deliverance ministry, or the like. You will need a healthy tension between biblical theory and real-world practicality. If the conversation skews too far to one side, prompt the group to explore the other. For example, if everyone is sharing stories, ask the group if they know what the Bible has to say about this subject. Or if everyone is spouting theories and arguments, ask if anyone has an experience that would help us think about a real-world application.

Once in a great while, someone wants to talk about something they think is deep, but it's actually fringe and will not benefit the attendees. Perhaps they want to talk about UFOs, the mark of the beast, or government conspiracies. Only talk about a subject for as long as Jesus seems to be in it. Sometimes it's sufficient to say, "That's a super interesting conversation, but it's not why most of us came tonight. Let's keep this focused on Jesus."

A new believer might identify with a political party that is different from most or all of the house-church members. Philosophies that everyone thinks are obvious may give the new believer a strong sense of "I don't fit in here." Remind the house church that within Jesus's twelve, he had Simon the zealot (an anti-government social-justice warrior) and Matthew the tax-collector (a Roman government shill). Somehow, these two men abandoned their differences to embrace a superior kingdom, and they served in unity while obeying Jesus. We gather to love one another and grow in Christ, not argue about politics. (This is not to say, however, that we should avoid difficult or controversial subjects like abortion or greed. We simply need to frame such conversations within the context of our mission and not the promotion of specific political parties.)

In short, identify the makeup of the group, and make sure everyone can connect with the conversation, loving each other along the way.

APPENDIX E:

TIPS FOR FACILITATING DISCUSSION

House-church facilitation is an art form. Some people are naturally gifted at it, and some people don't want anything to do with it, but everyone can be taught to do it well. Here, you will learn some of the best time-tested and proven tips and tools for leading small-group discussions.

Remember the purpose of the meeting: Keep in mind that this is not a church service in the traditional sense, so your goal is not to provide a stage production or a one-sided monologue. People are gathering for deep Christian fellowship and biblical discussion. Anything outside of that can be done another time in another setting.

Don't worry about needing to know everything: You don't need to have all the answers, and you don't need to fix every problem. Simply provide strategies for researching and finding answers. That way, people don't become dependent on you—they learn to be dependent on God, the Bible, and each other. Always point them to Jesus, and never be afraid to say, "I don't know."

Remember you're not teaching a class: The temptation for many of us—especially those who are really into the Word of God—is to dominate the discussion. The fact is, the more you allow others the opportunity to talk, the more they'll become involved and open up, and the more they'll learn too. Your level of interaction will be more than others in the group simply because of your role, so you'll need to be proactive about keeping people engaged in the discussion.

Be secure in your identity: The more you make your goal being liked, the worse you'll do. Be an ambassador of Christ. Don't be afraid to speak the truth or challenge points that others bring up. Scripture will defend itself. Encourage others to do even greater works than you ever have. Make your goal the ministry of reconciliation (bringing unity between God and a group of people) so that all can excel in the things of God.

Don't let legalism take over: Don't feel guilty if church went differently and you didn't get to do something you planned. The question is not whether the system was perfect or whether every planned element of the meeting took place. Rather it is this: Could God express His presence at our meeting? Make every effort to avoid man-made tangents, but keep your eyes open for Spirit-led detours.

Model preparation: Read your Bible regularly. Pray often. Study Christian books and listen to a wide range of sermons.

Journal. The more you engage yourself in learning and growing, the more people in your church will be challenged to do the same. Be a pacesetter. Try to come every week with your own testimony of something God did through you, and always be prepared to share a revelation from Scripture, even if it's short.

Don't let Jesus get trampled!: Some people are natural talkers and tend to dominate the discussion with trivial matters. Conversations about great movies and the hamburger someone ate last night might be interesting, but they do not bring people closer to God, and they don't accomplish the purpose for the meeting (which is why everyone set aside time from their week to come). If discussion starts drifting away from the planned topic, treat the situation according to the nature of Christ and draw attention back to the reason everyone came. Sometimes in our efforts to honor and cater to natural talkers, we end up dishonoring everyone else in the group who sacrificed time to come for an expected purpose. Natural talkers need to be taught consideration for others so that Jesus can accomplish everything he desires in the meeting. It may feel rude to shut down a side conversation, but what's ruder is wasting the time of those who came for the right purpose. Always divert side discussions to after the meeting.

Let people process their thoughts and feelings: Again, this isn't a class; it's a discussion and a fellowship. Some topics that may come up are emotionally stirring or bring up old wounds. Let people vent about those situations because part of becoming effective Christians is processing such thoughts and feelings. If they're bringing up this topic, it's because they trust you and the group members to help them process. Don't feel like you need to provide answers, simply provide a listening ear. Validate their feelings as real and understandable, offer to pray with the person after the meeting or right then (whichever is most appropriate), and assure them that we're all in this together so you and the church are here for them.

Honor the authority of Scripture: Many of us believe a lot of traditions that are not found in the Bible. The apostle Paul said that all Scripture is "useful for teaching, rebuking, correcting, and training in righteousness." If a dispute arises or tensions stir about an issue, turn the group's attention to Scripture—"Does anyone know what the Bible says about this?" If the Bible is silent on the matter, then invite the group to form their own individual conclusions and move on; but point out that since the Bible doesn't offer an answer, none of us should embrace our conclusions with the same certainty with which we embrace Scripture. And that means we don't need to argue.

Be grateful for every answer: This will significantly increase the interaction that takes place in your house church. Listen intently to everyone, maintain eye contact with the speaker, and throw in little encouragements whenever appropriate.

Keep the discussion moving: Feel free to ask questions about what people say—even if you know what they mean. Keep the group dynamics going and maintain the focus on what the Holy Spirit has been doing and saying at your meeting.

Hide behind the group when fitting: This may seem a bit strange, but sometimes the group is your most valuable asset as a leader. As the lead-personality in a group, people will often look first to you for approval. If someone says something that's absolutely wrong and you want to refrain from shooting them down publicly, turn it over to group discussion by asking, "What do you all think?" One of two things will happen: Either the issue will correct itself in the context of discussion, or everyone will agree with the wrong perspective, allowing you to bring biblical correction without singling out one individual as wrong.

Consider the makeup of your group: Some people may be quiet and reserved while others may be rather expressive. Don't be afraid to ask the talkative person to hold their answer as you direct the question specifically to the quieter people: "What do *you* think?" or "I'm interested to hear what ____ has to say about this." If people are noticeably intimidated by group interaction, it's okay to back off so they don't feel uncomfortable attending. Some people aren't interested in speaking at all, but that doesn't mean they aren't learning and growing. In time, they'll open up, so feel free to give these people space for as long as they need. You may consider asking them after a meeting why they don't say anything. Sometimes, it's just that they can't get a word in edgewise, and that will alert you to a need for better moderation of the discussion.

Use silence to your advantage: Give others (and maybe yourself) time to think and muster the courage to respond to questions. You don't need to fill every awkward pause. Let the silence continue for a full minute if needed—people will catch on! It's not always your responsibility to make noise—often, silence occurs because God is moving on someone's heart. This will also encourage a culture in which the group expects that you're not going to let them off the hook until someone answers, which will lead to faster responses in the future.

Involve God in the discussion: At various points, as the group interacts, something will be said or done that requires a response to God. For instance, talking about forgiveness is nice—especially if everyone shares an insight—but you would be missing the boat if you didn't ask something like, "Would it be all right with all of you if we took a moment and asked the Holy Spirit if we have anyone we need to forgive?" Then lead out in prayer or ask someone else to. Allow God to participate in the conversation by bringing topics to a time of speaking with him as a group. Much of this will happen during the application time at each meeting, but remain sensitive to the possibility of short prayers in the middle of the discussion time.

Pray daily for the people in your house church: Make a point to dedicate yourself to Christ's work in your fellow Christians. Ask God for insights that will help or challenge specific individuals in your church. Ask Him to give you words of encouragement and affirmation for various people. And if correction of some kind is necessary, ask Him for the right words, actions (or lack of actions), and attitude to convey the transformative love of Jesus in an effective and meaningful way.

APPENDIX F:

ADVICE FOR CONVENTIONAL CHURCH LEADERS

Those of you in conventional churches can possibly implement ideas from this book within your organizations. Understand that such a transition will likely be slow and complicated, but the payoff will be worthwhile.

Imagine a self-replicating small-group ministry that makes disciples who make disciples. Imagine a framework of training and equipping believers that runs without your direct intervention. It will require a certain amount of surrendering control, but a proper structure will mitigate some of the inherent risks.

Many pastors of conventional churches have asked me how I protect the people of my house-church network from heresy. My lighthearted but pointed response is, "How do you protect the people of *your* church from heresy?" In conventional churches, a pastor can say whatever they like, and if anyone disagrees, they're usually limited to complaining to their spouse in the car. The pastor doesn't really hear much pushback. But everything I say in a house-church meeting is immediately scrutinized by everyone who has a Bible and some history with the Lord. Many times, people have replied to my teaching with, "Wait. What about this Scripture?" A conversation then ensues that either proves me right or wrong, and we all grow as a result. My theology has grown and strengthened over the years because such debate was welcomed.

Relinquishing control requires noting that we are not the sole arbiters of truth. The Scriptures must be our foundation. In my network, we have a statement of faith that clarifies the essentials of our common message and shared core values that shape our culture, but we allow our house churches to exercise a great deal of diversity within those constraints. All our disagreements are brought to the Scriptures to either be settled or accepted as reasonable disagreements.

If you're willing to embrace the inevitable messes of diverse opinions and release authority to people in your congregation, I believe you'll see a movement of disciple making in your church.

Take Your Time

My former pastor, Brooks McElhenny, noted to me that he was a small rudder on a huge ship. Changes in the church needed to happen gradually or else either he would break or the ship would capsize and dump everyone out.

Many are hesitant to change. What you win them with, you win them to. People generally like things the way they are; that's why they come. Meaningful, sustainable change will take time.

Some people will also resist change entirely, but don't let stagnant people dissuade you from following the Holy Spirit. Too often, we in church leadership are tempted to cater to the dead rather than accommodate the living—perhaps because sometimes there are more of them. Another former pastor, Otis Buchan, once said, "If, as a leader, you're always leading people in the direction they already want to go, you're not necessary."

In the book *WikiChurch*, author Steve Murrell shared how he transitioned a church in the Philippines into a disciple-making movement. Over the course of two years, his staff began quietly developing home-based discipleship groups. Anytime someone in the church learned about what they were doing and wanted to participate, they would answer, "No, you can't join one, but if you will gather three church friends and three unchurched friends, we will teach you how to lead one. When would you like to start?"[72] (I highly recommend his book to anyone wanting to do the same.)

In other words, the transition you're looking for may need to look less like a sudden structural overhaul and more like a slow process of intentional disciple making that begins with church leadership and multiplies until it becomes the predominant culture of the congregation.

You may want to use *Gospel Houses* as training material for home-group leaders. This will help cast vision and clarify your

---

[72] Steve Murrell, *WikiChurch: Making Discipleship Engaging, Empowering, and Viral* (Lake Mary, Florida: Charisma House, 2011) Kindle Edition, 47.

goals. Bulk quantities can be ordered from the publisher at a discounted rate.

Dream with Me

Imagine your church five years from now. If nothing changes in your current structure and programs, what will everything look like?

If your projection indicates that your church will be stronger and healthier, then you may not need to change anything. Keep doing what you're doing. And if the principles of this book can accelerate that health, then implement those as well.

But if your projection indicates either stagnation or decline, it may be time to make a significant course correction. For reasons noted above, don't have a knee-jerk reaction or make sudden changes. Follow the Spirit's strategy. Pray for God's direction and take your time implementing the changes he prompts.

Empower and equip the people of your church to make disciples in their homes. Soon, they will be multiplying faster than you ever dreamed possible.

APPENDIX G:

RECOMMENDED RESOURCES

The following books are arranged by topic and have each played a role in the development of our culture at Roots Church.

Disciple Making

- *DiscipleShift: Five Steps that Help Your Church to Make Disciples Who Make Disciples* by Jim Putman and Bobby Harrington with Robert E. Coleman
- *The Master of Relationships: How Jesus Formed His Team* by Rick Zachary
- *Organic Discipleship: Mentoring Others into Spiritual Maturity and Leadership* by Dennis McCallum and Jessica Lowery
- *Family on Mission: Integrating Discipleship into the Fabric of Our Everyday Lives* by Mike and Sally Breen
- *With: A Practical Guide to Informal Mentoring and Intentional Disciple Making* by Alvin L. Reid and George G. Robinson
- *Hero Maker: Five Essential Practices for Leaders to Multiply Leaders* by Dave Ferguson and Warren Bird
- *Multiply: Disciples Making Disciples* by Francis Chan

GOSPEL HOUSES ~ Art Thomas

House-Church Principles

- *The Spirit-Filled Small Group: Leading Your Group to Experience the Spiritual Gifts* by Joel Comiskey
- *Groups that Thrive: 8 Surprising Discoveries about Life-Giving Small Groups* by Joel Comiskey with Jim Egli
- *Micro Church Networks: A Church for a New Generation* by Larry Kreider
- *MegaShift: The Best News Since Year One* by James Rutz
- *Letters to the Church* by Francis Chan

Leadership and Organizational Strategy

- *Teams that Thrive: Five Disciplines of Collaborative Church Leadership* by Ryan Hartwig and Warren Bird
- *Incomplete by Design: Team Ministry, A Characteristic of Revival Culture* by Steve and Sally Wilson
- *Managing Conflict Creatively: A Guide for Missionaries and Christian Workers* by Donald C. Palmer
- *Exponential: How You and Your Friends Can Start a Missional Church Movement* by Dave Ferguson and Jon Ferguson
- *Multiplying Missional Leaders: From Half-Hearted Volunteers to a Mobilized Kingdom Force* by Mike Breen

Healing Ministry

- *Paid in Full: God's Desire to Heal through Today's Believers* documentary film by Art Thomas and James Loruss
- *Paid in Full: 40-Day Healing Ministry Activation Manual* by Art Thomas, James Loruss, and Jonathan Ammon
- *Spiritual Tweezers: Removing Paul's Thorn in the Flesh and Other False Objections to God's Will for Healing* by Art Thomas

Children's and Youth Ministry

- *Children in Cell Ministry: Discipling the Future Generation Now* by Joel Comiskey
- *Redefining Children's Ministry in the 21st Century: A Call for Radical Change* by Becky Fischer
- *Youth in Cell Ministry: Discipling the Next Generation Now* by Joel Comiskey
- *Family-Based Youth Ministry* by Mark DeVries

Hearing God's Voice

- *Voice of God: Hear God, Know God, & Change the World* documentary film by Art Thomas and James Loruss
- *Voice of God: 40-Day Hearing God Activation Manual* by Art Thomas, James Loruss, and Jonathan Ammon
- *You May All Prophesy: Practical Guidelines for Prophetic Ministry* by Steve Thompson
- *The Word of Knowledge in Action: A Practical Guide for the Supernatural Church* by Art Thomas

Power Evangelism

- *The Adventure of Saying Yes* by JonMark Baker
- *A Practical Guide to Evangelism Supernaturally* by Chris Overstreet
- *Power Evangelism* by John Wimber with Kevin Springer
- *Immediate Obedience: The Adventure of Tuning in to God* by Rod Loy

Converting a Conventional Church to Small Groups

- *WikiChurch: Making Discipleship Engaging, Empowering, and Viral* by Steve Murrell

Spirit-Filled Theology and Practice

- *Empowered for Global Mission: A Missionary Look at the Book of Acts* by Denzil R. Miller
- *The Charismatic Theology of St. Luke: Trajectories from the Old Testament to Luke-Acts* by Roger Stronstad
- *Paul, the Spirit, and the People of God* by Gordon D. Fee
- *Two Views on Women in Ministry* by Belleville, Blomberg, Keener, and Schreiner (General Editor: James R. Beck)

Stewarding and Responding to Revival

- *Keeping the Fire: Sustaining revival through love – the 5 core values of Iris Global* by Rolland Baker

Tools for New Disciples

- *Rooted: Thriving in Your New Life* by Art Thomas
- *How to Read the Bible for All It's Worth* by Gordon D. Fee and Douglas Stuart

www.ingramcontent.com/pod-product-compliance
Lightning Source LLC
Chambersburg PA
CBHW070116100426
42744CB00010B/1847
* 9 7 8 1 9 5 9 5 4 7 0 1 3 *